ALSO BY FEN MONTAIGNE

Reeling in Russia

FRASER'S PENGUINS

FRASER'S PENGUINS

A JOURNEY TO THE FUTURE IN

ANTARCTICA

Fen Montaigne

A John Macrae Book
Henry Holt and Company
New York

Henry Holt and Company, LLC
Publishers since 1866
175 Fifth Avenue
New York, New York 10010
www.henryholt.com

Henry Holt® and ⬡® are registered trademarks of Henry Holt and Company, LLC.

Distributed in Canada by H. B. Fenn and Company Ltd.

Library of Congress Cataloging-in-Publication Data

Montaigne, Fen.
   Fraser's penguins : a journey to the future in Antarctica / Fen Montaigne. — 1st ed.
      p. cm.
   ISBN 978-0-8050-7942-5
   1. Adélie penguin. 2. Endangered species. 3. Climatic changes—Antarctica. 4. Global
environmental change. 5. Nature—Effect of human beings on—Antarctica. 6. Fraser, Bill,
1950—Voyages and travels. 7. Environmentalists—United States. 8. Antarctica—Description
and travel.   I. Title.
   QL696.S473M668 2010
   577.2'209989—dc22   2010007151

First Edition 2010

Designed by Meryl Sussman Levavi
Printed in the United States of America
1   3   5   7   9   10   8   6   4   2

To Claire and Nuni

CONTENTS

FRASER'S PENGUINS

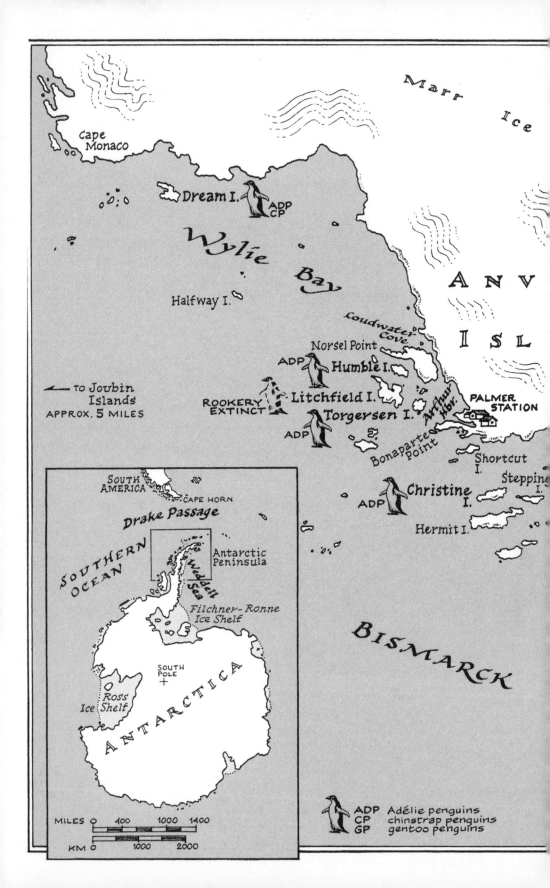

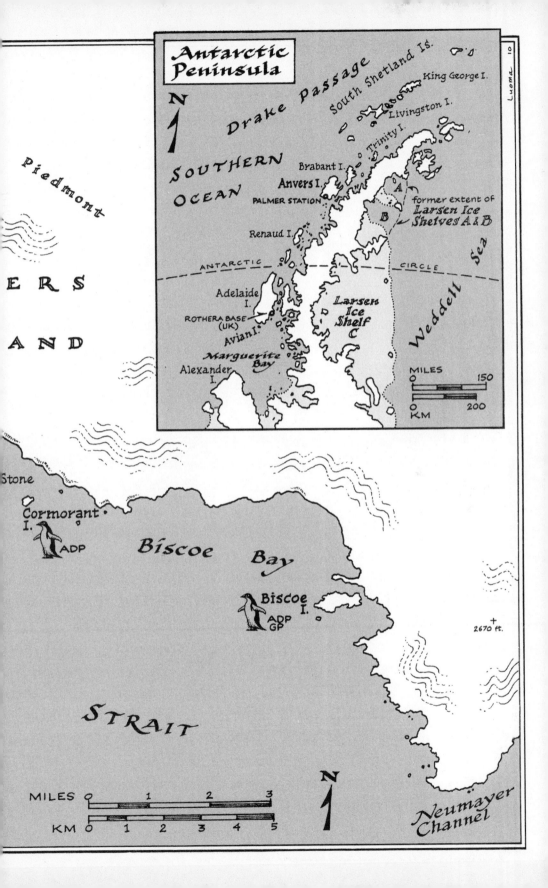

Antarctic Peninsula

N

Drake Passage

South Shetland Is.

King George I.

SOUTHERN

OCEAN

Livingston I.

Trinity I.

Brabant I.

Anvers I.

PALMER STATION

A

former extent of
*Larsen Ice
Shelves A & B*

B

Renaud I.

ANTARCTIC — — — CIRCLE

Weddell Sea

Adelaide
I.

ROTHERA BASE
(UK)

Avian I.

*Larsen
Ice
Shelf
C*

*Marguerite
Bay*

Alexander
I.

MILES
0   150

0   200
KM

Luoma

10

Piedmont

E R S

A N D

Stone

Cormorant
I.

ADP

Biscoe   Bay

Biscoe
I.

ADP
GP

+
2670 ft.

S T R A I T

Neumayer
Channel

MILES 0   1   2   3

KM 0   1   2   3   4   5

N

PROLOGUE

What we're looking at here is an entire ecosystem that is changing, and it's not changing in hundreds of years. It's changing in thirty to fifty years. To me this is foretelling the future across major parts of the planet. All those places we cherish are going to change.

—BILL FRASER, Torgersen Island, 2006

ON A STILL, SUNNY EVENING IN FEBRUARY, SCORES OF NEWLY fledged Adélie penguin chicks were arrayed on the cobblestone beaches of Torgersen Island, contemplating the next step in their brief lives. Only two months old yet almost fully grown, these twenty-inch-high, black-and-white seabirds milled about, some emitting the feeble, honklike call peculiar to adolescent Adélies, others standing and staring at the Southern Ocean. The temperature in this corner of the northwestern Antarctic Peninsula hovered just above freezing. The sun was making its slow descent toward the horizon, its rays casting a gentle light on the ice-draped mountains that run down the spine of the nine-hundred-mile finger of land.

I stood a few dozen feet from the beaches and gazed at the sea—frigid, remarkably clear, its surface broken by scores of icebergs—stretching before me. To my left, the peninsular mountain range—sheer black rock faces and vast fields of ice streaming to the Southern Ocean—dominated the eastern horizon. To my right, the great white dome of the Marr Ice Piedmont sloped gradually to the west. I had been in Antarctica nearly four months, but, as always, I felt incapable of grasping the scale and beauty of this place. To take it all in with a single glance, capture it in a photograph, or render it faithfully in words seemed impossible.

The tableau behind me was not quite so picturesque. Torgersen Island was then home to a rapidly diminishing rookery of 2,500 breeding pairs of Adélie penguins, and at the end of the reproductive season the penguin colonies were a scene of squalor and disarray. Not two weeks before, Torgersen had been the site of frenetic activity, with adult Adélies—the classic tuxedoed penguin and one of only two penguin species that breed exclusively in Antarctica—shuttling to and from the sea to sate the ravenous appetites of their rapidly growing offspring. Now the colonies were empty, with most of the adults at sea gorging on krill after the exhausting process of raising offspring, and the chicks piling up on the beaches. Recent rains had turned the colonies into rank swamps of guano, with trickles of red waste flowing out of the nesting areas and down to the ocean. Skuas—the main terrestrial predator of the Adélies— picked over the carcasses of penguin chicks and swarmed overhead.

Hundreds of fledged chicks had already slipped into the sea, and hundreds more were assembled along the shores of Torgersen and nearby penguin islands, summoning the courage to enter the water. Small groups of young Adélies gradually nudged their way to the ocean's edge, with the bolder among them hopping out onto rocks until they were five to ten feet from shore. Some of these chicks seemed poised to dive in, but after several minutes retreated to the beach. Others, however, displayed a greater intensity as they neared the water, eyeing the incoming waves with a certain focus. The bravest moved to the front, staring at the sea and letting the waves lap at their webbed feet. Then, suddenly, they took a step or two and dove in, prompting a dozen other chicks to follow suit. Looking half panicked and half playful, these newly fledged penguins dog-paddled in the shallows, splashed wildly with their flippers, dipped their heads underwater, and honked to their fellow swimmers. Within a minute, however, the stronger chicks began heading out to sea, diving and remaining underwater for five or ten seconds as they learned to swim.

While most of the chicks left the security of their terrestrial life in the company of other penguins, some young Adélies embarked on this new phase alone. That evening on Torgersen Island, I watched a single chick enter the water and swim into the channel between Torgersen and nearby Litchfield Island. The young bird splashed on the surface for a few seconds, dove, reappeared twenty to thirty feet out to sea, lifted its head high to get its bearings, emitted a clipped squawk, paddled awhile, and then dove again. Using my binoculars, I followed the penguin for several hundred yards as it made its way to the southwest. Soon, however, the chick was nothing more than a tiny dot on the surface of the sea. Then it dove once more, and I lost sight of the young penguin for good. As I watched the chick disappear into the expanse of ocean off Torgersen Island, I wondered how this solitary, untutored, seven-pound seabird would learn to feed itself and survive. My fears were not unfounded, for in the northwestern Antarctic Peninsula this was precisely the problem: The Adélie chicks were going to sea, but they weren't coming back.

IN THE AUSTRAL summer of 2005–06, I spent nearly five months at Palmer Station, a scrap of civilization grafted onto a rocky spit of land in a world of ice, snow, sea, and stone. It is named for an early-nineteenth-century American seal hunter, Nathaniel B. Palmer, who at age twenty had the audacity to leave Stonington, Connecticut, in command of a forty-seven-foot sloop, the *Hero,* sail the length of the planet, cross the wild stretch of ocean known as the Drake Passage, and enter foggy, uncharted, iceberg-covered Antarctic waters in search of fur seals. He found them, making himself and his fellow officers from the sealing fleet wealthy men. In the process, in just five years—from 1819 through 1823—the British and American flotilla wiped out virtually the entire population of half a million fur seals in the South Shetland Islands, on the northern tip of the Antarctic Peninsula. Today, Palmer is perhaps best known as the first American to have laid eyes on the Antarctic mainland.

The U.S. government research station named in Palmer's honor is a cluster of a half dozen corrugated metal buildings that, at peak operations during the austral summer, house roughly forty scientists and support staff. These days, the researchers are mainly engaged in studying how the rapid warming of Palmer's environs is cascading through this icebound world, affecting everything from the formation of sea ice, to the krill that depend on the sea ice, to the Adélie penguins (*Pygoscelis adeliae*) that depend on the sea ice and the krill. The northwestern Antarctic Peninsula, where the station is located, has heated up faster than almost any other place on earth, with winter temperatures rising 11°F in the past sixty years and average annual temperatures increasing 5°F since 1951—five times the global average.

While at Palmer, I worked as a member of ecologist Bill Fraser's research team during the breeding season of the penguins, skuas, giant petrels, blue-eyed shags, kelp gulls, and other seabirds that nest in the region. Fraser first came to Palmer Station in 1974, as a young graduate student. In the ensuing three and a half decades, he has watched this world start to melt around him, painstakingly documenting how a changing cast of seabirds—most notably the Adélie penguin—are reacting to their warming environment. His research, which brought him back to Palmer Station year after year, has paid off, as Fraser and his colleagues have assembled one of the most detailed portraits on earth of the impacts of rising temperatures on the natural world. Their work is of more than passing academic interest, however, for as Antarctica warms and its ice sheets begin to melt, the seas along our coasts will rise, and global weather patterns will change.

ONE MORNING IN early March, not long before the end of my stay at Palmer Station, I walked out of my dormitory and gazed upon a scene that never grew old: the pale blue palisades of the Marr Ice Piedmont, the enormous glacier that envelops the station; the waters of Arthur Harbor, filled this day with large rafts of brash ice shed by the Marr with thunderous rumbles; the rocky islands just offshore, dusted the night before with an inch of snow and home to a rapidly disappearing population of Adélie penguins; and the Antarctic sky, its brilliant blue hue occasionally visible through low, gray-bottomed clouds.

Striding down a short boardwalk and entering the galley, I glanced at two small calendars sitting on a shelf at the head of the serving line, their messages changing every morning. The first calendar contained the word of the day. The second displayed sayings of Buddhist sages and other enlightened souls. These aphorisms often sailed over my head, but on this morning a quote from Pythagoras, the ancient Greek mathematician and philosopher, caught my attention.

"Astonishing! Everything is intelligent!"

That day, and on many that followed, Pythagoras's declaration kept looping back through my mind. After months working in the Antarctic, spending my days among seals, whales, seabirds, and penguins, I had come to the same conclusion. How could I not? The Adélie penguins alone had exhibited an instinctual intelligence that was breathtaking. After migrating hundreds of miles from their winter feeding grounds, they marched off the ice in the austral spring and—even though their nesting territories were concealed under snow—headed to the very colonies where many were hatched or had raised chicks before. There the Adélies stood or lay patiently until the snow melted, exposing the pebbled ground underneath. If a mate from the previous season survived the winter, the pair frequently was reunited. Together they patiently constructed a cup-shaped nest of stones. They copulated. They took turns incubating two eggs, with the liberated penguin making a beeline for feeding grounds in the Southern Ocean, where it gorged on krill before returning to relieve its partner. Together, the couple guarded the chicks, and when their offspring's demand for nourishment became overwhelming, both parents took to the sea to feed. Upon their return, the parents recognized their chicks not by sight but by voice, identifying them by the slightest variations in their raspy calls.

Finally, as the chicks reached adult size, losing their down and gaining feathers, the entire raucous yet well-ordered process crescendoed. Sensing that they could no longer continue to feed full-grown chicks and keep themselves alive, the adult Adélies simply took off. The adolescent

Adélies clustered in packs and contemplated the fact of their abandonment for a day or two. Then, their hunger growing, they clumsily made
their way to the shoreline. They stared at the Southern Ocean for hours,
perhaps days, until making the ultimate instinctual leap of faith: They
dove in.

Astonishing indeed! Of course, these natural dramas are played out
every day, all over the world, from suburban backyards to the poles.
But never had I witnessed such elegantly instinctive behavior at such
close range. Never had I spent day after day, months on end, observing
wild creatures; nor had I followed this round of reproduction from
start to finish. And never had I observed the natural world in so
untouched a setting, a place whose beauty has beggared the descriptive
powers of explorers and visitors ever since the first Europeans laid eyes
on the continent nearly two centuries ago.

"It is impossible for me to render even a moderately fair description
of the other-worldly beauty and perfect uniqueness of the landscape,"
the Norwegian businessman and explorer Henryk Johan Bull wrote of
his 1895 visit to Victoria Land, on the Ross Sea. "The pinnacled mountains towering range beyond range in majestic grandeur under a cover-
let of matchless white; the glittering and sparkling gold and silver of
the sunshine, broken or reflected through the crystals of ice and snow . . .
but perhaps more than all, the utter desolation, the awesome, unearthly
silence pervading the whole landscape."

Palmer Station is lost in such an epic landscape, a place where
mountains—some reaching 9,000 feet and all draped in ice caps and
glaciers—tower over the frigid waters of the Southern Ocean. As spring
began, the sea's surface was locked in ice that had trapped innumerable
icebergs, their shapes running from massive, flat-topped tabular bergs
to whimsical, castle-like structures. On especially clear days, I could
stand atop the vast Marr Ice Piedmont that rose behind the station and
gaze through the dust-free Antarctic atmosphere at mountain summits
120 miles away, a line of the purest ice and the blackest rock unfurling
toward the South Pole. The scene was eternal and untouched, and I,
like many people who have spent time in Antarctica, was overcome
with an exhilarating feeling of insignificance.

"One's dear self becomes so miserably small in these mighty surroundings," said Lieutenant Kristian Prestrud, a member of Norwegian Roald Amundsen's 1910–12 expedition, the first to reach the South Pole.

To describe the power of this continent, its human interlopers inevitably have resorted to the language of the spirit. Bill Fraser is not inclined to such poetic musings, but nevertheless the beauty and grandeur of Antarctica are an important part of what has drawn him back to the continent for more than three decades. Early in his scientific career, Fraser made a decision to get to know one place well, to fully understand the relationships among all the creatures inhabiting a single spot on the planet. Such dedication is typical of many Antarctic scientists—including the small community of penguin researchers—who spend years working on the continent, often under harsh conditions. In Fraser's case, that patience has yielded important results, for he has found himself in a position to witness something that neither Ernest Shackleton, nor Robert Falcon Scott, nor any other of the legendary Antarctic adventurers had ever seen: In just a few decades, the Antarctic Peninsula and the seabirds and marine mammals that inhabit it have changed rapidly. Working with Fraser during just one birding season at Palmer, I, too, witnessed this transformation as colonies of Adélie penguins died out before my eyes.

It was hard to believe that anything could defeat the pugnacious Adélies, which stand no higher than a man's knee and thrive in the most inhospitable environment on earth. But the Adélie has met its match in man, for the forces we have unleashed—in the form of planet-warming greenhouse gases—have reached the world's wildest continent and begun altering it. The most deleterious effect on Adélies has been the steady disappearance of sea ice along the western Antarctic Peninsula. Like the polar bear's in the Arctic or the emperor penguin's farther south in the Antarctic, the Adélie penguin's existence is intimately intertwined with the sea ice that has long defined life at the poles. When sea ice markedly declines, so, too, do Adélies. The demise of these beloved birds in this part of Antarctica seems, at first glance, to be the work of unfathomable natural forces. But thanks to the research conducted by Fraser and his colleagues, it has become increasingly clear that humanity is every bit as responsible for the decline of Adélie penguins along the northwestern Antarctic Peninsula as Nathaniel

Palmer and his mates were for the near extirpation of Antarctica's fur seals nearly two centuries ago.

Fully 2.5 million pairs of Adélie penguins still exist in Antarctica, and although they are dying out around Palmer Station, Adélies will no doubt continue to exist on the continent for the foreseeable future. Whether they will continue to thrive is another matter. Steadily rising temperatures are now nibbling at the edges of the planet's coldest continent, most notably along the Antarctic Peninsula, the crooked sliver of land that juts toward the southern tip of South America and extends farther north than any other part of Antarctica. Yet if, as expected, global temperatures continue to rise as mankind pours more greenhouse gases into the atmosphere, warming won't merely be creeping across the periphery of the miles-thick dome of ice that is Antarctica. It will penetrate deeply into the continent, shrinking sea ice, shattering the great ice shelves that flow off the land and float on the Southern Ocean, and melting glaciers and ice sheets, which will lift sea levels worldwide. This melting will ultimately be bad news for Adélie and emperor penguins throughout much of Antarctica, as it will for all the continent's other ice-dependent species, such as krill and crabeater seals.

Over time, I came to see the saga of Fraser and the Adélies as a cautionary tale, a sign of what the rest of us will soon be experiencing worldwide. Fraser has worked in a particularly exotic part of the planet, but the fundamental changes he has witnessed in his Antarctic backyard will soon be coming to everybody's neighborhood. The birds that have long migrated through our regions will change, as will the species of plants, flowers, and trees. The snow that fell in the towns where we grew up will increasingly become sleet and rain. Some of these changes are already taking place. Some will occur gradually over generations. But scientists such as Bill Fraser, who work in icebound worlds, have had the opportunity to observe large-scale changes telescoped into a few decades. A gradual shift in the range of tree species is a subtle thing, but the disappearance of ice—or Adélie penguins—is hard to miss.

And so, although he had no inkling of it when he first came to Palmer Station, Bill Fraser has turned out to be a sentinel, working in a part of the planet that most of us will never visit and bearing witness to rapid changes that foreshadow our own futures. For that reason alone, I was convinced that Fraser's story was worth telling.

The Adélies around Palmer Station are already experiencing the effects of warming, and it seems that their relentless instinct and their natural intelligence can take them only so far. Today, in at least one corner of Antarctica, the continent's iconic penguin is starting to falter.

"Astonishing! Everything is intelligent!"

Well, not quite everything.

CHAPTER I

THE PASSAGE

These days are with one for all time—they are never to be forgotten—and they are to be found nowhere else in all the world but at the poles. . . . One only wishes one could bring a glimpse of it away . . . with all its unimaginable beauty.

—EDWARD WILSON,
Terra Nova expedition, 1910–13

IN OCTOBER 1975, BILL FRASER—A TWENTY-FIVE-YEAR-OLD graduate student at the University of Minnesota—sailed from Ushuaia, Argentina, to Antarctica aboard a 125-foot, wooden-hulled research vessel, the RV *Hero*, named in honor of Nathaniel Palmer's sloop. After weathering a gale in the Drake Passage, the *Hero* neared the relatively tranquil waters of the Bransfield Strait, sheltered from the Southern Ocean by the South Shetland Islands. Exhausted, Fraser went to sleep. The next morning he awoke to unaccustomed stillness. The ship pitched no more. The water was flat. The only sound the young graduate student heard was the drone of the *Hero*'s 760-horsepower diesel engine.

Walking on deck, he felt as if he had entered an alternate universe. "I stepped out into this gray world," Fraser later recalled. "It had been snowing heavily and the ship was silently moving through this three- to four-inch layer of snow and slush on the water. There was snow all over

the deck. It was incredibly foggy. And the ship was completely surrounded by snow petrels, one of the most beautiful birds in the world—
absolutely white. When you see them you know the ice is near. They fly
silently and just appear and disappear. I went to bed under reasonably
normal conditions and woke up in this world that was completely for-
eign and remote."

As the green-hulled *Hero* steamed into the South Shetlands, off the
northwestern tip of the Antarctic Peninsula, Fraser was treated to yet
more polar theater: The snow stopped, the fog began to disperse, the
sky lightened, and, for a brief time, he caught a glimpse of the peaks of
Smith Island, mantled in ice.

After stopping at King George Island, in the South Shetlands, the
Hero eventually steamed into the Bismarck Strait near Anvers Island,
on whose southern shore Palmer Station is nestled. The ship's progress
was soon blocked by thick sea ice. Specially built for the National Science Foundation to supply Palmer Station and work along the Antarctic Peninsula, the *Hero* had a two-inch-thick hull of white oak, overlaid
with a rock-hard layer of greenheart. The forward hull was sheathed
with metal plating. But nothing short of an icebreaker could penetrate
the sea ice surrounding the small American base. So Palmer Station's
manager and the *Hero*'s Dutch captain decided that the people, equipment, and provisions moving in and out of the station would travel on
skis and sleds.

Because 1975 had been a heavy sea ice year, the frozen Southern
Ocean surrounding Palmer Station had not yet begun to break up,
enabling Fraser to glide swiftly over the surface. As he skied, leopard
seals—sleek, spotted predators that devour everything from krill to
penguins—cruised under the ice, tracking his movements and those
of the other skiers. Fraser could sometimes hear the leopard seals—
(*Hydrurga leptonyx*)—trilling their low, droning calls, and occasionally
a seal would poke its reptilian-looking head through an opening in the
ice to observe the passing skiers. The ice-loving leopard seals were a
common feature around Palmer Station, lounging on floes, attacking
Adélie penguins, trailing the rubber Zodiac boats used by scientists,
and occasionally biting a hole in one.

Skiing to Palmer Station—where he would spend the next thirteen months—Fraser took in a panoramic view: the saw-toothed line of the peninsular range extending south to the horizon, the snow-covered islands just offshore, and the Marr Ice Piedmont—roughly forty miles long and twenty miles across at its widest point—covering much of Anvers Island. Palmer Station had been in operation for only seven years, replacing smaller British and American bases that had been in the area since 1954, and the outpost appeared to have only the most tenuous of footholds on the grand Antarctic landscape: a few buildings perched on rocks and engulfed by a limitless expanse of ice and ocean. The sense that the station was a speck of civilization in a frozen wilderness was captured by the well-known landscape photographer Eliot Porter, who visited Palmer Station in 1975 and 1976, sometimes accompanying Fraser as he carried out his ornithological studies.

"Behind the station the ice field of Anvers Island loomed up, a minatory presence that seemed to declare its implacable intention to wipe this insolent blot from the Antarctic landscape," Porter wrote in his photo book *Antarctica*. "Next to the enormous ice sheet, even the security and permanence of the rock on which the station was built seemed uncertain—as though the balance of forces could as easily tilt in favor of an advance as of a retreat by the ice sheet."

In the ensuing three and a half decades, that balance has swung decisively in the direction of the station: Decades of robust warming have caused the Marr Ice Piedmont to thin and retreat fifteen hundred feet from this sliver of civilization.

Bill Fraser arrived at Palmer Station at a time of rapid transition, both in the climate of the northern Antarctic Peninsula and in the scientific work being carried out at the base. Only a few years before, the station had been run by U.S. Navy personnel. Few scientists had worked at Palmer. The *Hero* was itself a symbol of an earlier era—a wooden trawler outfitted with an engine and four sails.

As for global warming, neither Fraser nor most other members of the scientific community gave much thought to the subject. In 1975, few scholars were linking human activity with rising global temperatures. One of Fraser's professors at the University of Minnesota had discussed climate change, but he'd told his students that it was unlikely they would witness its effects in their lifetimes.

It turns out, however, that Fraser came to Antarctica at a pivotal time, when both the global climate and the Antarctic Peninsula's were beginning to react dramatically to the staggering amounts of carbon dioxide and other greenhouse gases humanity was pumping into the air. In later years, a Russian study would show that the world's glaciers began to melt and retreat on a large scale in the mid-1970s. The Intergovernmental Panel on Climate Change (IPCC) would later conclude that human-induced global warming began to significantly affect the planet at about the same time.

Higher temperatures were also beginning to sweep down the Antarctic Peninsula and would only increase in the coming decades. In hindsight, Fraser realizes that as a graduate student he experienced the tail end of an older, colder climate regime that had long dominated this part of the Antarctic Peninsula. One thing, above all, defined this system: the formation of ice on the Southern Ocean. The sea, with its high salt content, freezes at 28.8°F, so warmer air temperatures—and an increase in sea temperature of just a few tenths of a degree—can make the difference between an extensive covering of sea ice in the winter and a considerably smaller one. And over millions of years, the creatures in this part of Antarctica—in particular, the shrimplike Antarctic krill, *Euphausia superba*—had evolved in a world with sea ice at its center.

In the mid-1970s, Fraser and his colleagues began to compile baseline data on the state of nearly everything in Palmer's environs: the glaciers, the seabirds, the krill, and the smallest of all the marine organisms, the phytoplankton and diatoms. In the coming decades, as the peninsula warmed drastically, these observations would prove invaluable in documenting the region's transformation.

THESE DAYS, THE trip to Palmer Station begins in Punta Arenas, Chile, at the southern tip of South America. A placid town of 125,000 people, its central square lined with handsome nineteenth- and early-twentieth-century stone buildings, Punta Arenas sits on the Strait of

Magellan at 53° S, its dwellings creeping up the surrounding hillsides. Home in the mid-nineteenth century to a penal colony, the Patagonian town has a decidedly end-of-the-earth feel, with winds howling much of the year, permanently bending the southern beeches and the other scrubby trees; heavy gray clouds advancing swiftly over the landscape; and, on the rare clear days, broad vistas of Tierra del Fuego, with its barren, fawn-colored hills directly across the strait and, far to the south, the glaciated peaks of the Cordillera Darwin, rising to 8,000 feet.

I spent three days in Punta Arenas, and the night before our departure about twenty scientists, field team members, and support staff enjoyed a raucous evening of drinking pisco sours—a delicious cocktail that goes down like limeade but whose high-alcohol wallop must be accorded due respect—and eating conger eel, crab, and other Patagonian delicacies. With the group were two other members of Fraser's birding team, Peter Horne and Jennifer Blum, who—along with me—would carry out the first month's fieldwork at Palmer. We had just spent four days together at Fraser's home and office in southwestern Montana, planning the season's work. Three others had joined us in the Rockies: Fraser's wife, Donna Patterson, an expert on southern giant petrels and an integral part of his operation; Brett Pickering, an experienced Palmer Station field-worker; and Kristen Gorman, an ornithological field-worker spending her first season at Palmer.

Fraser, then fifty-five, had started a second family with Patterson, and with the birth of a son in 2004 the ecologist's decades-long practice of working nearly half the year in Antarctica was coming to an end. He planned to join us briefly at Palmer Station in November, and then return again in January for the final two and a half months of the birding season.

I first met Bill Fraser in January 2004, when I traveled to Palmer Station under the auspices of the National Science Foundation to write about his research for a magazine. Fraser, who had already received substantial media attention for his groundbreaking work on the impact of rapidly rising temperatures on Adélie penguins, was a lean and handsome figure, slightly over six feet tall, with rapidly thinning, light brown hair, a ruddy complexion, blue eyes, thin lips, and a cleft in his chin. After three decades of working in Antarctica, he had perfected his field outfit, donning just the right clothes to protect him from the elements yet not leave him overheated as he moved swiftly across the terrain. He wore a fleece sweater covered by a royal blue windbreaker that was faded by the sun and had been ripped in places by birds' beaks and rocks; rugged black rain pants heavily stained by penguin and skua guano and crusty with sea salt; and ankle-high, leather hiking boots, deeply scarred by years of scrambling over Antarctic rocks. On his head he wore a pale gray, sun-bleached baseball cap, and over the hat he sported a gray fleece headband to keep his ears warm. His outfit was completed by sunglasses, leather gloves, and a brightly patterned fleece neck gaiter, ideal for keeping rain and snow from dripping down his collar and easily jettisoned on warm, sunny days. After experiencing varying degrees of discomfort, most members of Fraser's team soon learned to emulate his dress.

Fraser, who retains the thirty-two-inch waist he had in college and is in excellent condition, bounds easily over the rocks on the islands near Palmer. When I returned to spend the entire summer season with his team, the only day I could match him stride for stride was shortly after he arrived. That was because he had shown up on station with a cold and was not yet in peak field shape. As a result, when we trudged up a steep, snowy slope on Hermit Island to census southern giant petrels, both of us arrived at the summit huffing and puffing. Within a week, Fraser was scarcely winded as he made similar climbs.

The main reason Fraser had allowed me to join his team during the 2005–06 season was that he had observed me in the field when I first visited Palmer Station and had judged that I was in reasonably good shape and was not a troublemaker. From experience, he knew that prickly—or poorly conditioned—characters would not wear well during the long months of fieldwork and could ruin team morale. This also was a lesson he'd no doubt learned in the military, though he was reluctant to discuss his service. The more time I spent with Fraser, the more I sensed how he'd been shaped by his hitch in the military and imbued with the best of its traditions. He was fiercely protective of—and loyal to—his squad of birders; unlike many field biologists, Fraser provided health insurance to his seasonal field-workers and contributed to their pension plans. At Palmer, he was keenly attuned to the group's well-being and morale. Later in the season, as I began to grow tired after months of fieldwork, I made some sloppy mistakes. Once, lost in thought, I walked too close to some giant petrels and spooked them. A day or two later, I carelessly wandered next to a group of elephant seals wallowing at the edge of an Adélie penguin colony, prompting two of them to slither rapidly away in panic and nearly crush to death some penguin chicks.

Later that afternoon, Fraser pulled me aside, fixed me with a concerned yet stern gaze, and said, "I think you're getting burned out. I've noticed it for a while. You came out of the boat yesterday with a rope wrapped around your legs. The other day you got too excited when we were corralling chicks on Humble."

I apologized and told him I felt good.

"You don't even know it's happening to you," he continued. "I saw one person, after four months here, literally step off the boat right into the water. I had to talk to you because when someone is like this he can easily get hurt himself or hurt someone else on the team. And it's no good for morale. As the season wears on, I see my role here as keeping morale up. So if you need time off, just take it. It's no problem."

I apologized again. He smiled, patted me on the back, and said, "Just relax."

Fraser had no patience for pretension, and he wasn't keen, either, on scientists who rarely worked in the field. That summer, a well-known scientist who personified both those characteristics came to the station as a lecturer on a cruise ship. Fraser briefly chatted with the portly individual and was unimpressed. A few days later, as we sat on one of the islands, eating lunch and gazing at the sea and the mountains, the scientist's name came up.

"He's a desktop ecologist," said Fraser. "We bring him out here for twelve hours and I guarantee you we'll be dragging a body back."

In 2000, after Fraser left academia, he and Patterson formed the Polar Oceans Research Group, a nonprofit based in their home on a thirty-four-acre farm in southwestern Montana's breathtaking Ruby Valley. Their modest, century-old house sits at 5,000 feet and has panoramic views in all directions of the snow-covered peaks of the Tobacco Root, Ruby, Pioneer, and Highland ranges. Their county, Madison, is nearly half the size of New Jersey but has no stoplights, not quite seven thousand inhabitants, and a population density of two people per square mile.

Polly Penhale, the former program director of Antarctic biology and medicine at the National Science Foundation, told me that Fraser's single-minded dedication to his Antarctic work was a throwback to another era. "He's part of a generation of scientists we won't see again," she said. "How many people would give up their personal lives for four to five months a year for all those years?"

Hugh Ducklow, who heads a major long-term study at Palmer Station and is director of the Ecosystems Center, Marine Biological Laboratory, in Woods Hole, Massachusetts, said of Fraser, "When you think about Bill coming here and spending up to half of each year, having your life divided that way—very few people can do that. A lot of the work is really tedious and you have to have a vision of where this is going. He is also pretty stubborn—he knows what he wants to do and he is not really deterred from doing it. And he has a wonderful feel for the ecosystem. It goes beyond an intellectual approach. He has a connection to the ecosystem, which sounds kind of mystical, but it's true."

Fraser's devotion to the Antarctic has not been without its costs, both personal and professional. In one twenty-year streak, he spent three to five months every year in Antarctica—and occasionally seven or eight—as his first wife and two daughters stayed at home in the States. His prolonged absences were a source of friction in the marriage, which eventually ended in divorce, and his relationship with one of his daughters has been strained. (Once, as he was preparing to depart for another season at Palmer, one of his daughters told him, "Mommy says you love penguins more than you love me.")

"This is what I had decided to do with my life, and there was this very strong pull to go down there," said Fraser. "It was the only way to do the work I wanted to do, and I thought that with my first wife, it was understood from the beginning that this was what I was interested in. I might be away for four months, but then I was home for a long period. But it was a source of friction."

As I came to know Fraser better and read more about earlier generations of Antarctic explorers and scientists, I began to see how seamlessly he fit into the tradition of people who have devoted their lives to the continent. It was not only that he had committed himself to studying Antarctica at great personal cost, that he was a steady leader in the field, that he relished the sense of living on the edge, and that his work there was the defining aspect of his life; like many earlier explorers, he also seemed happiest in Antarctica and felt out of place in fast-paced civilization. I once asked Fraser if he could live in a city. He replied, "No way. I would die there. It's like oil and water. When I have to spend four or five days at a conference in a big city, I wither away. I become lethargic and depressed. It drives me insane. I hate it when I can't see the horizon."

It's no coincidence that Fraser has chosen to spend his life in two places—Montana and Antarctica—with plenty of horizon. In Montana, he and his wife kill virtually all their meat themselves, hunting elk, deer, and antelope in the surrounding mountains and high plains. One of Fraser's favorite pastimes is to set off alone into the snowy mountains, pick up the tracks of an elk, stalk it, shoot it, gut and quarter it, and drag it down from the high country.

This alienation from the bustle of civilization is a trait shared by many Antarctic explorers, including Ernest Shackleton. After his Antarctic expeditions, Shackleton was often unhappy back in England. He, too, chafed at city life and—because he was often short of money—conjured up financial schemes that rarely came to fruition. Alfred Lansing, whose book *Endurance* remains the best account of the legendary expedition of the same name, observed that in civilization Shackleton "was a Percheron draft horse harnessed to a child's wagon cart. But in the Antarctic—here was a burden that challenged every atom of his strength." In a letter to his wife in 1919, Shackleton wrote, "Sometimes I think I am no good at anything but being away in the wilds just with men."

THE *LAURENCE M. GOULD*—named for the American geologist and polar explorer who was second-in-command during Richard Byrd's first Antarctic expedition, in 1928–30—left the dock shortly before eleven A.M. on Saturday, October 22, in a cold, light rain. Chartered by the U.S. National Science Foundation's Office of Polar Programs to bring personnel and supplies to Palmer and conduct oceanographic studies in Antarctic waters, the *Gould* was a homely, snub-nosed, 230-foot vessel with a red-orange hull, high sides from amidships forward, and a creamy yellow superstructure.

We initially headed northeast, navigating the Strait of Magellan on our way to the Atlantic Ocean. Several species of seabirds—including southern fulmars, black-browed albatrosses, southern giant petrels, and Cape, or pintado, petrels—followed the ship. Commerson's dolphins—with a predominately white body, black head, and a black saddle from the dorsal fin to the tail—hurtled toward us through the flat waters of the strait, then frolicked in our bow wake before disappearing. Low, light-brown hills flanked the placid waterway, which was more than a dozen miles wide in places. Occasionally we would pass a solitary sheep station on the coastline of Tierra del Fuego, and in the evening we steamed past clusters of yellow oil-drilling platforms. The skies began to clear and the sun set spectacularly over a dark sea, gilding the clouds with brilliant gold and orange hues.

The next morning, the *Gould* was moving toward Antarctica at 13 knots in a calm and sunny south Atlantic, the rugged headlands and snowy summits of Tierra del Fuego a dozen or two miles off our starboard side. The air temperature was 45°F, and thick, white clouds, their undersides reflecting the blue-gray sea, drifted across the sky. Black-browed albatrosses skimmed over the water, gracefully riding the winds. With a wingspan of about seven feet and a white body and dark overwing, the black-browed albatross, belongs—as do most of the seabirds we would see over the South Atlantic and the Southern Ocean—to the order Procellariiformes; the name is derived from the Latin *procella,* for storm. All expertly ride the winds and air currents, none more beautifully than the wandering albatrosses, with a wingspan reaching eleven feet. We would soon see several in the Drake Passage.

I spent hours watching the aerial displays of the seabirds that accompanied us on our four-day voyage to Palmer Station, with only the species of Procellariiformes changing. At one point, close to forty charcoal-gray, immature southern giant petrels tailed our ship, the group performing an endless round in which the birds hovered and glided alongside the *Gould,* slowly made their way forward by changing the angle of their wings with scarcely a flicker of muscle movement, peeled off, wheeled, and rode the winds far behind the boat before rejoining the slow procession to the bow.

At midafternoon on the second day of the voyage, the *Gould* motored into the Le Maire Strait, which separates Tierra del Fuego from Isla de los Estados, a remote Argentinean outpost with a small navy base. As the wind rose and whitecaps filled the Lemaire, the Isla de los Estados passed a few miles off our port side. Although the day was sunny, the island looked forbidding—a windswept outcropping of fawn-colored hills and forests, with sheer rock cliffs looming over the sea. It was our last good view of South America—and of trees.

Later that evening, east of Cape Horn, we entered the Drake Passage, which separates South America from the Antarctic Peninsula. Like the rest of the Southern Ocean, the Drake Passage is a harrowing body of water, with waves that regularly reach thirty feet and occasionally tower ten stories high. The passage was discovered by Sir Francis Drake in September 1578, after his ship, the *Golden Hind,* was blown south from the mouth of the Strait of Magellan in a storm. The ship was carried into the passage as far as 57° S, about a hundred miles below Cape Horn, where, Drake wrote, "the Atlanticke Ocean and the South Sea (the Pacific) meete in a most large and free scope."

Drake was one of several English and Dutch seamen who, in the sixteenth and seventeenth centuries, were either blown off course or purposely sailed south of South America and New Zealand in search of a continent at the southern end of the earth. The belief that a great southern landmass existed can be traced back to Aristotle, Pythagoras, and other ancient philosophers and geographers. Aristotle theorized that in order to balance the landmass that was known to exist to the north—which the Greeks called Arctos, since it sat under the northern constellation of the Great Bear, Arctos—there must be land to the south, the Anti-Arctos. Ptolemy, who lived in Egypt in the first and second centuries A.D., labeled the landmass Terra Australis Incognita—the "unknown southern land."

Around A.D. 650, a Polynesian named Ui-te-Rangiora claimed to have sailed so far south that he encountered a frozen ocean. But it was left to the great English mariner Captain James Cook to sail closer to the continent than anyone yet had as he circumnavigated Antarctica during two voyages deep into the Southern Ocean from 1772 to 1775, in the *Resolution* and the *Adventure*. On January 17, 1773, Cook became the first person to cross the Antarctic Circle, sailing to within eighty-one miles of the continent. A year later, on January 30, 1774, he ventured farther south than anyone before—to 71°10′ S, where he reported in his journal that thick sea ice prevented his ship from proceeding "one Inch farther South."

Cook and his men never actually laid eyes on the continent, but they ceaselessly encountered the icebergs that had fractured off its glaciers and ice shelves. The great naval officer correctly surmised that the abundant ice had to originate from a southern landmass. He spent months in the Southern Ocean, his expedition's small wooden ships frequently battered by gales as they dodged uncharted reefs and countless icebergs. Maneuvering in appalling weather on decks and rigging slick with ice, the officers and crews of the *Resolution* and the *Adventure* lived with near-constant menace. Perhaps better than any explorer who came after him, Cook understood that humans in Antarctica were trespassers in an alien land.

In February 1775, the captain was nearing the end of his second lengthy voyage in Antarctic waters, and the biting chill coming off the frigid sea was a perpetual reminder of the swift death they could expect should their vessels sink. "The risque one runs in exploring a coast, in these unknown and icy seas, is so very great that I can be bold enough to say that no man will ever venture farther than I have done; and that the lands which may lie to the south may never be explored," wrote Cook. "Thick fogs, snow storms, intense cold, and every other thing that can render navigation dangerous, must be encountered, and these difficulties are greatly heightened by the inexpressibly horrid aspect of the country; a country doomed by nature never once to feel the warmth of the sun's rays, but to lie buried in everlasting snow and ice."

Ernest Shackleton experienced the Drake Passage at its worst, voyaging in a twenty-three-foot, sail-powered whaleboat across its eastern reaches and then farther into the Southern Ocean, to the island of South Georgia. Shackleton and five other men from the wrecked *Endurance* made the eight-hundred-mile trip in winter in sixteen days, pulling off one of the greatest small-boat journeys of all time. This feat led to the rescue of the remainder of the crew, who were surviving on seals and seabirds on Elephant Island, off the northern end of the Antarctic Peninsula. The most dangerous moment of the journey came one night at midnight, with Shackleton at the tiller. To the south and southwest, Shackleton saw something white that he at first mistook for a break in the clouds. He soon realized, however, that the pale streak on the horizon was actually a monster wave bearing down on them. He described what happened next in his book *South*:

> During twenty-six years' experience of the ocean in all its moods I had not encountered a wave so gigantic. It was a mighty upheaval of the ocean, a thing quite-apart from the big white-capped seas that had been our tireless enemies for many days. I shouted, "For God's sake, hold on! It's got us." Then came a moment of suspense that seemed drawn out into hours. White surged the foam of the breaking sea around us. We felt our boat lifted and flung forward like a cork in breaking surf. We were in a seething chaos of tortured water; but somehow the boat lived through it, half full of water, sagging to the dead weight and shuddering under the blow.

The Drake's towering waves are formed because, as author Nathaniel Philbrick has noted, the passage "is the only place on earth where the wind can circulate around the entire globe without ever touching land." And just as the winds blow unimpeded, so, too, do the waves build, driven by strong westerlies. The locked-in weather pattern of Antarctica—in which a never-ending series of low-pressure systems circulates clockwise around a massive high-pressure system centered over the South Pole—means that the passage and the Southern Ocean are subject to gale after gale.

Antarctica's uniqueness—defined, above all, by its enormous continental ice sheet, three miles thick in places—is inextricably linked with the insulating power of the Southern Ocean. Antarctica is a citadel of

cold, and the Southern Ocean is its moat. The continent became isolated at the bottom of the world roughly 30 million years ago, when the
Antarctic Peninsula parted company with the southern tip of South
America and began settling into its current position. (About 180 million to 200 million years ago, Antarctica, South America, Africa, Australia, and New Zealand all were joined together in the great southern
supercontinent, Gondwana, but eventually the continents began moving apart, or rifting. Africa was the first to go, about 170 million years
ago, with the Indian subcontinent rifting apart from Antarctica about
120 million years ago. Australia and Antarctica separated about 35
million to 40 million years ago, followed by the separation of South
America and Antarctica, which took place over a long period, perhaps
30 million to 35 million years ago. Gradually, those two continents
worked their way into their present positions, opening up the Drake
Passage and leaving Antarctica surrounded by water.)

With its polar position depriving it of the sun's strongest rays, and
with the Southern Ocean insulating it from moderating influences
from the north, the vast Antarctic ice sheet began to form, probably
reaching its current extent about 10 million to 15 million years ago.
Over the past 10 million years or so, Antarctica's ice sheets—roughly
divided into east and west—have grown and shrunk, thickened and
thinned. Today, those sheets form one of the earth's most remarkable
features: a great cloak of frozen precipitation, with an average thickness of 7,500 feet and a depth in some places of 16,000 feet, covering an
area one and a half times the size of the United States, including Alaska.
Scientists estimate that 90 percent of the planet's ice and 70 to 85 percent of its fresh water are locked up in Antarctica's ice sheets, which
cover virtually the entire continent except for thin strips of rocky coast.
The Antarctic ice cap is so large, and reflects so much heat back into the
atmosphere, that it plays a significant role in cooling the earth. Were all
that ice to melt, sea levels would rise by more than 200 feet, displacing
at least half of the earth's population.

Antarctica is so much colder than the Arctic (the lowest temperature ever recorded on earth was −128.64°F, at the Russian Antarctic
base Vostok, on July 21, 1983) for a simple reason: Antarctica is a

continent surrounded by water, while the Arctic is water—the Arctic Ocean—surrounded by land. The continental climates of Alaska, Canada, Russia, and Scandinavia temper the Arctic's cold, while the Southern Ocean cuts off Antarctica from moderating influences. The large temperature and air-pressure discrepancy between the Antarctic and the surrounding warmer waters of the Atlantic, Pacific, and Indian oceans sets off the procession of lows that spin ceaselessly around the continent and roil the Southern Ocean.

THIS TIME, HOWEVER, the passengers aboard the *Laurence M. Gould* had nothing to fear. On this late-October crossing, we had won the Drake lottery and could expect to experience what veteran Antarctic seamen dismissively call "Drake Lake." We had managed to hit the Drake not long after the passage of one low-pressure system, and the next low, as if on a timetable, was five hundred miles to the west and would not clobber the Drake until after we had sailed through. We had threaded the eye of the needle, which is not to say that all was dead calm. Shortly after emerging from the protection of Cape Horn and nearby islands, I lay in my bunk in the bow and could feel the power of oceanic swells rocking the top-heavy, graceless *Gould*.

The next morning, I awoke to a sparkling day and reasonably gentle seas. On deck, the sun bouncing off the cobalt-blue water was blinding. A light wind stirred up whitecaps, and low, widely spaced rollers rippled over the Drake from the west. Squadrons of Cape petrels—jaunty, pigeon-sized birds with distinctive white splotches on charcoal-gray upper wings—escorted the ship, hovering just off the sides of the *Gould* and dipping low over the water. One of the *Gould*'s two engines had died during the night, and the vessel chugged along at about 8 knots, churning a turquoise wake.

I took full advantage of the weather, spending hours on deck, mesmerized by the passage of the swells and the changing hues of the water in cloud and sun. I never saw another ship, which only heightened the sense that we were traversing a boundary that led to the most inaccessible region on the planet. Most of the scientists on board were participating in an exhaustive study of climate change along the western Antarctic Peninsula. Launched in 1990, this project is part of the Long Term Ecological Research (LTER) Network, an effort by the National Science Foundation to chronicle environmental changes—many of them driven by rising temperatures—in twenty-six important ecosystems in the United States, Puerto Rico, Antarctica, and Polynesia. Palmer Station is one of two LTER sites in Antarctica, the other being near McMurdo Station, on the Ross Sea. Fraser had been a member of the Palmer LTER from the beginning, his work focused on Adélie penguins and other so-called apex seabird predators at the top of the food chain.

Among those on board was Hugh Ducklow, the lead scientist on the Palmer LTER team and an expert on marine microbes; Langdon Quetin, an LTER scientist and an expert on Antarctic krill from the University of California, Santa Barbara; and Susan G. Trivelpiece, who was not part of the Palmer LTER team but who, together with her husband, Wayne Z. Trivelpiece, had long been studying Adélie, chinstrap, and gentoo penguins on King George Island, at the northern tip of the Antarctic Peninsula.

The community of Adélie penguin researchers from the States was tiny, consisting of four scientists: the Trivelpieces, working out of a small, government-funded station on King George Island; Fraser, based 250 miles to the south at Palmer Station; and David G. Ainley, who studied the far larger—and far more southerly—Adélie colonies on the Ross Sea. These three principal research teams had been working in Antarctica since the mid-1970s, funded by the National Science Foundation or the National Oceanic and Atmospheric Administration. Although the coterie of U.S. Adélie penguin scientists was small, it was not necessarily close-knit. Fraser and Wayne Trivelpiece had experienced a falling-out and were no longer on speaking terms, a rupture that may have had as much to do with scientific rivalry as with a clash of strong personalities. Beneath his affable exterior, Fraser possessed a certain reserve, and I sensed that this was not a man you would want to cross.

By the evening of October 24, as we passed 58° S, the air and sea temperatures began to drop. Below us, the Drake Passage was two miles deep.

I WENT TO bed in one world and woke up in another. During our second night at sea, we had crossed the largest and most abrupt ecological frontier on earth: the Antarctic Convergence. North of the convergence, the weather we encountered and the birds following our boat were typical of the far south Atlantic in spring, with the sea and air temperatures both hovering around 42°F. South of the convergence, we had entered the realm of the Antarctic, with the air and water temperatures around 32° to 34°F. On deck it was markedly chillier; the air, as Captain Cook noted after crossing the convergence in 1772, "begins to be pinching cold." The fair skies of the South Atlantic had given way to heavy gray clouds and spitting snow. As we moved through the convergence and deeper into Antarctic waters, we began to see small icebergs. No longer did albatrosses follow our boat. Now blue petrels and Antarctic prions were in the air, and chinstrap penguins arced in and out of the sea.

Crossing the convergence by boat is a stirring transition; in a matter of hours, the world to which I had grown accustomed gave way to the most alien and beautiful place on the planet.

At its most basic level, the Antarctic Convergence is the zone where the frigid ring of water and air around Antarctica meets the temperate world. More precisely, the convergence is a marine boundary where ice-cold Antarctic waters collide with warmer waters and sink below them. Dropping deep under the Atlantic, Pacific, and Indian oceans, this nutrient-rich Antarctic Bottom Water then spreads throughout the globe, affecting ocean currents worldwide and leading to cold, rich upwellings of nutrients that foster tremendous production of plankton and marine life. Two of the world's richest currents—the Benguela, off West Africa, and the Humboldt, off western South America—begin with the frigid waters flowing out from Antarctica, sinking, and rising again. These icy currents carry an abundance of protein, which supports penguin species living in warm climes in Africa and South America, including the Galápagos penguin, which lives on the equator and whose breeding cycle is based on the arrival of fish and squid riding cold currents. Although only two truly polar penguin species exist, the Adélie and the emperor, the remaining sixteen to nineteen penguin species (debate continues as to whether various populations, such as the little blue penguin in New Zealand and Australia, constitute one or more species) are nevertheless tied to Antarctica through the diffusion of its cold waters.

The Antarctic Convergence, also known as the Antarctic Polar Front, is generally located between 55° S and 60° S. But currents carrying great streams of frigid water from the Ross and Weddell seas, which both contain massive ice shelves, can push the convergence to 50° S. Whatever the convergence envelops, including South Georgia Island and numerous subantarctic island groups, it transforms into a world of ice.

Above all, as biologist David Campbell writes in *The Crystal Desert*, the convergence is "perhaps the longest and most important biological barrier on earth, as formidable as any mountain range or desert." On each side of the convergence are markedly different species, whether of phytoplankton, or krill, or penguins, or fish. But the greatest difference is this: North of the convergence there is a far wider variety of species, but south of this frontier, in Antarctica's hugely productive waters, are staggering numbers of birds, seals, and krill. No one knows for sure, but some scientists estimate that at the height of summer, approximately 75 million penguins and other seabirds nest and feed in Antarctic and subantarctic waters. The most common penguin in the region, the chinstrap, is estimated to number 7.5 million pairs. About 1 million pairs of chinstraps nest on Zavodovski Island alone, in the South Sandwich chain. So many seabirds have traditionally congregated around South Georgia that the dean of Southern Ocean ornithologists, Robert Cushman Murphy—visiting the island in 1912 on a whaling ship—described petrels and albatrosses "filling the air like the snowflakes of a blizzard." They were drawn, he said, by the "new butchery" of the island's then-thriving whaling industry.

In addition to seabirds are tens of millions of seals, mainly crabeaters. And then there is the two-inch-long shrimplike creature that feeds nearly everything in the Antarctic: *Euphausia superba*, the Antarctic krill. Billions of these crustaceans populate the Southern Ocean, with some experts contending that more *Euphausia superba* exist on earth than any other species of living thing. Great rafts of Antarctic krill, extending several miles across and six hundred feet below the surface, have been spotted in the Southern Ocean, tinting the sea pink. That abundance may be a thing of the past, however; with winter sea ice cover shrinking in parts of Antarctica, some studies have concluded that the ice-dependent *Euphausia superba* is already in decline.

Antarctica, the subantarctic islands, and the Southern Ocean are the marine equivalent of the now-lost terrestrial paradises of three centuries ago: America's Great Plains, with their millions of bison, and Africa's Serengeti, with countless beasts of all descriptions. To stand on the shores of Baily Head on Deception Island and watch 100,000 pairs of chinstrap penguins going about their business is to witness a display of nature's unfettered fecundity. The chinstraps return en masse from their feeding grounds, their porpoising forms exploding in and out of the water like the spattering of gunfire. They then waddle in procession off the black sand beach and march into a vast amphitheater, its steep slopes—rising hundreds of feet—covered with nesting penguins. Observing this chinstrap metropolis leads to an almost euphoric appreciation of the bounty of the wild world when left unmolested by man.

BY THE EVENING of October 25, we had nearly traversed the Drake Passage and were so close to the South Shetland Islands that Captain Robert Verret II was on deck, speaking on his cell phone by connecting with a relay tower from a nearby Chilean base. The weather was fickle, with bands of fog and snow squalls giving way to breaks in the clouds and glimpses of blue sky. At one point, a beam of sunlight pierced the overcast and bounced off the flat, silver sea. Soon, however, we were back in thick fog, with snow piling up on the anchor chains. Out of the mist, two jagged icebergs, several stories high, drifted past on our starboard side, emanating a faint, glacial blue color. Then, just as the gloomy evening light was fading, I saw, to port, an icy mass shrouded in clouds: King George Island.

These days, traveling in steel-hulled ships outfitted with sonar, radar, Global Positioning System satellites, Internet, and e-mail, the visitor doesn't approach Antarctica with foreboding. High technology and reliable nautical charts have banished the ignorance that once made sailing in these waters a near-death experience. The pervasive sense of peril that dogged earlier expeditions is gone. Nevertheless, to first catch sight of the continent on a foul day, taking in only a small portion of the impressive rock-and-ice superstructure hidden in the clouds, still stirs a primal sense of unease. On such a day, it takes a very small leap of imagination to appreciate the feeling of doom that swept over many early explorers as they maneuvered through treacherous seas in tiny ships and beheld massive, ice-draped mountains, their upper reaches cloaked in mist and clouds.

We dropped off Sue Trivelpiece and her team on the shores of Admiralty Bay, on King George island, where the Trivelpieces have, since 1976, documented the same downward trends in Adélie penguin populations that Bill Fraser has. The next morning, I awoke to the sound of ice scraping and clanging against the hull of the *Laurence M. Gould*. Leaning out of my bunk, I looked through the porthole at a placid, lead-gray sea on which floated scattered sheets of sea ice and rafts of sky-blue icebergs, sloughed off by the glaciers and ice streams that cloaked the Antarctic Peninsula to our port side and a chain of islands to starboard. Wheeling and gliding over the ice-strewn channel were a dozen lesser snow petrels, pure-white creatures fifteen inches long and with a thirty-inch wingspan.

We were at 64° S, entering the Croker Passage. Walking on deck, I looked at a scene composed of shades of gray: the darker hue of the sea; a low, smoke-colored ceiling of clouds; and, farther ahead, a lighter curtain of gray where a snow shower obscured the horizon. The band of clouds cut off the higher elevations of the islands—Liège to starboard, Two Hummock to port—leaving open to view only the vivid white ice fields that streamed over sheer black rock into the sea. The water was 31°F, the air 29. Large, wet flakes of snow drifted out of the sky.

A few hundred yards in front of us, a pod of eight to ten Antarctic minke whales surged through the water, their black backs arcing out of the sea before they dove in search of krill. The second smallest of the baleen whales—which feed by using hornlike plates to strain prey from seawater—Antarctic minkes can grow to thirty-five feet in length and typically weigh five to ten tons. They are the only whales still hunted in Antarctica, with the Japanese killing hundreds a year for alleged scientific purposes.

Around eleven A.M., we steamed into the Gerlache Strait, a major inside passage, roughly one hundred miles long, that separates the Palmer Archipelago from the Antarctic Peninsula. The strait was named for the Belgian adventurer Adrien de Gerlache de Gomery, who explored and mapped the area in January and February 1898 before sailing another five hundred miles south and—much to the consternation of most members of his expedition—getting stuck in the pack ice for thirteen months. Accompanying de Gerlache were two notable—and indispensible— men: Frederick Cook and Roald Amundsen, the Norwegian who would eventually be the first to the South Pole.

On a fair day, the narrow Gerlache Strait offers some of the most striking panoramas on the Antarctic Peninsula, with the glaciated peninsular mountain range—an extension of the Andes—dropping straight into the sea. But the view this morning was a murky half mile of fog, snow, and ice. On the bridge, Captain Verret—a forty-year-old Cajun with wavy dark hair flowing to his shoulders—was guiding his Louisiana-built vessel through a field of small icebergs.

Toward the bottom of the strait, at around five in the evening, the dismal weather dispersed. To the west, the thick cloud cover disintegrated, revealing swaths of vivid blue sky over the mountains of Anvers Island. Buoyed by the improving weather and excited at the prospect of soon arriving at Palmer Station, scientists and support staff came on deck to photograph and gaze upon the shifting patterns of sun and shadow on the fields of snow and ice encrusting the mountains. I have never been to a place where the appearance of a ray of sun or a streak of blue sky so completely alters the landscape—and a person's mood.

As we neared the end of the Neumayer Channel—an even narrower passage named by de Gerlache for the German scientist and polar explorer Georg von Neumayer—the leaden clouds returned. The Neumayer, which cuts between Anvers and Wiencke islands, is little more than a mile wide in places, and the looming mountains, lost in the clouds, were an eerie presence. The *Gould* plowed through the still waters of the channel, where Adélie penguins stood on icebergs and their cousins, the slightly larger gentoo penguins, porpoised in the sea. Several gentoos swam near the ship. I leaned over the bow railing and watched as they zigzagged underwater with astonishing speed, executing sharp turns in a fraction of a second and, alarmed by the passage of the *Gould,* bursting away, torpedo-like, leaving a trail of bubbles.

Captain Verret, speaking over the radio with Palmer Station manager Robert Farrell about the wind that was causing the Gould to run late, explained, in a heavy Cajun accent, "We got about fifteen knots comin' out da nordeast. Come on, buddy, you know ahm trawin' to git dar as quick as pos'ble." One reason for his sense of urgency was the party at the station scheduled for that night, to celebrate the relief of the winter's skeleton crew. Large quantities of alcohol would be consumed, the hard liquor served over glacial ice thousands of years old.

Around six P.M., the *Gould* emerged from the Neumayer Channel and entered the Bismarck Strait, which itself opens up to the Southern Ocean on the Pacific side of the Antarctic Peninsula. Palmer Station lay about a dozen miles to the west. Almost immediately, the ship encountered a field of loosely packed sea ice that stretched to the horizon. Cutting its speed from 9 to 7 knots, the *Gould,* with its steel-reinforced hull, pushed its way through the ice, muscling aside jigsaw-like pieces ranging in size from a manhole cover to a basketball court.

The formation of a great skirt of sea ice around Antarctica in the austral winter is one of the defining features of the continent and represents the most extensive seasonal change on earth. At the end of the Southern Hemisphere's summer, in February, the ring of sea ice girding the Antarctic continent shrinks to between 1 million and 1.5 million square miles. Seven months later, at the end of the austral winter in September, the circle of sea ice around the continent has expanded about 5 to 7 times, to between 7 million and 7.5 million square miles— more than doubling the size of the continent itself. Much of the sea ice is about three feet thick, but sea ice that has formed over many years can reach thicknesses of more than forty feet.

As the *Gould* plowed its way toward Palmer Station, the critical role that Antarctica's seasonal sea ice plays in the immense richness of the Southern Ocean was visible all around the ship. Surrounding us was pack ice breaking up with the rising spring temperatures. The ship's passage through the pack fractured the sheets, churning up a light brown substance encased in the ice. This was a mass of diatoms— single-celled algae that grow in profusion in the icy, nutrient-rich waters of the Southern Ocean and that form the basis of the entire food chain. In winter, the diatoms survive under the ice, providing food for juvenile krill, which scrape phytoplankton from the underside of the pack. In the spring and summer, as the ice recedes and disappears, the strengthening sun stimulates the growth of diatoms and other phyto-plankton in the water, creating blooms so immense that their cloudy signature is visible in satellite photographs from space. The krill feed on the plankton, and nearly all the seabirds, seals, and whales eat the krill.

The color of café au lait, the diatom-filled ice resembled mud-flecked floes during the breakup of a northern river in spring. To the stern, in the channel carved by the *Gould,* rafts of diatoms splashed against the ice, our trail resembling a truck's as it runs down a dirt road in Ver-mont during the spring thaw. Looking out upon this endless expanse of sea ice, I found it difficult to believe that, in this region of Antarctica, the winter pack was steadily shrinking, with troubling implications for the krill and all that eat them.

Just in front of us, about a dozen crabeater seals—inhabitants of the pack ice—burst out of a lead in the water at the approach of the ship and slithered across slabs of ice. Often colored a light taupe, weighing on average about 500 pounds, and growing to eight feet in length, crab-eaters account for more than 50 percent of all the seals, walruses, and sea lions on earth. Indeed, with their numbers variously estimated from about ten million to seventy million, the crabeater is one of the most common large mammals on the planet. It lives and breeds in the Antarctic and subantarctic, and contrary to its name—bestowed upon it by early explorers—it subsists not on crabs but almost entirely on Antarctic krill. The marooned, icebound expeditions from the heroic age of Antarctic exploration, including Shackleton's and de Gerlache's, survived in part by eating crabeater seals and penguins. During my time at Palmer Station, the long-snouted seals were common in the early season, when the sea ice was thick. As the pack ice disappeared, so, too, did the crabeaters.

Shortly before eight P.M., as the *Gould* drew within a half dozen miles of Palmer Station, the sea ice became so tightly packed that it seemed possible to walk across the floes to the base. Imperceptibly, the atmosphere assumed the ethereal hues found only in polar regions. To stern, the weather remained somber, but in front of us, where lighter clouds covered the sky, the tableau was a mix of pale blues and whites. On the western horizon, the underside of the clouds glowed a faint white, a phenomenon known as "ice blink," in which the color of sea ice is reflected back onto the clouds. The air everywhere seemed suffused with an otherworldly blue: the sea ice in front of us was tinged blue, the undersides of the clouds between the *Gould* and Palmer Station radiated the color of a robin's egg, and over Anvers Island the Marr Ice Piedmont was backlit by iridescent lavender.

Gradually, to the west, a band of clear sky appeared on the horizon and turned gold as the sun set. Silhouetted against the yellow-orange streak and embedded in the pack ice was a profusion of large icebergs in fanciful forms. One resembled a ziggurat. Another was shaped like a mesa. Yet another had the outline of a supertanker, and a fourth looked like a Gothic cathedral.

At eight-thirty, the *Gould* headed into ice-clogged Arthur Harbor. Ahead, in the dusky light, on a narrow spit of land, sat Palmer Station. We glided past Torgersen Island, off our port side, and on the blanket of snow on the island's southern half were two small, black circles: a few dozen Adélie penguins, waiting to nest.

Most of the *Gould*'s passengers—there to replace about a dozen of Palmer Station's small winter contingent and launch the summer science programs—were on deck now, in high spirits at the prospect of disembarking. The base was deep in snow, and most of the winter staff had come to meet the *Gould* at the tiny dock, with its three steel shipping containers and two Volkswagen-sized, capsule-shaped, black rubber bumpers. Many aboard the *Gould* waved and yelled to the people on shore; Palmer was a tiny station, and its scientists and staff were like family, reuniting in Antarctica year after year.

After three attempts to drive a wedge through the ice of Hero Inlet, Captain Verret finally docked his ship. We walked down the gangplank to much hugging and fanfare. As the neon-blue glow behind the Marr Ice Piedmont slowly faded, we carried our gear off the ship and into the two small dormitory buildings. Peter Horne, Jennifer Blum, and I hauled some equipment into the birders' hut, a tent set up just outside the station's corrugated-steel laboratory building.

The party that night did not disappoint. Around two in the morning, I wandered out to the wide, metal-grated veranda just off the station's bar. The thumping of music from the bar's voluminous, computerized playlist washed over the base through the cold Antarctic air. Someone shut the sliding glass door to the bar, and I was alone, sipping bourbon over chunks of a glacier. The balcony commanded a fine view of the Bismarck Strait and the Southern Ocean.

Leaning on the balcony railing, I gazed at a scene that was frozen in all directions. The ocean was an unbroken mosaic of sea ice slabs of all sizes, dotted with icebergs. The nearby islands, where the Adélies had come to breed, lay under a deep cloak of snow. Light clouds covered the sky, and through them glimmered the hint of a coming sunrise to the southwest. On that night, and for months to come, darkness never fully descended over this corner of Antarctica, the round-the-clock light illuminating a panorama of glaciers, icebergs, mountains, and sea.

CHAPTER 2

PENGUINS

All the world loves a penguin. I think it is because in many respects they are like ourselves, and in some respects what we should like to be. Had we but half their physical courage none could stand against us . . . [They are] fighting against bigger odds than any other bird, and fighting always with the most gallant pluck.

—Apsley Cherry-Garrard,
Terra Nova expedition, 1910–13

Although it was no more than a half mile from Palmer Station, Torgersen Island might as well have been on the other side of the continent, given the ice piled up in Arthur Harbor. Fraser's birding team travels to the Adélie rookeries—located on five islands within three miles of the station and on several others within fifteen miles—in small rubber Zodiac boats that cannot penetrate thick ice. And the jumble of floes blanketing the sea between us and the penguin rookeries left the impression that we would be confined to the station for days.

But as our first full day at Palmer Station progressed, signs of hope appeared. The westerly winds that had driven all that ice against Anvers Island switched to the northeast and picked up in intensity as the day wore on, pushing the broken pack ice away from the Marr Ice Piedmont and out to sea at a brisk pace. Smaller icebergs were shoved out, too, sailing by like schooners. Steel-gray clouds intermittently released wet snow that blew sideways. I cheered the rout of the sea ice, even though the force banishing it—high winds—would also prevent us from motoring to the Adélie rookeries. (Boating is prohibited when winds exceed 25 miles per hour, a wise restriction considering that capsizing in the Southern Ocean around Palmer, where water temperatures hover around 34°F in summer, can lead to swift death.) Still, sea ice is a far more implacable force than wind, which can drop in an instant, and I was delighted as it howled above 40 miles per hour, driving whitecaps across the pewter-colored waters of Arthur Harbor.

By evening, it looked like our time had come. Abruptly, the winds dropped so sharply that they barely registered on the anemometer. Our three-person team donned field clothes and put a Zodiac in the water; we were just about to step into it when the wind came up again, in a few minutes rising from 2 miles per hour, to 15, to 35. Gusts soon surpassed 45 as the wind direction careened from all points of the compass. We took off our rain pants and windbreakers and forsook all hope of fieldwork. Later, Langdon Quetin informed me that there was a name for such a seductive respite during a Palmer Station gale: sucker hole. Many a greenhorn team had leapt into one of these, only to be quickly beaten back to base—soaked, frozen, and chastened.

Wind gusts reached 51 miles per hour that evening, playing a symphony to which I grew quite attached at Palmer: the snapping of flags, their clasps clanging wildly on the aluminum pole; the heaving of the walls of the birding team's work tent; and the moaning and rattling of my bedroom windows as a storm flung itself against the dormitory.

Unable to get to the penguins, after dinner I grabbed a powerful spotting scope and, carrying it to the balcony outside the galley, trained it on some of the Adélie colonies on Torgersen, a roughly circular island about four hundred yards in diameter. It was a forlorn scene: a lowering sky; the air filled with fine snow being propelled off the glacier by the gale; the dark, agitated waters of the harbor; and, just offshore, the receding band of jumbled sea ice. The penguins were hunkered down. Many lay on the snow, facing north, into the wind. Others stood. Occasionally, when the wind eased slightly, a few penguins would engage in the so-called ecstatic display, a territorial and mating behavior in which the Adélie points his beak skyward, flaps his flippers up and down, and emits a long call.

I could see no bare ground; Torgersen and, beyond it, the penguin island of Litchfield were blanketed in snow, only the steepest portions of their ridgelines revealing the black of basalt and diorite. Viewing this bleak scene through the wind-buffeted scope filled me with admiration for the Adélies, whose stubborn character was a match for the environment that at the moment was pummeling them with a robust spring storm.

Three days after I arrived at Palmer Station, the forces that had conspired against us working in the field finally stood down. The wind quit. So did the snow and rain. The cloud ceiling lifted slightly. The barometer rose. The station's satellite weather service showed a large, cloudless gap opening between the two comma-shaped low-pressure systems churning up the western Antarctic Peninsula—one just passing us, the other well to our south. We had a lot of fieldwork to do, as that year's ship schedule had brought us to Palmer later than usual. And so, shortly after breakfast on the last day of October, the time had finally come to pay a visit to the Adélie penguins.

Not even a faint breeze blew as we jumped into our Zodiac and motored the short distance to Torgersen Island. Arthur Harbor was a mirror, its surface reflecting the crumbling, pitted cerulean-blue face of the Marr Ice Piedmont and the rapidly dispersing clouds overhead. Such perfect stillness was a rare thing at Palmer Station, and it presaged many calm, windless days ahead that season, a weather pattern that Palmer veterans said was unlike any they had seen before.

As we tied up our boat on Torgersen's rocky shore and walked the short distance to the penguins, I was struck first by the depth of the snow. Initially we tried to walk without snowshoes, but we soon found that we were postholing up to our knees and groins, the snow inside our imprints tinged a faint shade of blue.

The Adélies were arrayed on the gently sloping north side of Torgersen Island, an archipelago of dark shapes on an expanse of white. As I walked up an incline and the Adélie colonies opened up before me, I was impressed by the purity and tranquillity of the scene, characteristic of the early season: The snow hid centuries of guano that had accreted at the colonies, and the breasts of most of the Adélies were still a satiny white. For the most part, the birds had already paired off, and everywhere couples stood silently side by side, looking like partners at the start of a square dance. Occasionally one penguin would gracefully bow to its mate, while others would greet each other by issuing full-throated honks and weaving their heads back and forth in a form of Adélie air kiss. Some Adélies had been lying in the snow for so long that the warmth of their bodies had formed a bowl in the snow's surface. As they waited for the snow to melt and nest building to begin, the Adélies dozed in upright and prone positions, the white rings around the dark pupils of their flat eyes gently closing as they drifted off. The birds were rotund and in fine shape, having fattened up in anticipation of the long fast during mating and nest building.

The sound most commonly heard was that of males, often unattached, trying at this late date to attract a mate by performing the ecstatic display, during which the head points heavenward and the penguin fills its lungs and throat like a bagpipe before issuing a braying call in gulping, staccato bursts. As penguin biologists and explorers have observed for more than a century, the ecstatic display—which one French biologist called the *chant de satisfaction*—is contagious. Once one Adélie starts— the ecstatic display is performed mainly by males—the call often spreads to nearby penguins. Soon, the air reverberates with the racket of gulping, trumpeting Adélies.

The two largest colonies on the north side still held 800 and 600 breeding pairs during the 2005–06 season, but this was a mere vestige of the island Fraser had come to know thirty years before, when the Adélie colonies formed one nearly unbroken mass on the island's northern half. (Penguins are always counted as breeding pairs, since the birds are easier to tally by censusing nests at peak egg-laying periods.) The contrast with my first visit to a penguin rookery two years earlier could not have been sharper. (A rookery is a large area where birds breed. Adélie rookeries, often on islands, are made up of individual colonies.) I had arrived then in early January, at the height of summer. The snow had almost disappeared from the islands, many of the chicks were two weeks old, and the rookeries were at their most raucous: Adults trekked to and from the sea as they furiously tried to satisfy their chicks' appetites. The colonies themselves were awash in brick-red guano, which was smeared over young and old penguins alike.

On that occasion, my first close-up view of a penguin came on

Christine Island, when I clambered up from the boat landing over guano-slick rocks, stuck my head over a large boulder, and found myself face-to-face with a small colony of downy chicks and adult Adélies, which still managed to look dignified despite the general squalor of the nesting grounds. In front of me, just feet away, were the quintessential penguins—with the starched white front and officious waddle—whose coloring and bearing have elicited a similar reaction from every explorer or scientist who ever gazed upon an Adélie. "[A] smart and fussy little man in evening clothes," wrote the ornithologist Robert Cushman Murphy, nearly a century ago, "with the tail of the black coat dragging on the ground, and who walks with the roll and swagger of an old salt just ashore from a long voyage."

Two years later, as we walked around the colonies counting penguins, what was surprising was the nonchalance with which these well-studied birds reacted to our presence. The Adélies—named in 1841 by the French explorer Jules-Sébastien-César Dumont d'Urville in honor of his wife, Adèle—paid us little attention as long as we stayed ten feet away. Move closer, however, and you would be subjected to an array of elaborate threat displays, all exhaustively studied by scientists: a wall-eyed stare, or the raising of the feathers on the head into something resembling a flattop haircut. Move closer still and many Adélies would, without hesitation, charge and jam a sharp beak into your leg.

Like much scientific fieldwork, the studies performed by Fraser's birding team involved the patient execution of repetitious tasks. The group's main tools were small counters, the size of a whistle, which we used to tally the number of penguins in various colonies in Palmer's vicinity; the small, yellow, waterproof field notebooks in which we recorded data; a long steel rod to gauge snow depth; plastic calipers to measure the eggs, beaks, and primary feathers of Adélie penguins and other seabirds; a net bag and a scale to weigh eggs and birds; aluminum bands to place on the legs of skuas and giant petrels; and banding pliers. Arguably the most important tool was the counter, for it was the accurate enumeration of thousands of penguins in scores of colonies over dozens of years that told the story of Palmer's Adélies.

On that first day in the field, our goals were simple: to count the penguins in roughly fifteen so-called indicator colonies—spread over three islands—that we would track all season, and to measure the snow depth along well-established transects. The indicator colonies would give Fraser an idea of how representative colonies were faring in the annual struggle to reproduce successfully: how many pairs laid eggs, how many chicks those pairs produced, and how many chicks survived until the end of the season, fledged successfully, and went to sea.

The counting work had grown easier in recent years, for the simple reason that the steep decline in Adélie populations meant that there were many fewer penguins to tally. As we trudged through the snow on that first day, Peter Horne, who had worked with Fraser the past two seasons at Palmer Station, was struck by the sharp decline in penguins from the previous year. Several of the indicator colonies had nearly disappeared. Passing one colony, in which just a handful of nesting Adélies remained, Horne said, "I think we can all agree that we do not need clickers for this one."

As on all the islands, the snow was appreciably deeper on the south side of Torgersen's ridges and hills. This is because prevailing winds blow from the north, sweeping snow away on north-facing terrain and leaving it intact on south-facing territory, in the lee of hills. Where the snow is deep, Adélies do not do well; by the fall of 2005, the northern part of Torgersen Island was home to more than 2,400 breeding pairs, while the south side of the island held 63. Unraveling this south/north, snow/no snow dichotomy—a phenomenon exacerbated by the increase in snowfall along the warming peninsula—would prove to be a key discovery by Fraser.

As the team went about its work, we came across many Adélies in the midst of copulation, a delicate act that requires persistence and good balance on the part of the males. A pair may copulate numerous times in October—overkill, perhaps, but a healthy instinct that vastly improves the likelihood of a fertilized egg. In lovemaking Adélie style, the female lies down as the male mounts her and treads on her back; inexperienced males sometimes slip off, particularly if the colony is awash in guano. With the male shifting his weight from foot to foot, the female gradually raises and fans her tail, exposing her cloaca—the all-purpose opening possessed by all birds, reptiles, and amphibians that is the outlet for the genital, urinary, and intestinal tracts. (The term comes from the Latin word for "sewer.") The female raises her beak and the male lowers his and the pair rapidly tap their beaks together in a prolonged, quivering touch. The male then lowers his cloaca and covers the female's in what is known as the "cloacal kiss." He ejaculates, and in a few seconds the "kiss" is over. The male hops off as the female's tail gradually lowers and closes, her cloaca contracting in rhythmic spasms to draw in his sperm. Often, the male then stands quietly by his partner—a touching act, especially in contrast to the colony around them when other penguins are fighting or breaking into a round of ecstatic displays. With little difference in size between male and female Adélie penguins, the only sure way of quickly identifying a bird's sex is to spot the footprints on the females' backs during mating season.

But with all this lovemaking goes a great deal of fighting—not between mates, but among neighbors and potential suitors. On that first day—and many that followed—we witnessed numerous brawls in which Adélies chased, pecked, and pummeled one another with their flippers. Colony life has its evolutionary advantages, including better defense against predators, the assembling of a critical mass of birds for breeding, and greater ease of finding prey by following fellow colony members to feeding grounds. But with nests often only twenty-five to thirty inches apart from center to center, the close quarters ensure unceasing conflict. Adélies are renowned for their scrappiness, and some fights erupted when a bird strayed from its territory or had to make its way to a nest in the center of a colony, with the trespassing bird skittering rapidly through the colony exposed to a gauntlet of its peers squawking and pecking as it passed.

The more ferocious and prolonged fights occurred when an Adélie returned from the long spring migration to find its mate with another penguin. We witnessed several such battles that first day, with the aggrieved Adélie chasing the usurping penguin for dozens of yards in and out of the colony. Sometimes the penguins ran. Sometimes they tobogganed on their breasts as fast as a man could walk, digging up snow with their flippers as they went. Two Adélies stood and fought, delivering body blows with their flippers that reverberated like the thumping of a stick on a carpet being cleaned. They bounced off each others' chests, ricocheted backward, then took a few stutter steps before colliding again like sumo wrestlers. They pulled each other's beaks, yanked out feathers, and tumbled through the colony, eliciting a cacophony of protesting yelps from their neighbors. In its spreading chaos, the fight resembled a barroom brawl in a Hollywood western.

Like nearly every aspect of the Adélie penguin's life history, these love-triangle brawls have been well studied. Richard L. Penney—one of a handful of devoted twentieth-century Adélie penguin researchers—carried out an intensive, two-year research project on Adélies from 1959 to 1961 at Wilkes Station, a now-defunct base on the opposite side of Antarctica from Palmer Station. Working with Adélies marked by aluminum flipper bands, Penney painstakingly observed the behavior of Adélie penguins, an undertaking that was the basis for his 1964 Ph.D. thesis in zoology at the University of Wisconsin. Over the course of three breeding seasons, Penney placed flipper bands on 1,528 adult Adélies, 66 juveniles, and 217 chicks at Wilkes Station. Living in a small hut amid the rookeries, he logged more than fifteen hundred hours of Adélie observations, only occasionally returning to a nearby base to resupply himself or wait out howling windstorms.

Among the Adélie interactions Penney studied was brawling. He observed ten fights between females, and in seven of the ten cases, the row erupted when a female returned to her former territory to find her mate consorting with another female. (Since males almost always return first in the springtime, these early-season fights tend to involve females whose places have been usurped.)

Penney discovered that the longer the interloping female had been on the nest with the male, the worse the battle when last year's hen returned. If the new female had taken up with the male for less than two days, she would generally surrender her position to the former mate with little fight. But if the new hen had been there for many days, the rows were often fierce.

One of the pioneering students of Adélie penguin behavior was actually a physician, G. Murray Levick, who served as the Royal Navy doctor on Robert Falcon Scott's 1910–13 Terra Nova expedition. While spending a summer on the shores of the Ross Sea at Cape Adare—home to the world's largest Adélie colony, then probably numbering more than 200,000 breeding pairs—Levick undertook a study of Adélie penguin habits and behavior that became the basis for his classic book *Antarctic Penguins*. He witnessed ceaseless mêlées between returning penguins and usurpers on their territories. In anthropomorphizing the Adélies, however, he made the incorrect assumption that the clashes were invariably between rival males.

Levick came across one Adélie that had lost its eye in a clash and others with bloody flipper prints on their white breasts. However, neither he nor most other Adélie observers ever witnessed a fight to the death.

Levick and Penney were members of a small fraternity of twentieth-century penguin researchers who collectively spent years in Antarctica studying Adélies and other penguin species. The group also included the Frenchman Louis Gain, a zoologist and botanist who carried out Adélie and gentoo research not far from Palmer Station during the Second French South Polar Expedition under Jean-Baptiste Charcot, from 1908 to 1910, and William J. L. Sladen, an ornithologist who did pioneering Antarctic penguin studies at midcentury. Fraser's colleague David Ainley was a protégé of Sladen's.

Fraser, too, is a direct descendent of this coterie of earlier Adélie researchers, all of whom shared a willingness to endure harsh conditions for months or years at a time in pursuit of a deeper understanding of this iconic bird. Few, however, have spent as many years working in the field as Fraser and his colleagues David Ainley and Sue and Wayne Trivelpiece. Collectively, they have been studying Adélies and their cousins—chinstrap and gentoo penguins—for more than a century.

WHILE MOST COLONIES on Torgersen Island were still buried under snow in late October, a few on exposed ridges were partially snow-free. There, Adélies were already constructing cup-shaped nests by plucking pebbles from open ground and delicately placing them in a gradually accreting pile. Nest construction could also spark a row, as one Adélie stole pebbles from another. Scientists and explorers have long been amused by—and occasionally censorious of—the pebble thievery that is a hallmark of Adélie colonies. Spend any time observing an Adélie penguin colony and you will see penguins—usually males, since they do most of the nest building—marching up to a neighbor's nest, pilfering a stone, and carting it to his own nest. Sometimes the theft goes unnoticed. Other times it will elicit a peck or a full-fledged chase.

Levick performed an ingenious experiment in 1911 when he painted some nesting pebbles red and wrapped others with green cloth. He placed them in a pile near a colony. In short order the penguins picked up the red pebbles—apparently their favorite color—and then the green ones. Levick watched as the colored pebbles were carried back to Adélie nests, where, through thievery, they were continuously redistributed to new nests throughout the colony. The Adélies also had a fondness for shiny items, snatching tin, glass, and the head of a teaspoon from the expedition's scrap heap and carting these baubles to their nests.

The Adélies' fondness for shiny trinkets and their predilection for squabbling and larceny have led to many comparisons with humans, like this one from the natural historian George Gaylord Simpson: "They fight with their neighbors; steal from each other; quarrel with their wives but also give them gifts of rare stones."

Levick also humanized the pebble larceny, describing guilty-looking Adélies sneaking up to nests and stealing pebble after pebble from unsuspecting penguins incubating eggs. "Here could be seen how much individual character makes for success or failure in the efforts of the penguins to produce and rear their offspring," wrote Levick. "There are vigilant birds, always alert, who never seem to get robbed or molested in any way: these have big high nests, made with piles of stones. Others are unwary and get huffed as a result."

More often than not, however, the widespread pilfering balances out in the end. This was the conclusion reached by Charles Laseron, a member of Sir Douglas Mawson's 1911–14 Australasian Antarctic Expedition, as he watched Adélies engaged in a continual round of stone stealing. "So it went on in an endless cycle, by which none was better off, yet all were evidently convinced that their wealth steadily grew," Laseron wrote in *South with Mawson*.

As our team walked around Torgersen Island, we saw some penguins engaging in the early stages of nest building by lying on their stomachs and scooping out an indentation for a nest using their pink webbed feet. Where the ground was exposed, melting snow mixed with guano from previous years to form the brown gumbo that is a fixture of Adélie colonies. Here, the breasts of some penguins were soiled with brownish-red mire. Elsewhere, however, there was little guano in sight. Many of the Adélies had been on Torgersen for two to three weeks, fasting the entire time. Their digestive tracts were empty, so instead of guano tinted red with krill, the Adélies excreted greenish feces—from the bile in their systems—onto the snow.

By early afternoon, bands of clear sky opened up and the sun occasionally shone. The air remained uncommonly still as we boated to Litchfield Island, just behind Torgersen. Nearly three-quarters of a mile long and a half mile wide, Litchfield—three times the size of Torgersen—is a highly restricted zone because of the rare, deep moss beds that grow on and around its ridges. When Fraser arrived at Palmer in the mid-1970s, the island was home to roughly 900 pairs of Adélies. But that number had steadily dwindled, and as we leapt out of our boats and walked across snow many feet deep, we discovered that the island's sole remaining colony had fallen to 36 birds—15 breeding pairs and 6 non-breeders. Studies of Adélie bones buried under layers of guano have shown that penguins have nested on Litchfield Island for at least six hundred years, and possibly much longer. (Judging by the empty expanse of nesting pebbles, Fraser believes that in earlier eras—exactly when, and under what climatic conditions, is unclear—thousands of Adélies probably nested on Litchfield.) Now the island's Adélie penguin population was on the verge of disappearing.

As Peter, Jennifer, and I motored among the three islands closest to the station—Humble lay opposite Litchfield, nearly a mile from Palmer—we cruised over the clearest sea I had ever seen. Brown ribbons of kelp swaying in the currents, the multicolored rocks on the ocean bottom, starfish—all were as vivid as if viewed through the Antarctic atmosphere. The reason was simple: With the sea ice not yet in full retreat, Antarctica's summer sun had not catalyzed the photosynthetic process that leads to the Southern Ocean's seasonal plankton blooms, which cloud the water. Within a few weeks, the water's limpid clarity would be gone.

Later that afternoon, the ocean's transparency only heightened the intensity of a close encounter with a leopard seal. Cruising slowly in shallow water off Humble Island, we had just passed a small iceberg when we heard a loud expulsion of breath right behind us. An enormous leopard seal, the biggest we were to see all season, had raised its head out of the water and begun to follow our Zodiac. The leopard seal looked close to 12 feet long—nearly the length of the Zodiac—and was so thick it seemed like a man would be hard-pressed to get his arms around it. The seal was undoubtedly a female, which are considerably bigger than male leopard seals and can grow to more than 13 feet in length and weigh eleven hundred pounds.

The leopard seal's sinister appearance comes in large measure from its head—a sloping, wide-jawed visage that has frequently been described as reptilian or snakelike but that struck me as positively prehistoric. It is a sleek, predatory head with rows of large teeth, made even more evil-looking by being placed atop a massive body. As Peter throttled back on the engine, the dark-backed seal circled us, occasionally sur-facing to emit a powerful exhalation. And then, dropping behind our Zodiac once again, the seal rolled over on her back and swam under our boat. I leaned over the side and gazed at this predator from just inches away as she cruised by us underwater. Her pale, spotted under-side looked turquoise just under the surface of the Southern Ocean. The seal moved with ease, eyeing us blankly as she passed. She swam with us for a minute or two more in a manner more playful than threat-ening. But I was relieved, nevertheless, to note that if she did decide to attack and puncture our boat—which leopard seals have done previously at Palmer and at other locations along the Antarctic Peninsula—we were less than twenty-five feet from the shore and would have time to scramble there before spilling into her world.

By evening, the skies had largely cleared and there was not a trace of wind. I stood on the quiet south side of Torgersen Island, home to two tiny Adélie colonies, and watched and listened. The silence was so com-plete that I could hear the swish of an Adélie tobogganing past me in the snow along a well-worn penguin highway. Nearby, grounded ice-bergs glowed a heavenly shade of blue, their color formed by thousands of years of compaction.

THE ADÉLIES I observed that first evening on Torgersen Island had come off the ice in mid-October, right on schedule. The band of frozen ocean enveloping the northwestern Antarctic Peninsula had begun breaking up unusually early, in August, but persistent winds from the west and northwest had packed a wide swath of the decaying ice tightly against Anvers Island. In light ice years, or years when winds push the ice away from the peninsula, the Adélies can use their preferred method of locomotion—swimming—to arrive at the doorstep of their ancestral islands. But this year the Adélies had to either walk, or toboggan on their bellies across many miles of frozen sea.

In early October, Glenn Grant, a science technician who had spent the winter at Palmer Station, first saw several long strings of Adélies threading some islands a few miles offshore. A procession of black dots on a white background, the penguins seemed to be following a leader, maintaining column formation like a battalion of cadets. "They moved along like a line of ants," Grant told me. "They were traveling amazingly fast, heading for Torgersen Island. They knew where they wanted to go."

The Adélies came in waves over several weeks. Grant would go to bed in the evening with no penguins on the move and wake up the next morning to the sight of hundreds more of the upright birds fanning out across the sea ice as they headed for the five islands near the station with Adélie rookeries. Once on their home islands, the Adélies waddled and slid on their bellies to the colonies where they had been hatched or had bred the year before. And there they began to set up house, a process requiring a brand of patience that perhaps can be summoned only by a creature with the brain of a bird. For many days, often several weeks, they stood or lay steadfastly over the site where they intended to procreate, waiting for the spring sun and the warmth of their bodies to expose the small, battleship-gray pebbles that would become their nests.

From the earliest days of the continent's discovery, explorers have remarked on the stirring sight in spring of masses of Adélie penguins heading with great determination—over ice and through water—to their native colonies. James Clark Ross, the discoverer of the Ross Sea and the Ross Ice Shelf, wrote in 1841 of the "wonderful instinct, far beyond the powers of untutored reason, that enables these creatures to find their way . . . several hundred miles, to their place of usual resort."

In October 1915, Ernest Shackleton described the joy of seeing life return to the Antarctic after a long, dark winter during which his ship, the *Endurance,* was locked in the pack ice of the Weddell Sea. "Spring was in the air," wrote Shackleton, "and if there were no green growing things to gladden our eyes, there were at least many seals, penguins, and even whales disporting themselves in the leads."

The spring journey to their breeding grounds is the culmination of an elaborate migratory cycle that provides, at different seasons, the three things Adélie penguins need to survive: Ice- and snow-free nesting grounds, which they find on the narrow strip of rocky shoreline and coastal islands of Antarctica. (Less than 5 percent of the continent's coast is rock; the rest is buried under ice.) Open water, so they can forage. And sea ice, which in winter becomes their platform for resting and plunging into the sea to hunt for krill and fish.

The Adélies' migratory cycle begins in the fall when, after rearing their chicks, the penguins seek tranquil, less windy refuges on land or sea ice to undergo their annual molt, replacing their worn set of feathers with a new one. Afterward, as winter approaches and the continent's circle of sea ice expands rapidly outward from south to north, the Adélies follow the sea ice as it spreads. In the dead of winter, Adélie penguins will always be found north of the Antarctic Circle, for they need at least a few hours of daylight to forage. (The Antarctic Circle, at 66°33' S, is the latitude at which the sun never rises on June 21 or 22, the austral winter solstice.)

During the winter, the Adélies are rarely found at the ice edge, a transitional zone where ice freezes and thaws and is subject to breakup from the swells of the Southern Ocean. Instead, they hang back at least several miles, and often as far as thirty to fifty miles, from the sea. Bill Fraser saw this firsthand during a scientific cruise to the Weddell Sea in the midwinter—July and August—of 1988. Fraser and his fellow researchers penetrated several dozen miles into the pack, along the way encountering huge numbers of Adélies assembled on the frozen ocean. "The ice was black as far as you could see with Adélies," he recalled.

The Adélies were clustered on so-called gray ice, its color indicating that it had frozen more recently than the solid white ice deeper in the pack. Channels frequently opened in this young ice, and on several occasions Fraser saw lines of thousands of Adélies marching toward the leads, through which they disappeared into the Weddell Sea in pursuit of prey.

As the days lengthen in late winter and early spring, Adélie penguins, like most birds and animals, react to the waxing light. The longer days stimulate the pituitary and other glands, releasing hormones that cause the birds to enter a period of overeating, known as hyperphagia. Around the vernal equinox (the first day of spring), the penguins gorge on krill and fish in preparation for the long migration, the last days or weeks of which, particularly in high latitudes such as those of the Ross Sea, might be over impenetrable sea ice, forcing the Adélies to fast. Given that Adélies are flightless, the distances they migrate—swimming in open water, Adélies can travel at a steady pace of four and a half miles per hour—are impressive. Adélies nesting at high latitudes, such as on Ross Island, sometimes complete annual round-trip migrations of more than 3,500 miles. Satellite tags placed on Adélies near Palmer Station show that some make round-trip migrations of more than 1,500 miles as they travel to the ice edge at the top of the Antarctic Peninsula and north of the Weddell Sea, where they enjoy access to undersea canyons rich with krill.

Even more striking is the accuracy with which they wend their way back to their native colonies. The most impressive proof of this came fifty years ago, when Richard Penney conducted an unconventional yet ingenious experiment, not unlike the efforts of suburbanites who trap bothersome squirrels, drive them many miles away, and release them, only to discover that somehow they find their way home. On December 3, 1959, Penney snatched five male, nonbreeding Adélies from their rookery on Wilkes Land, in eastern Antarctica. He affixed numbered bands to their flippers, placed the Adélies in cloth bags, and had them flown halfway across Antarctica to McMurdo Sound, on the Ross Sea. There, they were released.

Ten months later, three of the five returned to the Wilkes Land colonies from which they had been taken. (Two of the birds retained their bands; a third had a line of worn feathers where the band had fallen off.) The penguins had swum 2,400 miles along the Antarctic coast, passing many Adélie rookeries along the way. Their average speed was eight miles per day. What was most remarkable was that the birds managed this feat after being flown overland and turned loose in a place they had never been before. It is sufficiently impressive that, driven by instinct, birds such as Arctic terns can migrate annually from the Arctic to the Antarctic and back again. But to be flown thousands of miles away, released, and then swim home on a route that the penguins had never traveled demonstrates a keen homing ability.

In another experiment, Penney and a colleague plucked more than a hundred nonbreeding male Adélies from Cape Crozier, on the Ross Sea, and flew them to a half dozen locations 200 to 900 miles away. Released on flat, featureless polar ice sheets or sea ice shelves that offered the penguins no visual migratory clues, the Adélies invariably headed north-northeast or north-northwest. In doing so they demonstrated a sound survival instinct: Any penguin heading north would eventually hit the open ocean and food, after which they would head for their colonies. The birds plainly used the sun as an aid to navigation, as they oriented themselves more quickly under clear skies than in cloudy weather.

Perhaps the most remarkable statistic that emerged from Penney's studies of the Adélies' homing instinct is this: 99 percent of the time, breeding Adélies returned to the same colonies where they had reproduced the year before, often winding up within a few feet of their previous territories.

What guides Adélie penguins and many other creatures—salmon, monarch butterflies, Arctic terns, albatrosses—is still something of a mystery to scientists. What is known is that the bodies of migratory birds contain a type of iron crystal called magnetite—often stored in the beak—that functions like an internal compass. More recent research has suggested that the brains of migratory birds have molecules called cryptochromes that may help them determine how far they are from the equator by detecting the angle of magnetic field lines.

The resolute homing behavior of Adélie and emperor penguins has impressed many Antarctic explorers who've observed the birds on the move over the ice, sometimes in small groups, sometimes in strings that stretched to the horizon. Robert Cushman Murphy, in his classic *Oceanic Birds of South America*, described the Adélie migration: "Travelling is continued only during daylight; when night overtakes the birds, they bivouac in line until dawn. The period of the ice passage may run to two weeks, or even more, throughout which the formation remains unbroken, even though miles of rough ice may wear or cut through the leathery soles until the army is leaving a ribbon of blood in its wake."

No matter how Adélie penguins get where they're going, the fact remains that, across Antarctica, at widely varying latitudes, they arrive home to mate at about the same time in late September and early to mid-October. The drive to procreate, and the instinctual knowledge that they must mate promptly so that their chicks hatch just as prey abundance peaks in summer, brings them to their natal colonies with Swiss punctuality and GPS-like precision.

As the Adélies stream into their rookeries in spring, the peace and martial order of the migration give way to the jostling and territorial spats of colony life. Levick described the long lines of migrating Adélies drawing to within a half mile of the rookery, after which they began to run, resembling a gaggle of schoolchildren dashing for a playing field. "Arrived at the rookery, and plunged suddenly amidst the din of that squalling, fighting, struggling crowd," Levick wrote, "the contrast with the dead silence and loneliness of the pack ice they had so recently left, was as great a one as can well be imagined; yet once there, the birds seemed collected and at home."

When penguins arrive at their former nesting spot, whether it's empty or a mate is already there, the Adélie will let loose with what is known as the "loud mutual display." The penguin either leans over the former territory or leans in on a potential mate and uncorks a raspy, staccato trumpeting sound. The call issued during the loud mutual display is the defining sound of an Adélie penguin rookery; during the reproductive season, the air in large colonies is rent with this harsh din. It's primarily a greeting, issued by males in early spring to an empty nest site as a way of reinforcing the bird's connection with that territory. A pair of Adélies, whether reunited after a brief foraging trip or eight months of winter, will greet each other with the loud mutual display. Standing close together, the Adélies bob their heads back and forth as they issue the strident call again and again, for ten seconds or more. In this case, the call is both a greeting and an identification tool, as Adélies recognize each other and their chicks by voice. Adult Adélies will lean over the eggs they're incubating and issue the call. Returning from a foraging trip, Adélies will blast the call into the ears of their chicks, an act that soon enables the young penguins to identify their parents. The display looks and sounds frantic—a fitting anthem for the hectic breeding season of these tough little birds.

OUR SECOND DAY in the field, November 1, opened as tranquilly as the previous one. We took full advantage, counting penguins and doing more snow measurements. The harbor waters were so calm that swimming penguins generated a wake that traveled a hundred yards before dissipating.

Late that afternoon, the wind picked up slightly and blew from an unwelcome direction—the southwest. Shortly after the shift in the wind, our Zodiac's fuel line became entangled in our rudder and broke as we traveled from one island to another. Sitting on Torgersen Island trying to repair the problem, we could see the once-banished swath of sea ice moving steadily back toward shore. With much work to be done in the field, the reappearance of the ice was like the return of some malevolent force.

Soon, it became clear that fixing the motor was going to require someone with greater mechanical skills than Peter, Jen, or I possessed. But even with the mosaic of sea ice creeping back in, slowly infiltrating Arthur Harbor, Peter was reluctant to call for help; getting towed back to the station is a distinction field teams try hard to avoid. When Peter did call, it was in the laid-back code that is part of the Palmer culture. "We're having a little trouble with the engine," he said over the radio to Toby Koffman, the boating coordinator. Toby got the message and was there in a few minutes, ready to pull us home.

Heading to the station, our Zodiacs bumped through chunks of sea ice streaming back into Arthur Harbor. Over the next few weeks, the ice would be a near-constant presence, keeping us away from the Adélie penguins.

CHAPTER 3

ICE

When to the beautiful tints in the sky and the deep deli-
cate shading on the snow are added perhaps the deep
colours of the open sea, with reflections from the ice foot
and ice-cliffs in it, all brilliant blues and emerald greens,
then indeed a man may realize how beautiful this world
can be, and how clean.

—APSLEY-CHERRY GARRARD,
Terra Nova expedition, 1910–13

By ANTARCTIC STANDARDS, THE MARR ICE PIEDMONT WAS A
tiny ice sheet, not quite forty miles long and twenty miles wide. But the
Marr loomed large at Palmer Station, its gently sloping dome forming
our backyard, and its frequent cannonading—with chunks of the glacier breaking off and cascading into Arthur Harbor—provided the
soundtrack to which we all worked and lived. Most importantly, the
Marr was an escape hatch; a thirty-minute trek up the ice piedmont
transported you from the twenty-first-century atmosphere of Palmer
Station to a timeless place that offered one of the most breathtaking
vistas on the planet. I can think of no other walk that, in the space of
half an hour, offers such an abrupt and exhilarating transition.

I made that hike nearly every night of the fifteen days in early
November during which we were iced in. It was not a heroic climb. The
way to the top wound from the main dormitory building, past a white

geodesic dome that held the station's satellite equipment, and finally beyond a corrugated metal structure housing sensors that sniffed the air for radioactive fallout. (The sensors are part of a global network designed to detect nuclear tests.) From there, in the early season, you walk several hundred feet over snow-covered ground that, only a few decades ago, was part of the Marr Ice Piedmont before it began its current retreat. The path then heads downhill into a small ravine before climbing up onto the ice piedmont. In springtime the snow is several feet deep and the gently inclined hike to the top is best done in snow-shoes. As the glacier has melted and retreated, its edges above the station have become noticeably more scalloped and its surface split by more crevasses. The area on which it is safe to walk has steadily narrowed, forcing the members of Palmer Station's search-and-rescue team to move the boundary markers—frayed black flags on wooden poles—closer together nearly every year.

The weather during the first few days of November was stunningly clear, and as I headed up onto the glacier in the evenings I felt compelled to halt every few minutes, turn around, and take in the view. The climb takes you no more than three hundred feet above sea level, but it is hard to imagine anywhere else on earth where so low a vantage point delivers such a panorama. I made the hike after nine P.M. and often stayed past eleven, enjoying the protracted sunsets that lit up the countless icebergs and the peaks of the peninsular chain in rich shades of gold, violet, and magenta. Often, toward the end of my walk, with the warm colors draining into cool hues of silver and cobalt, I would be alone atop the glacier, and I would think: When the time comes to leave this earth, I'd like to lift off from the Marr Ice Piedmont. It seemed like a small leap from there to eternity.

Frank Hurley, the photographer on Shackleton's *Endurance* expedition, experienced a similar sentiment as his ship, trapped in the ice, drifted across the Weddell Sea. "There were times," he wrote in *Shackleton's Argonauts,* "when the sky was a rainbow, flaming with radiant mock suns, and one's very heart and soul cried out in rapture, 'These things are not earthly; this is heaven.'"

In all directions, the landscape and seascape were encased in ice. Indeed, the limitless plain of sea ice that kept us locked in at the station was what gave the scene such power. The panorama changed not only by the day but by the hour. On one particularly clear evening, the sheer face of nearby Mount William, 5,249 feet tall, was thrown into vivid relief in the gilded light, its razor-edged ridges softened by thick layers of snow and ice. Twenty-five miles away, halfway up the length of Anvers Island, was 9,055-foot Mount Français. Less than a dozen miles in front of me were the pillowy ice domes burying the Wauwermans Islands, which were once connected to the peninsula by floating ice shelves. To the east, brilliantly lit, was a line of jagged peaks in the peninsular range, with tombstone-like black faces. These mountains were dozens of miles away, but in Antarctica's limpid atmosphere they looked as if they were little more than a short boat ride from Palmer Station. Visible 120 miles to the south were the 6,000- to 7,000-foot summits rising from the glaciated plateau that runs down the middle of the Antarctic Peninsula.

Close to shore, the sea ice was loosely packed and the open patches of water at the base of the Marr Ice Piedmont were placid, chrome-colored pools, reflecting the pale blue walls of the glacier. Beyond the nearby islands, whose black ridges were streaked with snow, the sea ice was a cool, blue-white table that ran to the horizon.

The tracks of a lone, tobogganing penguin ran across the ice piedmont, its flippers slicing knifelike slits in the sparkling snow. Other than the occasional shriek of a kelp gull or the sonorous boom of an iceberg calving off the Marr, the silence was complete. Indeed, the silence was a powerful force of its own, and it took time for this raggedy-nerved American to learn to stand there and take it all in.

Nearly a century before, looking at this same landscape in the evening light, Frederick A. Cook—the physician on the *Belgica* expedition—described it this way: "There is a solitude and restfulness about the whole scene which can only be felt; it cannot be described."

In November, icebergs locked in sea ice filled much of the horizon, creating a skyline of castles, mesas, and one particularly striking iceberg with a tall column capped by a figure that looked like a silhouette of Queen Nefertiti. The Nefertiti berg hung around for many weeks, the wind and ocean currents shoving it in all directions until it was finally blown close to Palmer, where the summer's warmth and the gentle swells eventually toppled it. Ernest Shackleton, steaming toward the Ross Sea in 1907 during the *Nimrod* expedition, likened sailing through a field of tabular icebergs—ranging in height from 80 to 150 feet—to traveling "the lanes and streets of a wonderful snowy Venice."

The towering chain of mountains that forms the backbone of the Antarctic is, by far, the most dominant geographical feature in northwestern Antarctica. Yet, strangely, no one at Palmer Station seemed to know the proper name for the mountain range, nor did the Antarctic maps on station identify the chain. I took to calling it the peninsular range and decided, on my return home, to learn its official name.

To my amazement, a top official at the United States Geological Survey's Board on Geographic Names—the committee that decides what names are formally attached to places in the U.S. and Antarctica—later informed me, "There is no specific name of which we know that applies to the mountain chain that forms the core of the . . . Antarctic Peninsula." He said I was welcome to officially propose one.

No matter what you call the peninsular range, the volume of glacial ice it harbors is staggering—thick mantles of ice that spill through the passes in great, frozen streams and flow to the Southern Ocean, forming massive headlands. On more than one occasion, I stood atop the Marr, gazed at the immeasurable tons of ice, and thought: If this ever starts to melt in earnest, the world will be a sorry place in which to live.

THOSE EARLY WEEKS of November were not all spent contemplating infinity from atop the glacier. Indeed, the mundane tasks of the iced-in birding team could bring a person swiftly back to earth, and none more so than sifting through bird shit looking for fish ear bones. Bill Fraser gauged the changes in the environment around Palmer Station in many ways—by counting and weighing penguins, censusing other seabirds, measuring snow depth, and noting shifts in seal populations. But to figure out what food could be found in the nearby waters of the Southern Ocean, nothing was as effective as collecting the droppings of penguins and skuas and sorting through it with a pair of tweezers. We also picked apart blue-eyed shag boluses—pellets of bones, scales, feathers, moss, and other indigestible material regurgitated by this species of cormorant. Fraser's team was primarily looking for otoliths—in this case, the pearly, triangular-shaped inner ear bones of fish. Often half the size of a lentil, an otolith revealed the species of fish and its age; the bone can be read like the rings of a tree.

So as the sea ice remained hard against the southern coast of Anvers Island, we sometimes sat in the lab at Palmer Station examining shag boluses or the poop of South Polar skuas that had been scraped off rocks and moss with spoons during the previous season, then frozen for nearly a year. Unthawed, this bird excreta did not smell all that bad, and there was strange satisfaction in striking a mother lode and extracting a few dozen otoliths from one little plastic bag of bird drop-pings. Over the years, Fraser had sent more than nine thousand oto-liths to a laboratory in Seattle, and the story they told was, in its own way, as revealing as the rapidly disappearing colonies of Adélie pen-guins all around Palmer Station.

What the otoliths disclosed was this: Over the last few decades, Antarctic silverfish (*Pleuragramma antarcticum*)—the most important species of fish in the Antarctic food chain and one whose life history depends on the presence of sea ice—had declined precipitously around Palmer Station. Five to fourteen inches long, this slender, homely fish— its blood, like that of other Antarctic fish species, contains glycoproteins that act like antifreeze—made up nearly half of the diet of the Adélie penguin around Palmer station in the 1970s. Now, apparently, the sil-verfish had largely disappeared in the Southern Ocean around Palmer.

Peter, Jen, and I also spoke frequently by phone with Bill Fraser and Donna Patterson. Sitting in the birders' tent, we would put them on speakerphone, with Fraser mainly commiserating with us about being shut in on station and reminding us that heavy sea ice in early November was not uncommon. Fraser was due to join us briefly in mid-November, as he traveled with a group from the National Science Foundation that was evaluating the Palmer Long Term Ecological Research program.

Horne, a thirty-one-year-old with a bachelor's degree from Duke University and a master's in environmental science from Western Wash-ington University, was the leader of our three-person early-season team. A gentle, easygoing Virginian with receding, curly, light-brown hair, Horne set the tone for a season so collegial and free of tension that I left

Palmer after five months convinced that I had seen the closest thing on earth to a commune. Peter was the repository of an impressive storehouse of bird-team argot, which consisted of saying things like "We're done-dee" whenever we had completed a task. His patience was boundless. Two months into the season, Peter displayed saintly understanding and compassion as he showed me, for the hundredth time, the proper knot to use when tying the boat to shore. He played the guitar and sang beautifully, did a dance at parties in which he went through the motions of reeling in his partner like a fish, and had a fondness for bourbon. All of these qualities endeared him to me.

Peter was assisted by Jennifer Blum, a native of Colorado and a graduate of Western State College of Colorado. In her late twenties, Jen displayed inexhaustible enthusiasm and competence. She equaled Peter in the patience department, and far outdistanced everyone with her stamina. A former college basketball player, Jen walked faster, snowshoed more rapidly, and climbed ridges more adroitly than the rest of us. After a twelve-hour day in the field, when most team members wanted only to have dinner, a drink, and an early bedtime, we would often find Jen in the Palmer gym, engaging in a long workout. She was considering getting a master's degree. The year before coming to Palmer, Jen had spent a summer season in Antarctica near McMurdo Station, on the Ross Sea, working for David Ainley, the most widely published of the troika of U.S. Adélie penguin scientists.

The birders' hut—the sanctuary of Fraser and his field team—was a small tent shaped like a Quonset hut, located just in front of the laboratory building, steps away from the dock and the boathouse. The hut was a cramped yet comfortable space where we spent most of our time when not in the field. Fraser had moved his group into the tent in part because Palmer Station was overflowing with researchers in the austral summer, in part because the birding team tended to give off the unpleasant odor of seabird guano, and in part because Fraser liked his team being off on its own.

The heavy-duty, laminated cloth tent—about fifteen feet long, eight feet wide, and seven feet high—was a faded, sky-blue color with a thick, silver tarp tied over the outside. The cluttered, tightly packed space had a plywood floor and two tables running along each wall. The group's computers sat on the tables, above which were shelves crammed with binders labeled "Diets," "Repro Sites," "Adélie Data," and "Marine Mammals." Underneath the desks were cardboard boxes stuffed with seabird leg bands, sleeping bags, beef jerky, dried apricots, boot wax, hand warmers, satellite and radio transmitters, scales, calipers, mechanical counters, and other tools of the birding trade. Bottles of wine and whiskey sat on a table at the back of the tent, which was adorned with photographs of team members from past seasons. Strung from one of the roof poles was a small stuffed penguin doll with a noose around its neck—a gift from one of the other scientific teams at the station.

Peter, Jen, and other two team members who would soon join us—Brett Pickering and Kristen Gorman—were typical of the field assistants Fraser liked to select: fit, easygoing, and bright young people who had previous experience as field biologists and who, in some cases, were working at Palmer as they pursued master's degrees or PhDs. Many returned year after year to work with Fraser.

By far the smallest of America's three year-round stations in Antarctica—the others are at the South Pole and on McMurdo Sound, on the Ross Sea—Palmer Station was a great leveler. Although there were two cooks, who prepared superb food in a range of cuisines from Mexican to Thai, cleaning the galley and the station was everyone's responsibility. Each night after dinner, a rotating team of five or six people would thoroughly scour the kitchen in a ritual known as "gash," performing their chores to deafening rock and roll. On Saturday afternoon, all station personnel gathered in the galley and picked a slip of paper out of a hat; the chit listed which part of the station he or she would be cleaning that week.

The station attracted an offbeat crowd, many of them outdoors enthusiasts from the West. Some worked half a year in Palmer as carpenters or on scientific field teams, then traveled for much of the rest of the year. Most of Palmer's residents were young, which meant that there was much pairing off and romantic intrigue. Some of those who met and fell in love at Palmer eventually got married. Indeed, one of the best parties during my stay at Palmer was a celebration of the engagement of just such a couple. The highlight of the evening was the unveiling of a four-foot-long penis sculpted from glacial ice with a chain saw. The frozen member was so anatomically correct that it contained a urethra and could be made to ejaculate, spectacularly, by taking a bottle of cheap champagne, shaking it, and attaching it to a tube at the base of the ice penis.

Over the years, Palmer Station had given rise to many peculiar customs. Although everyone had a comfortable bed in a warm room, about a dozen of the station's inhabitants pitched tents during the summer amid the rock rubble behind Palmer that bordered the upper reaches of Arthur Harbor. Securely anchored by large stones to withstand roaring winds, the tents offered a quiet refuge in Antarctica's pure air, and sleeping near the glacier's terminus meant that throughout the night tent residents could, at close range, listen to—and feel—the rumbling of the calving Marr glacier.

Then there was the tradition of diving off the dock into the freezing sea as a farewell salute to those heading north on the *Gould*. This ritual was mainly perpetuated by Palmer's younger residents, the bolder of whom would do flips into the ice-studded waters of Arthur Harbor. I tried it twice; the entry into the 34-degree sea sucked the air out of my lungs and so seized up my muscles that swimming ten feet to a metal ladder was an ordeal.

As THE SECOND week of being iced in on the station began, with no sign of an imminent wind shift to chase the pack ice out to sea, I began to worry that I would miss Adélie egg laying. Horne also was concerned about documenting the peak of egg laying, an important date in establishing both the timing and the success of the Adélies' reproductive season.

I had to content myself with hauling a spotting scope out to the balcony of the galley and observing the penguins on the south side of Torgersen Island. I could see the snow beginning to melt on higher ground. A handful of Adélies were lying down, and I wondered if some females had already laid their eggs and gone off to forage at sea, leaving their partners to take the first incubation shift. Other Adélie pairs stood next to each other, stock-still, waiting for the female to lay her pair of eggs. The reproductive season was clearly in full swing.

Although it would not be obvious to a casual observer, the penguin scene I was observing from afar underscored an intriguing fact about Adélies: Males demonstrate more pronounced domestic tendencies than females. The cocks show up first at the colony in spring, usually three to four days before the females; the males do most of the nest building; and after the female lays two eggs, she departs immediately to gorge on krill and fish, leaving the male to incubate the eggs for another week or two as he continues to fast.

The average age at which females first breed is five years, and for males it is around six years. This is a late reproductive start for birds that often die before the age of ten and only occasionally survive to age twenty, but mating is delayed for a good reason: In the unforgiving Antarctic environment, it takes Adélie penguins several years to learn to feed themselves well enough to survive the prolonged fasting of the breeding season and to successfully nourish two offspring.

Some debate has occurred in recent years about the monogamy of penguins, but as far as the faithfulness of Adélies is concerned, this much can be said with certainty: Given the neighborhood they live in, and the commute they endure, their fidelity is astonishing.

As they return to their colonies, Adélies are searching for a territory, not a specific mate, but if the former partner has survived the winter and reappeared, then the pair will almost always reunite on the old nest site. A study by Richard Penney of 282 banded pairs of Adélies showed that when both members of a couple returned, they reunited 83 percent of the time on the same nest site, leading Penney to conclude that "Adélies are essentially monogamous." He believed that Adélies fell somewhere between pairing for a single season and pairing for life. Other penguin researchers have described Adélies as "serially monogamous."

What drives Adélies to mate with the same partner year after year is pure instinct, for the breeding success of experienced pairs is considerably higher than that of younger birds or pairs that have not mated previously. Age and experience give an Adélie the edge it needs to pull off the feat of successfully raising chicks in such a hostile environment. This is because veteran Adélies arrive on the nesting grounds earlier and with more body fat to survive the fast. They choose a more propitious territory for their nest site—located on higher, snow-free ground and not on the periphery of a colony, where it would be vulnerable to skua predation—and build a better nest. They hook up with a mate more quickly, copulate more successfully, and, once the chicks hatch, will be more skilled at finding schools of krill and fish.

But what instinct and evolution dictate, the Antarctic environment conspires to undo. In Penney's fidelity study, 100 of the 282 pairs did not reunite because one of the members failed to return. Studies by David Ainley at Cape Crozier, on the Ross Sea, showed that no Adélie remained with the same partner for more than four years. Out of 100 pairs studied by Ainley, only 6 managed to breed for three seasons with the same partner—a direct result of high annual mortality.

Adélie penguins spend 90 percent of their lives in the Southern Ocean, where starvation, predation by leopard seals, and exhaustion brought on by being forced, in spring, to migrate long distances during heavy ice years all extract a heavy toll. Some studies suggest that annual mortality among young Adélies can be as high as 75 percent. Annual mortality rates among older Adélies are considerably lower, ranging from 10 to 40 percent, depending on the study. But the very act of procreation can be deadly; in one study, nearly 40 percent of Adélies that bred did not survive the following winter, presumably because they were in a weakened condition after feeding and caring for their chicks.

Adélies that have mated previously tend to reunite and copulate with little fanfare and great dispatch. Whereas a young Adélie pair might engage in various displays—what passes for Adélie foreplay—the veteran Adélie couple gets right to it. And let no one doubt the sex drive of an Adélie penguin—at least that of the males. Perhaps no one has documented the Adélie libido more thoroughly than William J. L. Sladen, the English scientist who conducted groundbreaking penguin studies on the South Orkney Islands and at Hope Bay, on the northern Antarctic Peninsula, from 1948 to 1951. One of the most influential penguin biologists of the twentieth century, Sladen—who eventually worked at Johns Hopkins University—conducted exhaustive research on Adélie, gentoo, and chinstrap penguins. The investigation into their sex lives was a minor part of his work, but Sladen nevertheless managed to document some memorable sexual behavior.

In one instance, Sladen observed a male Adélie mounting a female and making cloacal contact in a 60-mile-per-hour gale, a feat the bird managed by working his flippers vigorously to maintain his balance on her back. In another case, Sladen watched as a pair valiantly tried to mate during a blizzard. The temperature was 22°F, the wind was blowing up to 30 miles per hour, and snow had been falling continuously for twelve hours when, at one P.M. Sladen came upon the penguins. The female, who had laid a first egg the day before, was buried under the snow, with only the top of her head and bill showing. The male was standing next to her when Sladen walked away. He returned at 3:45 P.M. to see the male just finishing coitus with the female, a feat he had apparently accomplished by trampling the snow around her, exposing her back and cloaca in the midst of what Sladen called "a bleak white waste."

Five hours later, Sladen returned again. Even though it was snowing so hard that visibility was limited to a few yards, the male penguin had managed to expose the female's back and was repeatedly trying to balance on it and copulate. Four times he slipped off his mate's icy feathers, encouraged in his efforts by the female, who kept pointing her beak skyward, a sign that she was in the mood. Finally, the male gave up.

"The sexual impulse must be great," Sladen wrote, "when these acts are performed under such adverse conditions."

Being packed into a colony with hundreds or thousands of sexually charged neighbors provides many temptations and opportunities for Adélie penguins. One way the birds hold on to a mate and strengthen pair bonds is through displays of all kinds, ranging from silent bowing, to depositing stones on the nest, to mutual displays, loud and quiet. On numerous occasions Levick observed Adélies rocking their heads back and forth, almost brushing cheeks, in the quiet mutual display. "It is difficult to convey in words," wrote Levick, "the daintiness of this pretty little scene."

I observed penguins greeting each other in this fashion many times, as well as merely standing quietly side by side in the days before their first egg was laid. Watching these scenes, I found it difficult not to detect tenderness and a strong bond. Yet another, less gauzy way to view the Adélies' courtship and pairing is that it is merely the end result of a finely honed evolutionary process that improves their chances of procreation.

Perhaps the best description of the Adélie reproductive season was supplied by Robert Cushman Murphy, who wrote, "The period of the year during which the Antarctic penguins are on the nesting ground can be summed up as one of feeding, fighting, courting, thieving, and philandering."

THE ICE REMAINED an immovable force. I would wake up in the dorm room I shared with Peter Horne, open the shades expectantly—initially with optimism, then with resignation—and be greeted by the same scene: Arthur Harbor clogged with sea ice. The weather would change—wet snow one morning, blue skies the next—but the presence of sea ice, extending far offshore, never varied. Walking to the galley for breakfast, I would look at the propeller wind vane atop the station's main building, and it always seemed to be facing in the same general direction: west. The satellite photos we viewed on our computers confirmed the bad news: a tightly compacted wedge of sea ice extended most of the length of the western Antarctic Peninsula, disappearing just five to ten miles north of us off Anvers Island.

We sat in the birders' tent and wondered: Was it a heavy sea ice year? A normal or light sea ice year in which the winds had driven the ice inshore? The answer came in 2008, when a team of scientists, led by the Australian sea ice expert Robert Massom, released a paper on the anomalous 2005 season. What the researchers found was that the unusual juxtaposition of a strong high-pressure system off the northwest Weddell Sea, to our east, and a powerful low-pressure system in the Amundsen Sea, to our west, created winds that drove the ice inshore during that austral spring. Indeed, following the pattern of recent years, as warming swept down the Antarctic Peninsula, the ice extent in 2005 was lower than average, and it broke up earlier than usual. But the steady winds compacted the sea ice against the peninsula, creating one of the most impenetrable ice barriers in years. And although the winds were well below average in November and December—accounting for the many freakishly still days at Palmer Station—the dense ice did not disperse.

And so the birding team and the other researchers at Palmer

waited—and waited. Chafing one morning at our inability to visit the Adélie colonies during peak egg laying, I griped to Hugh Ducklow, the head of the Palmer LTER program. Reassuring me that the average date when boating teams at Palmer could reliably get out on ice-free water was November 23, Ducklow gave me some sound advice on surviving a season in Antarctica: "This is a marathon, not a sprint."

Two days before the expected arrival of Fraser and the LTER review team aboard the *Laurence M. Gould*, I stood outside the birders' tent and spoke with Langdon Quetin, the krill biologist who had been coming to Palmer for three decades. We both looked at the ice-clogged harbor. Then we glanced at the wind vane, slowly spinning in the ice-compacting westerly winds.

"I'm not optimistic," said Quetin.

I thought he was speaking about our chances of getting out in Zodiacs anytime soon, and answered that I hoped the ice would clear by Thanksgiving.

"I don't mean when we're getting out," replied Quetin, a research professor at the University of California, Santa Barbara. "I'm not sure the ship is going to make it in, with only one engine and all the snow that fell last night. It creates drag coming through the ice."

On the bright side, Quetin said, it was helpful for me to get a sense of the sort of sea ice that once was a regular fixture at Palmer Station. He recalled that station residents routinely walked over the sea ice in the winter and early spring to visit Torgersen Island and the remnants of the old British station on Norsel Point. Now the sea ice is rarely solid enough to go traipsing anywhere.

"A few degrees warmer," said Quetin, "makes a big difference."

That night, the wind howled outside my dormitory window, gusting in excess of 45 miles per hour. The next morning, the temperature was 25°F. The barometer rose during the day, the skies cleared, and the wind dropped. Snow fell heavily that night. The betting at the station was that the *Gould*—with one of its two engines broken—would not make it through the sea ice.

The following morning, November 14, the *Laurence M. Gould* steamed out of the Neumeyer Channel and into the Bismarck Strait. It cruised unimpeded for a couple of miles, then hit the pack. The ship continued to push ahead through the ice for another half mile before coming to a halt. At Palmer, station manager Bob Farrell announced that the ship might be returning to Punta Arenas.

In early afternoon, under brilliant blue skies, I grabbed one of the station's radios and once again walked up the Marr Ice Piedmont. Looking east, in the direction of the Neumayer Channel and the peninsular range, I initially saw nothing on the white surface of the sea. Then, peering closer, I spotted an orange speck on the ice, five to six miles away. The *Gould*'s insignificance in this landscape was total. Through my binoculars, I could see the ship maneuvering out of the ice.

Heidi Geisz, a longtime member of Fraser's field team who would go on to do research into pesticide levels in Antarctic penguins, was on the *Gould*. Her voice came over the radio: "I think I might be in heaven. Everything's white."

The Gould had stopped a mile or two short of the point where Fraser, thirty years before, had been forced by heavy sea ice to disembark from the RV *Hero* and ski into Palmer Station. This time, the only way out was backward, not forward, and I watched as the *Gould* headed north out of the pack and into the open waters of the Neumayer Channel.

The mood on the ship was dark. I could only imagine how disappointed and angry Fraser must have been, given how much he disliked the Drake Passage and the *Gould*. It had taken him a week to get from Montana to within a half dozen miles of Palmer Station, only to have to turn around and spend another week getting home. Other passengers had squandered just as much time. Scientists and support personnel were on the ship, including two members of our birding team. Langdon Quetin was expecting badly needed diving equipment that had been lost in October on his way down from the United States. Seven people at Palmer had been scheduled to leave. Peter, Jen, and I had been looking forward to Fraser's early-season visit, and now would have to wait another six weeks, until he could return in early January.

The inability of the *Gould* to make it to Palmer Station was a reminder that, even in this era of GPS navigation and reinforced, steel-hulled ships, Antarctica remains a place where the elements still reign. The rout of the *Gould* also showed us that, despite satellite communications with the outside world, Palmer was an isolated outpost, generally accessible only by boat. The rare exception arose in a medical emergency, when pilots from the United Kingdom's Rothera base, farther to the south, would risk landing with a ski-plane on the increasingly crevassed surface of the Marr Ice Piedmont.

That night, there was heavy drinking in the bar. As people lamented the winds that had packed in the ice around Palmer Station, someone shouted, "Sixty shots for sixty knots!"

IN DOZENS OF crossings spanning three decades, Bill Fraser had acquired an intense dislike for the trip from South America to Antarctica. The stormy voyage had become a reviled means to a beloved end.

Fraser began working in Antarctica under the tutelage of David F. Parmelee, his mentor and adviser at the University of Minnesota. An authority on Arctic seabirds, Parmelee arrived at Palmer Station in 1972 with a handful of graduate students. Little was known about most of the creatures that nested around or migrated to Palmer Station. Penguins—and particularly the Adélie penguin—had been the subject of extensive studies in other parts of Antarctica, but the habits and life histories of other seabirds, from the kelp gull to the giant petrel, remained largely mysterious.

Parmelee and his students began to collect data on nearly everything in Palmer's environs. He insisted that his graduate students observe and record the habits of every living thing they came across: penguins, seals, whales, skuas, blue-eyed shags, southern giant petrels, Antarctic terns, Wilson's storm petrels, and any errant species that happened to pass through the Palmer area. A classically trained ornithologist, Parmelee did not fancy himself an ecologist, although the designation was then coming into vogue in academia. But his emphasis on spending countless hours in the field, observing and understanding an entire ecosystem, appealed to Fraser.

"With Parmelee," recalled Fraser, "you never, ever allowed details to go unnoticed."

Under Parmelee's guidance, his graduate students selected different Antarctic bird species as subjects of study for their master's degrees or PhDs. Fraser chose the kelp gull, *Larus dominicanus*, also known as the southern black-backed gull and the Dominican gull. A hardy bird with a wingspan of about four feet, it is the only one of fifty-five gull species that breeds in the Antarctic. Some winter over on the Antarctic Peninsula, and Fraser's charge was to find out everything he could about the kelp gull's habits and life history during his thirteen-month stay in Palmer, beginning in October 1975.

Over the course of a year, he discovered a trove of new information about these birds, which also breed on subantarctic islands and in South America, Australia, and New Zealand. He documented their relationship with their favored prey, limpets—a snail-like marine mollusk—and banded hundreds of gulls to track their migrations. Fraser reveled in carrying out groundbreaking work in a majestic setting. "I absolutely fell in love with the landscape and the feeling of sheer wildness that existed here—just the overwhelming sense of being in a place that was utterly empty of human beings," he said. "It hooked me badly."

At the peak of the brief Antarctic summer, in January 1976, twenty-five to thirty scientists and support personnel were working at Palmer Station. As fall arrived, in late February and March, and the *Hero* shuttled them back to South America, the station's population began to dwindle. By June, in the depth of winter, Fraser found himself at Palmer Station with only five other men—a station manager, a cook, a paramedic, a communications technician, and a mechanic.

Like the previous winter, 1976 was a heavy sea ice year. Fraser often skied on the frozen Southern Ocean, traveling miles along the coastline of Anvers Island. On clear days, in the afternoon, Fraser would watch the sun barely rise above the horizon and then set in lingering, dramatic fashion, casting an orange glow across the landscape and lighting up the peaks of the peninsular chain. When the moon was full, Fraser would stand alone on the sea ice, miles from the station. As his breath rose like smoke into the night, he would listen to the stillness, broken occasionally by the report of cracking ice. Pausing for a few minutes, he absorbed the vast tableau around him: the Marr Ice Piedmont, the mountains heading south, the white Southern Ocean, extending over the horizon in the direction of New Zealand. All was ice, tinged a ghostly blue by the moonlight.

During his countless hours alone in nature that winter, Fraser felt another of the Antarctic's great attractions: the sense, oddly thrilling, of being dwarfed by a landscape virtually untouched by man. "It was a place where you could still feel inconsequential," he recalled. "You were part of a working system that paid you no mind."

At one point that winter, Fraser noticed that hundreds of seabirds were circling a large grounded iceberg several miles from the station. After observing this for a day or two, Fraser decided to investigate. He and two companions skied to the iceberg. As they drew closer, Fraser saw snow petrels, Antarctic petrels, and kelp gulls swarming around the berg, pecking at it and dipping into a narrow circle of open water encircling it. Skiing up to the moat, Fraser discovered what was causing the frenzy: Antarctic krill were in the water and were attached to the side of the iceberg, apparently grazing on phytoplankton.

Before long, it grew dark. Then, an ice fog, made up of frozen ice crystals, drifted in. Fraser and his companions had decided not to bring a compass because, in the limpid Antarctic atmosphere, the iceberg had looked far closer than it actually was. They discussed their options as temperatures dropped and darkness began to fall. Leaving the berg would be foolhardy, as they might be heading away from the station; but staying could lead to hypothermia. Nevertheless, they decided to remain where they were. And then, out of the fog, came the sound of music. They listened closely and soon picked up the strains of "Morning Has Broken." Station manager Larry Miyoda, worried that the men were lost, had hauled a large pair of stereo speakers onto the balcony of the Palmer galley and turned on Cat Stevens full blast.

The three men followed the music. It took them three hours to ski back to the station.

Looking back on his full year at Palmer, Fraser said, "That winter was a life-changing experience."

THAT BILL FRASER would wind up working in the Southern Hemisphere and devoting his career to the study of wildlife seems almost preordained. He was born William Ronald Fraser in Argentina in 1950. His grandfather, an American of Scottish heritage, was a race-car driver who moved to Argentina, where he eventually opened an import-export business. He married an Englishwoman living in Argentina, and Fraser's father—William Andrew Fraser—grew up there, joining the family business after earning an engineering degree in the United States. The Frasers moved in upper-class circles where Argentines and English expatriates frequently intermarried and socialized; Bill Fraser's aunt married into a prominent Argentinean-Uruguayan family, a union that cemented the family's position in society and pulled Bill Fraser deeper into a world of privilege.

It was an idyllic life for a boy, especially one with an affinity with the outdoors. During the winter, Fraser, who was bilingual, lived in Buenos Aires and attended private school. During the summer, he and his sister visited family estancias in the vast pampas, or grasslands, not far from the Argentine capital or at coastal homes in Argentina and Uruguay. Fraser fished, swam, rode horseback, and explored the ubiquitous marshes. In the fall and winter, he went hunting with his father and uncles. The estancia of his sister's godfather, a mosaic of tall grass and wetlands, was so large that it took six days to cross by horse; five decades later, Fraser still vividly recalls its vastness and solitude.

Early one spring, he was fishing on a beach in Uruguay with his father when he saw his first penguins. They were Magellanics, which breed in Argentina, Chile, and the Falkland Islands and may have been migrating from Brazil when Fraser spotted them. "I have a distinct memory of the Magellanics being on the beaches and then moving into the water and just completely disappearing," he recalled.

Fraser's family moved to the States in 1961, and he spent his teenage years living in the suburbs of Daytona Beach, Florida; Richmond, Virginia; and Princeton, New Jersey. His boyhood haunts have long since been gobbled up by suburban sprawl, but back then Fraser was surrounded by woods, fields, and wetlands. He took full advantage, devoting nearly all his spare time to fishing, hunting, and trapping.

Many of his Princeton High School classmates headed to Ivy League and eastern schools, but not Fraser, who went west and matriculated at Utah State University. He chose Utah State because it had one of the country's best wildlife management departments and was nestled in the Rockies, among the Wasatch, Wellsville, and Bear River mountains.

Surrounded by wilderness, immersed in the study of wildlife biology, and hanging out with fellow students who were cowboys from nearby Idaho, Fraser had found his niche. He graduated in 1973 with a BS in wildlife management.

IN THE MID-1970S, spending a winter at Palmer Station had more in common with Antarctica's so-called heroic age of exploration than with the Palmer Station of today. The station's isolation was nearly complete; for five to six months, ships could not penetrate the ice to reach the American outpost. As the sea froze around Palmer, darkness closed in. High winds and blizzards rattled the corrugated metal buildings. The only means of communication with the outside world was the short-wave radio, which was used infrequently. Unlike today, when satellite Internet and telephone connections keep the winter station manager and roughly fifteen personnel in constant touch with the outside world, Palmer Station then felt utterly sundered from civilization.

The six people who wintered at Palmer Station in 1975–76 each had their own methods of maintaining their sanity. Bill Fraser's lifeline was his work. No matter how inclement the weather, he usually spent several hours a day in the field studying kelp gulls. Back at the station, he would read and study for hours in the lab. He frequently skied for recreation and exercise.

"You begin not to withdraw so much as, well, you're taking care of your sanity," he recalled. "You start doing what you know you need to do to get through the winter. You knew you were there for the long haul. And the winters were a lot colder then."

For the most part, the men wintering with Fraser at Palmer adapted well—with one exception. Two winter residents had been at odds for months, and the tension finally came to a head during the men's one reliable social outlet—the Saturday night poker game. One of the feuding men offered to fix his antagonist a drink. Within moments of downing it, the man became violently ill. The man who had fixed the drink later denied poisoning his station mate and said his fellow resident had been stricken by a stomach bug. However, Fraser recalls that at the time the suspected poisoner withdrew into an almost catatonic state. He remained that way for several weeks until, at the station manager's request, an Argentine plane landed atop the Marr Ice Piedmont and armed officials whisked away the suspected troublemaker.

BILL FRASER'S THIRTEEN months in Antarctica came to an end in late October 1976. Despite the bizarre poker incident, it had been one of the best years of Fraser's life, launching him on a trajectory to becoming a field scientist. What he did not realize at the time was that he was witnessing the end of an era at Palmer Station, one in which extensive sea ice formation was common and ice-dependent Adélie penguins still thrived. Fraser has never forgotten the sight of Torgersen Island at the peak of summer in the mid-1970s. At that time, the island was home to roughly 9,000 pairs of breeding Adélie penguins. On a January evening, when many of the adults were on the island feeding their chicks, more than 20,000 Adélies of all ages mobbed Torgersen, their calls creating a cacophonous din.

"You'd see thousands of Adélies walking to and from the sea," said Fraser. "It was like ants in the forest—there was a constant stream of birds. Torgersen was an absolute mass of life. It just manifested the incredible productivity of this ocean and its ability to support life. You couldn't possibly fathom a day when you would fast-forward thirty years and there would be just a fraction of them left."

In the end, the ice nearly prevented Fraser from leaving Palmer. The Bismarck Strait was frozen, and as Captain Peter Lenie of the *Hero* emerged from the Neumayer Channel, the boat ran into impenetrable pack ice in the Bismarck Strait, about ten miles east of the U.S. base. On board were oceanographers and other scientists doing research on the Antarctic Peninsula, and Lenie radioed the station to say that he could wait no more than twenty-four hours for the ice to break up. Hiking up the Marr Ice Piedmont, Fraser could see the *Hero* in the distance, a dark dot on an endless white plain. After more than a year at Palmer Station, he was ready to leave.

He went to bed that night discouraged, believing he would be at

Palmer for many more weeks. And then Fraser's own *kamikaze,* or divine wind, appeared—a hard, steady blow from the north that continued all night. The next day, the miracle Fraser and the other members of the station's winter crew had been hoping for appeared: a long, narrow lead in the ice, opening up a passage from the mouth of the Neumayer Channel to Janus Island, about one and a half miles from the station. Fraser remembers Lenie saying over the radio, "I don't know what happened here, but we're going to come in. I'm going to turn around instantaneously because I don't want this lead to close in behind me, and you need to be ready to go."

It was growing dark as the *Hero* maneuvered into position near Janus Island. Miyoda placed flares on the ice to mark a safe path to the boat. Fraser worked furiously, hauling suitcases and boxes of books and gear to the *Hero.* When the work was finally done, he stowed his belongings on the ship as Lenie hurriedly turned the *Hero* around.

As the boat pulled away, Fraser stood on deck, clutching a gift from the first mate: a pint of Wild Turkey bourbon. Watching the lights of Palmer Station until they disappeared from view, the young biologist was flooded with conflicting emotions. He was tired. It had been a long year. Above all, he was relieved to be escaping the claustrophobic winter station. Heading inside to drink his bourbon, he found himself thinking: *I hope I never see this fucking place again.*

CHAPTER 4

THE PENINSULA
DISCOVERED

The will that gives man might to rule and dominate avails nothing here. The breeze which wafts the snow-flake, the ripple which stirs the lead, the tiny crystals which in countless millions build this gleaming ice-world, are all indifferent to a man's word or will.

—Frank Hurley,
Shackleton's *Endurance* expedition, 1914–16

Living for a year in Antarctica in the mid-1970s, Bill Fraser experienced the isolation but was spared the deprivation that was the hallmark of the heroic age of exploration. The miseries suffered by those adventurers were summed up by Apsley Cherry-Garrard, a young Englishman who, along with two other men from Robert Falcon Scott's 1910–13 *Terra Nova* expedition, successfully completed a harrowing nineteen-day trip in complete winter darkness, temperatures of –77°F, and hurricane-force winds to fetch a few emperor penguin eggs from a rookery on the Ross Sea.

"Polar exploration," Cherry-Garrard famously wrote in *The Worst Journey in the World* "is at once the cleanest and most isolated way of having a bad time which has been devised."

Dominated by legendary figures such as Ernest Shackleton, Roald Amundsen, and Robert Falcon Scott, the heroic age began in 1895, when the Sixth International Geographical Conference in London called for a coordinated campaign to map and study Antarctica, saying that the continent represented "the greatest piece of geographical exploration still to be undertaken." The era came to a close, in the minds of most historians, with the completion in 1917 of Shackleton's remarkable Imperial Trans-Antarctic Expedition, better known by the name of his ship, the *Endurance.*

By the time Fraser got to Antarctica, the continent had been well mapped and widely explored. Adventurers looking for a challenge in Antarctica could still find plenty of them—traversing the continent, scaling its highest mountains—but by the last quarter of the twentieth century, the most important work taking place in Antarctica was not exploration but the expansion of scientific research. In that sense, Fraser and his colleagues were the heirs to two centuries of adventurers who had probed the continent's defenses, exploited its seals, whales, and penguins, and endured terrible suffering as they ventured into its remotest corners, from the Weddell Sea to the South Pole itself.

AFTER CAPTAIN JAMES Cook's voyages of discovery around Antarctica, it was nearly a half century before an explorer actually set eyes on the continent. That the event occurred in January 1820 is indisputable, although there is some debate over who can rightfully claim the honor. Some say it was Captain Edward Bransfield of the British Royal Navy, who ventured south from Chile and explored the South Shetland Islands, at the northern end of the Antarctic Peninsula. But it seems almost certain that the Russian explorer Captain Fabian Gottlieb Thaddeus von Bellingshausen—the second man, after Cook, to circumnavigate Antarctica—was the first person to see the continent proper, spotting the mainland several days before Bransfield did.

In the wake of Bransfield's voyage, the exploration of Antarctica—in particular the Antarctic Peninsula, which was closer to civilization than any other part of the continent—began in earnest. What brought large numbers of men to the peninsula for the first time was the prospect of wealth, derived from the hide of one creature: the Antarctic fur seal, *Arctocephalus gazella.* Along with its cousin the South American fur seal, _Arctocephalus australis_, the Antarctic fur seal had already made many British and American sealers wealthy as they extirpated populations in the far South Atlantic and South Pacific oceans, as well as the Southern Ocean. The skins were prized by the Chinese, particularly for making felt, and this demand drove a frenzy of hunting from 1775 to 1825 during which millions of fur seals were slaughtered in the Southern Hemisphere. The trade spread from the Falkland Islands to South Georgia Island, where sealers killed an estimated 1.2 million Antarctic fur seals from 1778 to the early years of the nineteenth century. Initially unafraid of man, the seals blanketed South Georgia's beaches, allowing the hunters to quickly dispatch them with blows to the head from clubs. While sealing in South Georgia in 1785, a captain from Stonington, Connecticut, wrote that "the seals are so numerous I declare that if many thousand were killed overnight their loss would not be noticed in the morning."

By 1819, the sealing fleet had exhausted the known supplies of fur seals. Then, in February of that year, William Smith, a twenty-eight-year-old English sea captain making a run to Valparaiso, Chile, rounded Cape Horn and, encountering stiff westerlies, decided to head south into the Drake Passage in search of favorable winds. The gale blew Smith's brig, the _Williams,_ all the way to Antarctica. On February 19 and 20, with the storm still howling, Smith—an experienced ice captain who had been whaling in Greenland—spotted land. His position, 62°17′ S, 60°12′ W, put him just off the coast of Livingston Island in the South Shetland chain. The weather was so foul that he dared not explore, but when he arrived at Valparaiso he reported his discovery to the top Royal Navy officer there, who expressed skepticism. The sealers in the port, however, had faith in Smith's account, and a group of Yankee seal hunters offered him a handsome sum to divulge the location of this newly discovered land. Smith refused.

The following October, in the austral spring of 1819, Smith returned to the South Shetlands, taking possession of the land for the English crown and reporting that the terrain was "very high and covered with snow, (and) vast quantities of seals, whales, penguins." This time, when he returned to Valparaiso, no one doubted Smith's claims. The Royal Navy chartered his brig and placed Captain Edward Bransfield in charge, with the task of exploring the region discovered by Smith. Bransfield left Valparaiso in December 1819 and reached the South Shetlands on January 16, 1820.

Bransfield and the crew of the *Williams* were not alone in the South Shetlands. Acting on Smith's reports, an English brig, the *Espirito Santo,* had braved the Drake Passage and its crew was slaughtering fur seals on three-mile-long Rugged Island, west of Livingston Island. The Americans were determined to get in on the action as well. In July 1819, the sixty-eight-foot brig *Hersilia* left Stonington, Connecticut, carrying cargo for South America. Somewhere on the southerly voyage, possibly in the Falklands, the *Hersilia's* captain, James Sheffield, learned of Smith's discovery. Sheffield, whose second mate was young Nathaniel Palmer, decided to sail to Antarctica, arriving on January 18, 1820. Coincidentally, they, too, landed on Rugged Island, where there were ample fur seals for the *Hersilia* and *Espirito Santo.* In sixteen days, Palmer and his mates killed 8,868 fur seals, stopping only when they ran out of salt for the skins.

The Antarctic fur seal slaughter had begun. During the season of 1820–21, at least sixty American and British sealing vessels descended on the South Shetland Islands, including eight from New York and New England, commanded by Benjamin Pendleton of the Stonington fleet. Palmer was part of the fleet, serving as captain of the forty-seven-foot sloop *Hero,* designed to explore shallow waters and collect fur seal skins. The Americans arrived in the South Shetlands in November 1820, and by the twelfth of that month Pendleton was sufficiently worried about conflict with the growing number of British sealing vessels that he sent Palmer and the *Hero* to find new sealing grounds. In his tiny boat, Palmer probed southwest, sailing first to Deception Island. A volcanic caldera, Deception is roughly nine miles in diameter, its outer rim ringing a perfectly protected harbor that can be entered only through a narrow passage, about a quarter of a mile wide, in the basalt cliffs. The *Hero* entered the passage, now known as Neptune's Bellows, on November 15 and sailed around the harbor, past shores lined with steaming black volcanic sand.

With clear skies and excellent visibility, Palmer scrambled up the rim of the caldera and looked south. He plainly saw, sixty miles to the southeast, the white ramparts of the peninsular chain, becoming the first American to set eyes on the Antarctic mainland. On November 16, in clear weather, the *Hero* sailed south, heading for the mountain range Palmer had spotted. Later that day, the sloop approached Trinity Island, just off the Antarctic Peninsula at 63°40′ S. The following day, Palmer reported in his log that he "found the sea filled in immense Ice Bergs—at 12 hove to under the Jib Laid off & on until morning at 4 AM made sail in shore and Discovered a strait." That strait may well have been what is now known as Orleans Strait, which lies between Trinity Island and the peninsula and flows into the Gerlache Strait. But Palmer saw no seal rookeries on the ice-covered, inhospitable shores and, with icebergs all around, decided to head back to the South Shetlands.

In late 1820 and early 1821, the fur seal slaughter continued apace. By some estimates, the combined British and American sealing fleets may have collected 250,000 fur seal skins in the South Shetland Islands during that spring and summer. The business was dangerous and repugnant, with the sealers braving rough, frigid seas as they rowed small whaleboats from their ships to the fur seal rookeries on rocky beaches. Once on the shore, the men would herd the seals together, clubbing hundreds in a day and plunging up to their elbows in gore as they skinned the animals and cleaned their hides for salting. All of the adults were killed, leaving the mewling pups to starve to death from lack of their mothers' milk. In frigid, often gloomy conditions, the men lived in makeshift shelters heated and lit by fur seal oil, which coated them in black soot.

From January 14 to January 28, 1821, Pendleton sent Palmer on another exploratory cruise along the Antarctic Peninsula in search of additional seal rookeries. The logbook for the voyage long ago disappeared, but Palmer reported having reached 68° S. One account, written by Captain Edmund Fanning of New York, based on conversations with Palmer, accurately describes the coastline along the western Antarctic Peninsula that Palmer is said to have surveyed. "He found it to be extensive mountainous country, more sterile and dismal, if possible, and more heavily loaded with ice and snow than the South Shetlands," wrote Fanning. "There were sea leopards on its shore but no fur seals; the main part of the coast was icebound, although it was in the midsummer of this hemisphere, and a landing consequently difficult."

Shortly after midnight on the morning of February 5, Palmer was on the deck of the *Hero* at about 62° S, the boat barely moving in dense fog. He struck the ship's bell at 12:30 and through the fog heard two bells ring in reply. "The response startled me," Palmer later recounted, "but I soon resumed my pace, turned my thoughts homeward and applied myself to building castles in the air."

Thirty minutes later, he struck the bell twice more. Within seconds, two more bells answered his call.

"I could not credit my ears," Palmer said. "I thought I was dreaming." Other than the seabirds, he recalled, "I was sure no living object was within leagues of the sloop."

At 3:30 A.M., one of the *Hero*'s mates reported hearing voices through the fog. Shortly afterward, the fog began to clear and the mystery was solved: Nearby, off the *Hero*'s starboard bow, was a frigate, and off the port quarter was a sloop. It was the *Mirny* and the *Vostok* of Bellingshausen's fleet, as Palmer would soon learn when a small boat came to pick him up for a meeting with the Russian captain.

Palmer later recalled that Bellingshausen was incredulous "that I had come from U States in so small a vessel." Bellingshausen's journal only briefly mentions the encounter with Palmer, saying that the young American told him that he was "engaged in killing and skinning seals, whose numbers were perceptibly diminishing." The most detailed account of the encounter comes from the later writings of Fanning, who said Bellingshausen asked to see Palmer's logbooks after hearing that he had made it to 68° S in the tiny *Hero*. Fanning maintains that after examining the logs, Bellingshausen rose and said, "What do I see and what do I hear from a boy in his teens? That he is commander of a tiny boat of the size of the launch of my frigate, in which he has pushed his way to the pole through storm and ice; has sought and found the point I, in command of the best appointed fleets at the disposal of my august master, have for three weary years searched day and night for . . . what shall I say to my master? What will he think of me? But be that as it may, my grief is your joy. . . . I name the land you have discovered in honor of yourself, noble boy, Palmer Land."

The chain of islands off the northwest Antarctic Peninsula is today named the Palmer Archipelago. Far to the south, the lower half of the peninsula is called Palmer Land, in honor of the young American.

Within two days of Palmer's chance encounter with Bellingshausen, an American sealer from New Haven apparently became the first person to set foot on the Antarctic mainland. He was John Davis, the captain of the tender *Cecilia;* he had also gone in search of new fur seal rookeries late in the season, as tensions flared in the South Shetlands between British and American sealers. Heading south from Smith Island, Davis passed Hoseason Island, near the Antarctic Peninsula, and kept pushing on to 64° S. Finally, on February 7, 1820, the experienced captain ran into the peninsula and went ashore in a rowboat in search of seals, apparently near present-day Hughes Bay, at the top of the Gerlache Strait. Davis's log from that day reads: "Commences with open Cloudy Weather and Light winds a standing for a Large Body of Land in that Direction SE at 10 A.M. close in with it our Boat and Sent her on Shore to look for Seal at 11 A.M. the Boat returned but found no sign of Seal at noon our Latitude was 64°01′ South. Stood up a Large Bay, the Land high and covered intirely with snow. . . . I think this Southern Land to be a Continent."

Flush with profits from the 1820–21 sealing season, Palmer and the American fleet returned to the South Shetland Islands the following summer, as did the British. During the 1821–22 sealing season, the combined fleet reported killing 320,000 fur seals, essentially extirpating the entire population in the South Shetlands.

"This valuable animal, the fur seal, might, by a law similar to that which restrains fishermen in the size of the mesh of their net, have been spared to render annually 100,000 fur seals for many years to come," the British sealing captain James Weddell wrote. "This would have followed from not killing the mothers till the young were able to take to the water. . . . The system of extermination was practiced, however, at Shetland; for whenever a seal reached the beach . . . he was immediately killed, and his skin taken; and by this means, at the end of the second year, the animals became nearly extinct."

In 1823, the final good year of fur seal hunting, Weddell, an Englishman as interested in science and exploration as he was in accumulating fur seal skins, made an extraordinary voyage into the normally ice-bound sea on the eastern side of the Antarctic Peninsula. This body of water, which would eventually be named for Weddell, is the same one that drew Ernest Shackleton in 1914, only to trap his vessel, the *Endurance,* in the ice. But in February 1823, in what was certainly one of the most anomalous weather and ice years of the nineteenth century, Weddell was able to guide his brig, the *Jane,* to 74°15′ S, over a largely ice-free ocean. On February 18, as the *Jane* neared its most southerly point, with whales and seabirds cavorting around the ship, Weddell wrote in his log: "NOT A PARTICLE OF ICE OF ANY DESCRIPTION WAS TO BE SEEN."

In 1829, a ship visiting the South Shetlands found no fur seals. To this day, the island chain's once-teeming populations have not fully recovered.

IN THE 1830S and 1840s, several major expeditions explored the Antarctic Peninsula and other regions of the continent, mapping large stretches of coastline and further defining Antarctica's boundaries. From 1830 to 1832, John Biscoe, a young merchant mariner and former master in the Royal Navy, became the third man to circumnavigate the Antarctic as he searched for whales and seals. Working for Enderby Brothers, an English whaling company, Biscoe sailed close to land along an extended stretch of coast in the continent's Indian Ocean sector and explored large areas of the Antarctic Peninsula. His voyage—made in two ships, the *Tula* and the *Lively*—led him to correctly surmise that these two shores constituted "the headlands of a Southern Continent."

Sailing up the Antarctic Peninsula in February 1832, Biscoe discovered Adelaide Island and then, at 64° S, he came upon what would eventually be known as Anvers Island, a landmass so large he thought it was part of the mainland. On February 21, 1832, he is believed to have sailed into what is now called Biscoe Bay, about five miles east of the future site of Palmer Station, landing on a narrow strip of rocky shore in the bay—not far, apparently, from present-day Adélie and gentoo rookeries at Biscoe Point. In front of him were two mountains, one of which he called Mount William for his king; the other, at 5,036 feet, he named for Captain John Moberly, a former superior officer in the Royal Navy.

In the 1830s and 1840s, three major expeditions—one led by the Frenchman Jules-Sébastien-César Dumont d'Urville, one by the Englishman James Clark Ross, and one by the American Charles Wilkes—explored extensive areas of Antarctica's coast, including along the Antarctic Peninsula. Ross is famed chiefly for the discovery of the vast floating ice shelf named in his honor. All three explorers discovered unfathomable numbers of penguins, seabirds, and marine mammals. Wilkes encountered so many whales, according to historian Nathaniel Philbrick, that their spouting "reminded the men of smoke curling from the chimneys of a crowded city."

For the next three decades, not a single expedition, commercial or otherwise, visited the continent, in large part because the fur seal populations had been extirpated and whalers, with ample prey in more northerly climes, did not venture beyond the Antarctic Convergence. By the middle of the nineteenth century, after scores of sealing and scientific voyages to Antarctica, the world knew nothing about the continent beyond a few of its cobble beaches. One of those urging the continuing exploration of Antarctica and the Southern Ocean was renowned U.S. Navy oceanographer Matthew Fontaine Maury. Calling for an international scientific expedition to the continent, Maury noted in 1856 that "most of this immense area is as unknown to the inhabitants of the earth as is the interior of one of Jupiter's satellites."

In the summer of 1873–74, with whales in the Arctic in decline, Eduard Dallmann, a German sea captain and explorer, voyaged down the western Antarctic Peninsula in search of new whaling grounds. Traveling in the steamer *Grönland*, Dallmann explored and mapped much of the northwestern Antarctic Peninsula, including Anvers Island and lands to the south. Dallmann named numerous geographic features around present-day Palmer Station, including the Bismarck Strait.

The first major scientific expedition to answer the call of the Sixth International Geographical Congress was led by a little-known Belgian naval officer, Lieutenant Adrien de Gerlache de Gomery. He extensively explored the region around Palmer Station in the *Belgica* before sailing farther south along the Antarctic Peninsula and becoming trapped in the ice for thirteen months. The *Belgica* expedition was notable because it was the first to winter in the Antarctic and it made numerous scientific discoveries. But what is most intriguing about the voyage today is the crucial role played by two men who went on to achieve glory and—in one case—ignominy in polar exploration: Roald Amundsen and Dr. Frederick Cook. Lieutenant de Gerlache was a brave man, but he lacked the steel and competence of great polar explorers, such as Shackleton. Amundsen and Cook stepped in to fill the leadership void, preventing the mission from coming to pieces as the *Belgica* drifted across the Southern Ocean during the polar winter, locked in the ice.

The *Belgica,* a three-masted, ninety-eight-foot converted whaling vessel with a hull made of rock-hard greenheart, left Antwerp in August 1897, so laden with provisions and scientific equipment that it was nearly shipping water. Backed by the Royal Belgian Geographical Society and funded with government monies and a public subscription campaign, the expedition was staffed by an international crew that—after several defections in South America—consisted of nine Belgians, six Norwegians, two Poles, one Romanian, and one American. De Gerlache, thirty-one, had spent most of his adult life at sea, either in the merchant marine or the Belgian navy, and had consulted with the great Norwegian polar explorer Fridtjof Nansen about the *Belgica* expedition. Amundsen, a twenty-five-year-old Norwegian, was the second mate on the *Belgica*. Supremely confident on skis and a veteran of one sealing trip to Greenland, Amundsen had dreams of becoming a great polar explorer and leapt at the chance to participate in de Gerlache's expedition. The *Belgica* voyage proved a fine training ground for Amundsen, imparting lessons—both good and bad—that would prove invaluable as he became the first man to reach the South Pole in December 1911.

Cook, thirty-two, was a restless, widowed New York City physician who had accompanied Lieutenant Robert Peary on his first expedition to Greenland in 1891–92. Cook was keen to undertake more polar exploration but, unable to raise funds himself, he avidly joined de Gerlache as the *Belgica*'s doctor.

Also on board were several scientists, including the Polish chemist and geologist Henryk Arctowski, the Romanian biologist Emile G.

Racovitza, and the Belgian geophysicist Émile Danco. Most of the officers and crew had never been to the polar regions, and several would eventually crack under the strain of wintering in the Antarctic. In their defense, however, spending a winter below the Antarctic Circle in their small ship, trapped in the ice, had never been part of de Gerlache's announced plan. Letters to his family and other comments, however, indicate that de Gerlache may have been intending all along to winter in the pack ice aboard the *Belgica.*

On January 14, 1898, the *Belgica* set sail from Isla de los Estados, at the southern tip of South America, and crossed the Drake Passage, reaching the South Shetland Islands within a week. On January 22, a powerful storm struck the ship at 63° S near Low Island, and coal was washed into the scuppers that drain the deck. A popular young Norwegian sailor, Auguste-Karl Wiencke, went over the side on a rope to clear the scuppers, but as he worked a huge wave hit the ship, flinging Wiencke into the sea. Although he drifted away from the *Belgica,* Cook tossed Wiencke a log attached to a rope, which he managed to grab. One of the officers was lowered with a rope around his waist to pull Wiencke from the freezing water, but right before the officer reached Wiencke, the seaman—exhausted, his arms rigid from the cold—lost his grip on the log and disappeared beneath the waves.

With the officers and crew in mourning, the *Belgica* steamed south and spent the next three weeks, until February 12, exploring islands and the mainland flanking a one-hundred-mile channel they called "Belgica Strait"; eventually, the channel would be named in honor of de Gerlache. The expedition named three islands on the west side of the strait—Anvers (Antwerp), Brabant, and Liège—for three provinces in Belgium, made twenty landings along the strait, and mapped the area. In late January and early February, de Gerlache, Amundsen, Cook, Arctowski, and Danco undertook a treacherous, weeklong sledding journey along the crevasse-riven ice piedmont that streamed through the Solvay Mountains, on the southern end of Brabant Island. It was the first sledding trip in Antarctica.

On that journey, the men climbed higher in Antarctica than anyone had before, and from the top of the ice cap, amid mountains that rose more than 5,000 feet, they enjoyed a spectacular view of the peninsular range, stretching unbroken to the southern horizon. Taking geological samples at stops along the strait, Arctowski also began to formulate a theory that the mountain range running along the peninsula was an extension of the Andes Mountains, connected to the tip of South America by the Scotia Ridge, which runs under the Drake Passage and surfaces to form active volcanoes and mountains in the South Sandwich Islands, the South Shetlands, the South Orkneys, and South Georgia. He called the ice-smothered peninsular range the "Antarctandes" and theorized that the Andes and the peninsular range were formed by similar geological processes, with heavier tectonic plates from the Pacific forced under lighter continental plates. The resulting geology—a landscape of diorite, granite, granodiorite, quartzitic diorite, and basalt—is common around Palmer Station, generally dating back about 85 to 95 million years.

As the *Belgica* steamed down the strait, Arctowski made other major discoveries, including identifying new mosses, a vascular "hair grass" plant, more than fifty kinds of lichens, and one of the few insects living on the continent—the small, wingless Antarctic midge, now called *Belgica antarctica.*

In their journals and memoirs, the officers and scientists commented at length about the beauty of the strait, a wide, often placid body of water flanked on both sides by steep, black-faced mountains capped by massive fields of ice. "The whole panorama unrolling before our eyes, unseen as yet by any others, was of a tremendous grandeur," de Gerlache wrote. "The glaciers, like great congealed rivers, leaned over the sea, or vanished into it, a sea that seemed black in the face of so much whiteness."

In mid-February, the *Belgica* steamed farther south, traveling through fields of icebergs that rose and fell on what Cook called the "gigantic heave" of the Southern Ocean. Soon, the *Belgica* was skirting the edge of the pack ice. Drawing close to the northern tip of Alexander Island, beyond 68° S, Cook confessed that a "sense of chilly loneliness is more and more forced upon us by the passing panorama of snow, and ice, and deserted rocks." On February 28, 1899, as the ship hovered at the edge of pack ice extending to the horizon, a major storm swept in and opened up expanses of navigable water. Cook and the scientists advised de Gerlache that it was too late in the season to plunge into the pack, but de Gerlache ignored them and steamed ahead. For nearly ninety miles the wooden ship maneuvered deep into the sea ice. Then, on March 6, at 71°31′ S and 85°16′ W, the pack closed in and embraced the *Belgica*. It did not let go for another thirteen months.

Enduring sixty-seven days of complete darkness, temperatures plunging to −45°F, and claustrophobic conditions aboard the cramped, frigid ship, the officers, scientists, and crew drifted with the pack across 335 miles of the Southern Ocean. In the depth of winter, on June 5, Émile Danco died of congestive heart failure; his body was wrapped in sailcloth, weighted down at the feet, and dumped through a hole in the ice. Two men experienced breakdowns. So did the ship's cat, Nansen—named for the Norwegian explorer—which became reclusive and ill-tempered before finally expiring. De Gerlache and his second-in-command, Georges Lecointe, felt poorly and often withdrew.

Cook and Amundsen filled the vacuum. They had tried to convince de Gerlache that the men's mental and physical ailments—heart palpitations, chronic weakness, severe depression—were due to two things: a lack of fresh penguin and seal meat, which de Gerlache and some of the others refused to eat because of its strong taste, and a lack of light. Cook began to insist that all the crew eat fresh seal and penguin, which was often available, and the men obliged—even though the taste, as Cook later wrote, was akin to "a piece of beef, an odiferous codfish, and a canvas-back duck, roasted in a pot, with blood and cod-liver oil for sauce." Cook also initiated a regime of requiring the men to stand in front of the ship's stove, with its door propped open, to benefit from the heat and the light. This new regimen began to improve the collective health of the party, as did the return of the sun on July 22, 1899.

Meanwhile, Amundsen was enjoying the ordeal, viewing every experience as preparation for his goal of one day being first to the North or South Pole. As the *Belgica* began to force its way into the pack, eliciting a worried response from the expedition's scientists, Amundsen wrote in his diary, "Unfortunately the scientists are very frightened. They do not want to sail further into the ice any longer. Why did we come here then? Wasn't it to discover unknown territory? That cannot be done by staying at the edge of the ice and waiting."

A few weeks later, on March 11, 1899, as the ship became solidly encased in the sea ice and the temperature plummeted, Amundsen wrote, "Things are starting to get interesting."

Amundsen began to hatch plans to leave the *Belgica* with a companion in a two-man kayak. They would carry a sled and six months' worth of provisions—penguins and seals would supplement this fare—and head southeast toward the pole, camping on an iceberg during the winter before traveling farther southeast in the spring. Once they reached the other side of Antarctica, on the Ross Sea, Amundsen intended to kayak across the Southern Ocean to Australia. The plan was outlandish, but when discussing it in his diary, the young explorer stated, "This would of course take a number of years but I do not doubt this is possible."

Amundsen spent a great deal of time on the sea ice, killing seals and Adélie and emperor penguins for the crew. He discovered that by using a trumpet he could lure the penguins in for the kill. Once, after attracting and dispatching two emperor penguins, Amundsen wrote, "It seems that penguins are musical animals."

In the darkest part of the winter, not long after Danco died, Amundsen confided to his diary, "This is the life I have always wished for."

Much that Amundsen learned during the *Belgica* expedition played an important role in helping him beat Robert Falcon Scott to the South Pole. From Cook, he picked up good designs for snow goggles and for a light, warm, multilayered tent. Indeed, the tent Amundsen left behind at the pole, which was discovered by Scott and his men, was made, in part, according to Cook's design. While sledding on Brabant Island, Amundsen also soon realized that having men haul sleds in polar environments was far inferior to harnessing dogs for the task, reinforcing a conviction formed when he had first seen dog-sled teams used by the Inuit in Greenland. Amundsen's use of dog sleds during the South Polar race in 1911–12 proved to be the decisive factor in his victory.

Most important, however, was a negative lesson. After witnessing de Gerlache's disorganized planning and uncertain goals, after watching him wither as the ordeal dragged on, and after seeing some of the crew go to pieces, Amundsen realized the importance of exerting strong leadership, picking men who were mentally and physically tough, and planning for every contingency. The near disaster of the *Belgica* helped forge Amundsen's credo of exploration, as expressed in his autobiography, *My Life as an Explorer:* "Whatever I have accomplished in exploration has been the result of lifelong planning, painstaking preparation, and the hardest kind of conscientious work.... Victory awaits him who has everything in order—luck people call it. Defeat is certain for him who has neglected to take the necessary precautions in time—this is called bad luck."

Despite the suffering of the crew, the thirteen-month trial in the ice did result in several important scientific achievements—most notably, the first year-round meteorological records from the Antarctic. Arctowski, Lecointe, and Racovitza also gathered data on ocean currents and temperatures, wildlife, polar magnetism, and atmospheric phenomena.

Through the summer of 1898–99, the men waited expectantly for the ice to loosen and free the ship. But as the season began to draw to a close in early February, the *Belgica* remained trapped in the ice. The men used explosives to open up leads, to little effect, and, urged on by Cook, made a 2,300-foot channel by sawing through the ice. Not far to the north, they could see water reflected in the sky, indicating the presence of open ocean. Finally, on March 14, 1899, thanks both to their own efforts and to the late-season loosening of the sea ice, the *Belgica* was released from the pack. Two weeks later, the ship cruised into Punta Arenas.

De Gerlache and the crew returned to a hero's welcome in Belgium, and despite the loss of two men and the long ordeal in the pack, the *Belgica* expedition was—and is—viewed as a success because of its scientific achievements. While Amundsen went on to glory as the first man to reach the South Pole and the North Pole, Cook is chiefly remembered today as falsely claiming to have reached the North Pole in 1908; as is now known, he fell 410 miles short of his goal. Later, he was sentenced to fourteen years in prison for perpetrating a fraud in the oil business.

To the end of their days, Cook and Amundsen remained loyal allies, each crediting the other with holding together the *Belgica* expedition. Cook called Amundsen "the biggest, the strongest, the bravest" man on the expedition. Although acknowledging in later years that Cook was regarded as "one of the greatest humbug makers the world had ever seen," Amundsen nevertheless wrote of his former companion, "He, of all the ship's company, was the one man of unfaltering courage, unfailing hope, endless cheerfulness, and unwearied kindness. . . . And not only was his faith undaunted, but his ingenuity and enterprise were boundless."

As for the other men aboard the *Belgica*, the fifteen months in the Antarctic remained the single experience against which everything else in their lives was measured. Even Jan Van Mirlo, one of the sailors who became unhinged during the polar winter—for a while he wrote notes claiming that he could neither speak nor hear—looked back with affection on the voyage. This passage in his unpublished memoirs gives some idea of the grip that Antarctica can exert on a person's soul:

> However hard it was . . . sailing the Cape Horn Seas, the
> pack ice, the long winter, and comrades downing or dying
> in the polar night . . . however hard, it was one big pleasure
> trip, as well, a huge God-given holiday! For me, poor sinner,
> it was fun all the way. . . . And I remember that when even-
> tually we broke free unexpectedly from the ice's grip, free to
> set sail and fly home . . . I tell you that I suddenly was sad to
> see the place that held us for a year disappear.

BEFORE THE HEROIC age of exploration came to an end, two more expeditions—led by the same man, the French physician Jean-Baptiste Charcot—carried out extensive explorations along the western Antarctic Peninsula. From 1903 to 1905, aboard the *Français*, Charcot charted six hundred miles of coastline, spending the winter on Booth Island, just off the Danco Coast on the mainland, about twenty miles south-east of Palmer Station. The *Français* conducted numerous scientific experiments and—learning from the mistakes of the *Belgica*—Charcot ensured that the expedition's work was undertaken amid far more comfort than the *Belgica* voyagers had enjoyed. The *Français* was stocked with French wines, and the ship's cook baked fresh bread and croissants several days a week. The ship had a pet pig, named Toby, and on Christmas Day Charcot and his men picnicked on Booth Island, serenading the penguins with songs from a gramophone.

Upon Charcot's return to France, his wife—the granddaughter of Victor Hugo—promptly sued for divorce, claiming desertion. In 1907, Charcot remarried, this time with a prenuptial agreement that his second wife would not object to his polar expeditions. Charcot was the son of Jean-Martin Charcot, a renowned physician—and mentor to Sigmund Freud—who is now considered the father of neurology. The younger Charcot had inherited 400,000 gold francs from his father, much of which he used to fund his Antarctic expeditions.

His second journey to the western Antarctic Peninsula, aboard the *Pourquoi-Pas?*—the "Why Not?"—took place in 1908–10 and involved even more extensive exploration, during which Charcot surveyed 1,250 miles of coast and discovered a large, picturesque bay, between 68° S and 69° S, which he named for his new wife, Marguerite. Charcot and the *Pourquoi-Pas?* spent the winter on Petermann Island, about twenty-five miles southeast of Palmer Station, hard against the peninsula. Among the more notable scientific achievements of Charcot's second expedition was the penguin research of the zoologist Louis Gain, who studied and banded Adélies on Petermann Island. Gain's censuses also have proven to be a valuable record of the climate-induced changes in the region's penguin populations, for—like Fraser's work—they have helped document the precipitous drop in Adélie penguin populations and the arrival of large numbers of gentoo penguins.

With the end of the Ernest Shackleton's *Endurance* saga in 1917, the heroic age of exploration came to a close. Indeed, some of the subsequent expeditions along the western Antarctic Peninsula at times seemed more comic than heroic. One of those was the grandly named British Imperial Antarctic Expedition, which in fact consisted of only four men led by a highly disorganized leader, John Lachlan Cope. The plan had been to land the party at Hope Bay, on the northeastern side of the Weddell Sea, and then explore southward. When the Weddell Sea was, as usual, iced in, Cope changed plans, intending to set up a base on the western Antarctic Peninsula, not far from Palmer Station, and cross the towering, glaciated mountains on foot to reach the Weddell Sea.

Transported by a whaling ship, the men landed at Paradise Harbor, at the south end of the Gerlache Strait, on January 21, 1921. Cope soon recognized the impossibility of crossing the imposing peninsular chain with enough supplies remaining to launch an exploration of the Weddell Sea. He and the aviator he had recruited to survey the Antarctic Peninsula by air, Hubert Wilkins, decided to pack it in and head back to Montevideo, Uruguay, on a whaling ship. (Seven years later, Wilkins returned to Antarctica, flying the length of the Antarctic Peninsula and becoming the first person to survey and photograph the continent from the air.)

The two junior men on the expedition, nineteen-year-old Thomas Wyatt Bagshawe and twenty-four-year-old Maxime Charles Lester, elected to stay, because, as Bagshawe said, they did not have "the sense to know when they were defeated." The pair made their home in an overturned water boat—twenty-seven feet long, ten feet wide, and nearly four feet high—left by a whaling ship eight years before. They lived in the boat for 366 days before being retrieved by a whaling captain, who was not at all sure he would find the foolhardy pair alive. In fact, despite great hardship, the men flourished, even carrying out a detailed study of the gentoo penguins that shared Waterboat Point with them, roughly twenty-five miles due east of present-day Palmer Station.

The last, great foray along the western Antarctic Peninsula—forging a link between the heroic age of exploration and the modern era—was the British Graham Land Expedition, led by the Australian John Rymill. From 1934 to 1937, Rymill and fifteen men—traveling in a 103-foot schooner, the *Penola,* and making use of a de Havilland Fox Moth biplane for surveying and depot-laying—explored hundreds of miles of the Antarctic Peninsula. Members of the expedition made a 340-mile sled journey during which they discovered that Alexander Land, at 72° S, was in fact an island. Rymill's men also became the first to make the dangerous climb to the plateau atop the Antarctic Peninsula, where peaks rise to 10,000 feet.

The expedition's greatest achievement was proving conclusively that—contrary to mistaken reports from earlier air surveys—the Antarctic Peninsula was indeed a peninsula and not an archipelago with channels connecting the Weddell Sea with the Southern Ocean off western Antarctica. That finding, one of the most important geographic discoveries in Antarctica in the twentieth century, showed how little was known of the Antarctic Peninsula as late as 1934.

After World War II, exploring Antarctica and establishing bases became the work of governments and their militaries. In 1946 and 1947, the U.S. Navy's Operation Highjump—organized by the polar explorer Richard E. Byrd—used thirteen naval ships, twenty-three airplanes, and 4,700 men to map and take aerial photographs of the continent's 16,000-mile coastline. Even at that late date, Byrd remarked that existing maps of Antarctica had "little more relation to reality than some of the grotesque sixteenth-century maps of America used by pioneer explorers who crossed the Atlantic."

Other large expeditions followed, including the U.S. Navy's Operation Deep Freeze I and II, during which its commander, Rear Admiral George J. Dufek, landed at the South Pole in October 1956. He was the eleventh man to do so, as no one had set foot on the pole since the five men of Amundsen's expedition and the five accompanying Scott. In advance of the International Geophysical Year (IGY), which spanned 1957 and 1958, the United States began building stations at the pole and at Ross Island, on McMurdo Sound. The United Kingdom, the Soviet Union, France, Argentina, Australia, Chile, and five other nations built fifty other bases on the continent, as well, for the IGY. Worried about Cold War competition spreading to Antarctica, twelve countries signed the Antarctic Treaty in 1959, vowing to use the continent for peaceful, scientific purposes.

Palmer Station, finished in 1968, was by far the smallest of the United States' permanent bases. It was located about thirty miles from a larger British station, Faraday, in the Argentine Islands, a few miles off the Antarctic Peninsula. The dangers of living and working in Antarctica have greatly diminished since the heroic age of exploration, but events in the winter of 1982 at Faraday showed that the continent is still an exceptionally dangerous place.

On July 13, three young men working for the British Antarctic Survey decided to ski six miles from Faraday to Petermann Island, where Jean-Baptiste Charcot had wintered seventy-three years before. The men were planning to climb Mount Scott, a 2,887-foot peak located on the Antarctic Peninsula across the narrow Penola Strait from Petermann.

Scott was a reasonably low, yet steep peak with a small ice cap at its summit and ice streams flowing down its sheer, charcoal-gray face. The men intended to summit Scott and spend some time on Petermann, living there in a wooden hut stocked with food and firewood. A picture, taken with ten colleagues at Faraday, shows three jaunty young men standing in front of a snowy hut. John Coll, a clean-cut diesel mechanic wearing a heavy sweater, is smiling slightly, his arms folded across his chest. Kevin Ockleton, a meteorologist dressed only in jeans and a shirt, has a dark beard, longish hair, and a wide grin. Ambrose Morgan, a radio operator dressed in jeans and a sport coat, stands with his legs spread wide and his hands tucked into the front pockets of his pants. His dark hair falls over his ears and his forehead.

After their arrival at Petermann, things quickly went wrong, as described in the group's diary, part of which is now on display at the hut:

> 13th July 1982. Party of three arrived on 13th intending to climb Scott. John Coll, Ambrose Morgan, and Kevin Ockleton aborted the attempt on Scott on 14th due to failing light and poor condition of [Duseberg ice] ramp. Temp −25 C [−13°F]. Scott south face gully avalanched during afternoon. . . . Storm blew up on evening of 15th, 80 kts [92 mph winds] recorded at Palmer and 58 kts [67 mph] at Faraday. Two Peterman [sic] outhouses severely damaged during storm. Sea ice broke up enforcing prolonged stay. Estimated 50 days food supply. 90 days paraffin and considerable amounts of firewood! No booze and very few fags, but lots of tea and penguins.

Among this litany of mishaps and natural calamities, only one counted: "sea ice broke up." Hurricane-force winds had banished the thick blanket of sea ice over which the men had skied from Faraday to Petermann. They did, however, have sufficient stores to survive for weeks in the Petermann hut—firewood and some food, including the possibility of eating gentoo penguins. As soon as the sea ice reconstituted itself, the men could ski the short distance back to their base.

By August 1, however, salvation was not at hand. On that day, their diary read: "Still no sign of sea ice with wind blowing strongly from north. Radio contact with Faraday reduced to one sked per day due to failing radio batteries."

Two weeks later, with ice once again covering the sea, the men made the decision to ski back to Faraday. They never arrived. On September 13, their colleagues at Faraday sent a party on sleds to Petermann, but the rescue team found no sign of the men. Their exact fate is unknown, but they likely met their end in one of two ways: by plunging through thin ice into the sea or by being marooned on an ice floe and freezing to death as they drifted into the Southern Ocean. No doubt fed up with living in a primitive hut with meager food supplies and limited heat in the middle of the Antarctic winter, the three men chose to take their chances by skiing on sea ice that had not been fully reconstituted. Had they endured another month at Petermann, they would have been rescued, but fatigue, cold, and isolation clouded their judgment and they set off on their own. They are memorialized today by a five-foot-tall wooden cross that rises from a cairn by the water's edge. A small bronze plaque lists the men's names and summarizes their fate: "Lost on sea ice. August 1982."

Faraday Station remained part of the British Antarctic Survey's network of bases until 1996, when the United Kingdom transferred it to the Ukrainian government and it was renamed Akademik Vernadsky Station. Although Faraday and Palmer are relatively small Antarctic bases, their importance in studying the earth's swiftly changing climate has proved to be large. The Faraday temperature record, dating back to 1950, has documented the precipitous warming of the northwestern Antarctic Peninsula over the past sixty years. And Palmer Station turned out to be at ground zero for studying how these rapid temperature increases have transformed this maritime Antarctic environment and the creatures that call it home.

CHAPTER 5

INCUBATION

No matter how melancholy a man may feel, if he sees
one of these jolly little fellows he cheers up.

—W. G. Burn Murdoch,
Dundee Antarctic Whaling Expedition, 1892–93

Two days after the *Laurence M. Gould* turned around in the face of impenetrable sea ice, the wind shifted at last and blew in our favor. Howling out of the northeast at 40 miles per hour, the gale began driving the sea ice offshore. I nervously watched the water, afraid the wind would stop or shift again, allowing the ice to return. But the blow kept up, slowly shoving the great raft of ice away from the southern shore of Anvers Island. That night, in the birders' tent, I looked at the whiteboard that chronicled our fieldwork. Marked on the board's calendar, for fifteen days in a row, was the same word: "In."

That was about to change.

The next morning, I looked out my bedroom window and the sea ice was gone, banished to the Bismarck Strait a mile or two offshore. Walking down the station boardwalk, I was pelted with wet snow driven by wind gusts of 35 miles per hour. By 9:45, as the winds fell below twenty-five miles per hour, Peter, Jen, and I were in our Zodiac, heading to Torgersen Island.

In the last sixteen days, the scene had changed dramatically. The blanket of snow that had covered most of the island was now full of holes—ever-widening circles of lead-gray pebbles and brick-red muck, upon which Adélie penguins stood and lay. The immaculate tableau of late October had been replaced with the filth and stink of an Adélie rookery on a wet day. The Adélies' satiny white breasts were soiled. Everywhere were cup-shaped nests constructed of small stones; the most solid and commodious nests were six inches tall and resembled wide-mouthed volcanoes. And on the nests lay male Adélie penguins, incubating one or two cream-colored eggs, tinged faintly green and roughly three inches long. From time to time a male would stand and delicately adjust the eggs with his beak before nestling back down and covering them with his brood patch, a four-inch gap in his thick abdominal feathers that allows him to warm the eggs with bare, blood-engorged skin. Even on cold Antarctic stones, the heat of the brood patch enables Adélies to incubate their eggs at about 86°F.

The hens had been laying eggs for at least a week and were continuing to do so. It takes an Adélie an average of twenty-one days to gestate an egg, after which the eggs are incubated for thirty to thirty-nine days. Many nests contained two eggs, the customary Adélie clutch; the second is laid two to four days after the first. After the hen lays the eggs, she departs for the sea to feed, leaving her mate to handle the first incubation shift. Neither male nor female has eaten since arriving at the colony, meaning that the females have often fasted for several weeks, many losing a third of their body weight during this period, dropping from roughly 10 or 11 pounds to 6.5 or 7 pounds. The females usually spend a week or two at sea, replenishing their spent reserves, then relieve the males, who by this time often have been fasting for four to five weeks, losing up to 40 percent of their body weight. The males then take to sea for a week or two before returning to relieve their partners.

The shift changes then occur far more frequently, and by the end of the incubation period and during chick rearing, the Adélies relieve each other every day or two. But as David Ainley has pointed out, once the hen ambles down to the ocean after laying her eggs, an Adélie pair spends little time together; they resemble nothing so much as a harried human couple with husband and wife working different shifts, around the clock, to keep food on the table for their children.

Throughout the colonies on Torgersen, penguins continued to construct nests. Some were cocks whose mates were still waiting to lay a second egg; these males marched around the colony and its perimeter, carefully selecting a pebble before waddling back to the nest and depositing the rock with great delicacy. Other younger, nonbreeding males were building nests, a form of playing house. They often took less care, snatching stones and walking back to their unoccupied abode, where they tossed the pebble in an unruly pile with the nonchalance of a teenager flinging a wet towel on the floor.

On that day, and the two following, we hurriedly carried out the tasks that had accumulated during our two-week absence from the penguin rookeries. Working on the three closest islands—Torgersen, Humble, and Litchfield—we performed one of the key penguin counts of the season, known as "peak egg." This was a tally of all Adélie pairs that had successfully laid eggs, and it was used as the standard census of penguin populations. Counting penguins may sound like a task any simpleton could perform, but when some colonies contain hundreds of nesting pairs you can quickly go cross-eyed making sure you have neither missed a few pairs nor counted a pair twice. Our team performed three counts for every colony, and if the tallies were within 5 percent of each other, we used the average of the three. If not, we recounted. Jen and Peter also spent many hours during those three days choosing so-called repro sites—dozens of specially selected nests that the team would monitor for the rest of the season. How many eggs did the female lay? Did the pair lose eggs and, if so, when? How many chicks hatched, and when? Did any chicks perish, and when? And how many chicks grew to adolescence and then joined the unruly pack of young Adélies known as a crèche? These repro sites told the story, in microcosm, of the Adélie reproductive season at Palmer. Jen, who was especially meticulous, brought with her color photographs of repro sites taken by the team the previous season so that she could attempt to establish her repro colonies in the same locations.

This early in the season, the challenge was to see how many eggs lay under an incubating Adélie. Sometimes the penguin would make the job easy by standing and readjusting its eggs. But if the penguin was sitting resolutely on the nest, we would use long bamboo poles to prompt it to stretch its legs. Peter Horne was particularly skilled at coaxing the Adélies off their eggs. His preferred method was dangling one end of the pole just above a bird's head, which would often cause it to rise up and nip the pole, exposing the eggs.

One thing Fraser's team—and other Adélie researchers—knew for sure was that the more experienced penguins tended to nest deeper into the colonies and to have greater success raising chicks to the fledging stage. As I walked by a colony on Torgersen Island on that mid-November day, I was given a good demonstration of why this was so. Gliding low over the island was a brown skua (*Catharacta skua lonnbergi*), a predator that is technically in the seagull family but whose bold spirit and hooked beak more readily bring to mind a raptor. I watched as the brown skua glided over the colonies, causing the Adélies to rise in unison and blurt out loud warning squawks, a reaction that always brought to mind a wave cheer at a baseball game. As the skua flew over the largest colony on Torgersen, spreading its mottled brown and soot-colored feathers, it spotted a partially exposed egg near the colony's edge, probably belonging to a less experienced breeder. Dipping down, the skua snatched the egg in its beak without touching the ground and flew twenty-five yards away. The skua was soon joined by its mate, and the pair quickly devoured the contents of the egg. As we walked from colony to colony on Torgersen, we saw the shells of many Adélie eggs that had been eaten by brown skuas. The skuas had not been in evidence two weeks ago; there had been no reason for them to be there, as neither Adélie eggs nor chicks were yet on the menu. But in the ensuing two weeks, the brown skuas had arrived, exhibiting the same exquisite, evolutionary timing as the Adélies: Just as the skua hens needed nourishment to gestate their eggs, the Adélies would lay theirs. And when the skua chicks arrived, so, too, would the Adélie chicks, some of which, by way of skua parents, would then be fed to the young skuas. Bird eats bird, closing the circle of life in the Southern Ocean.

So, thanks largely to the depredations of skuas, the outer ring of a colony is not an auspicious spot for an Adélie nest. But veteran breeders instinctively realize that establishing a nest too deep inside the colony is not a good idea, either: too many cranky neighbors to pass on their way to and from the sea. That predicament was evident in Torgersen's two large colonies, where penguins in the interior had to wade through a mob of pecking Adélies, causing the travelers to sometimes carom around the colony like pinballs as they were assaulted by neighbors at every turn.

The speed with which the Adélies moved ahead with the business of reproduction depended on a colony's location. Penguins in colonies on the windswept northern side of Torgersen, especially on ridges, were well advanced, with many males incubating two eggs and the females already at sea. But the smaller population on the snowy south side, in the lee of a low ridge that bisects Torgersen Island, was lagging behind. In these modest colonies, sometimes only ten feet wide, it looked as if the snow had only recently melted, and fewer nests held two eggs. Snow—how much of it falls, when it falls, and where it accumulates—is a changing force on the northwestern Antarctic Peninsula, and the shift was having an ill effect on the Adélie populations.

Nowhere was that more evident than in Colony 19, on the southwest side of Torgersen, where melting snow had flooded low-lying nests. Approaching Colony 19, I could see dozens of Adélies standing in and around two murky ponds of snowmelt about six inches deep. The water was a putrid brown color, and under the surface were a half dozen penguin eggs, resembling large golf balls resting in a shallow water hazard. Adélies were standing belly-deep in the water, dunking their heads under the surface to try to move their eggs or their collapsed nests. Several of the more industrious penguins had managed to rebuild their nests high enough so that they just poked above the ponds, looking like castles in the middle of a lake. One or two even had succeeded in placing an egg atop the pile, after which they attempted to brood the egg. Other Adélies were sitting on eggs on the edges of the ponds, acting as if inhabiting lakefront property was a natural thing for a penguin.

The eggs submerged in ice water were, of course, addled, and there was little hope that the few eggs perched atop the rebuilt, waterlogged nests would produce a viable chick. But the nesting and brooding instinct is a powerful one, and these Adélies were determined to see the process through to its conclusion, even though the reproductive season was over for most of them. The behavior of the birds at Colony 19 was an example of what could be viewed as either the tenacity or the stupidity of Adélie penguins. I am partial to the first interpretation.

Previous scientists and explorers had witnessed an abundance of such behavior among Adélies. At Cape Adare in 1911, G. Murray Levick observed a spirited rescue operation in an inundated Adélie colony, a scene reminiscent of Mississippi River residents piling up sandbags to protect their homes from a flood. As meltwater trickled into the small colony from higher ground, the Adélies busied themselves wading across the small pool, retrieving stones from dry ground, and piling them up on their nests. One particularly diligent Adélie managed to raise the height of his nest a foot above the rising water and save the eggs.

Once, Levick saw hundreds of incubating Adélies buried during a snowstorm, the penguins dwelling in snow caves for days, popping their heads out to breathe. He witnessed one incident in which an Adélie approached its mate, which was entombed up to its head. The Adélie on the surface, wanting to trade places with its mate and commence the incubation shift, began pecking at the head of the snowbound Adélie, which seemed unable to free itself. The attack worsened to the point where Levick felt compelled to rescue the buried penguin. He did so by digging away the crust of snow, at which point the Adélie burst forth; the bird had been lying in a pool of guano-tainted meltwater, its eggs addled.

The stubborn determination to forge ahead with the continuation of the species was on display during another incident at Cape Adare. Many Adélies there nested under a high cliff that occasionally unleashed rock slides. One day, a rock-and-scree avalanche occurred, killing and injuring hundreds of Adélies at the base of the cliff and causing, in Levick's words, "the most sad havoc." The surviving Adélies suffered severe injuries, including broken legs and flippers. Some had been disemboweled; others had had the skin ripped off their backs. Levick and his men moved through the colony, rescuing those that could be saved and dispatching with ice axes those too injured to recover. Yet amid the carnage, the rest of the Adélies still sat quietly, incubating their eggs.

"I saw several badly injured birds sitting on their eggs," wrote Levick, "some of them soaked in blood, so that they looked like crimson parrots."

After several decades working with Adélies, Fraser has formed an opinion on the subject of the Adélies' mettle. "They are the toughest animals I've ever encountered," he told me when we first met, in 2004. "To see Adélie penguins that have almost been cut in half by leopard seals still coming back every day with a stomach full of krill for their chicks—it sets the standard for toughness. They are a courageous little animal."

THEY ARE ALSO superbly adapted to their frigid marine environment, occupying a unique ecological niche, thanks to tens of millions of years of evolution. The story of the Adélies and their sixteen to nineteen fellow species of penguins goes back 140 million to 160 million years, to the Jurassic period, when birds branched off the evolutionary tree from reptiles, their scales gradually changing into feathers. At some point around 100 million years ago, the ancestors of today's penguins were closely related to the forebears of the Procellariiformes seabirds of today, which include albatrosses, petrels, and fulmars. Then, approximately 55 million to 100 million years ago, penguins evolved into a flightless order of birds in the Southern Hemisphere as the southern supercontinent Gondwana was continuing to break apart into the continents of today.

Conditions in the southern seas were ideal for the emergence of birds that would make their living foraging at sea rather than ranging far and wide in the air. As the paleontologist George Gaylord Simpson has pointed out, birds developed the ability to fly so that they could evade predators and travel long distances in search of food. But as Simpson noted in his book *Penguins: Past and Present, Here and There,* "If all these functions become useless to a group of birds, flight will tend to be lost just because there is no natural selection favoring it."

That is precisely what happened with the ancestors of today's penguins. As it turned out, no penguin predators existed on many of the islands of the Southern Hemisphere where the proto-penguins lived. In addition, the southern oceans were rich in food. Slowly, over millions of years, natural selection favored a bird that could swim long distances, fattening up to the point where it could no longer take to the air. Flying birds need hollow bones and must remain relatively light in order to fly. But with no land predators threatening proto-penguins and with ample food in the ocean, it became advantageous for these southern birds to eat to the point where their wings could no longer lift them off the ground. Over time, their wings evolved into powerful flippers supremely suited to propelling them rapidly through the water.

The oldest known penguin fossils, found in New Zealand, belong to a species that lived roughly 60 million years ago. The first penguin fossil to be discovered was unearthed in a New Zealand limestone quarry in 1858 or 1859 and sent to the eminent English biologist Thomas Henry Huxley. It was clear that the bone came from a penguin larger than any in existence, and later studies estimated that Huxley's penguin—which probably lived 23 million to 34 million years ago—was about four foot nine and weighed close to two hundred pounds. The largest fossil penguin ever discovered was found by the Swedish geologist Otto Nordenskjöld during his 1901–04 Swedish Antarctic Expedition to the Weddell Sea. This ancient bird, unearthed on Seymour Island and eventually named *Anthropornis nordenskjoeldi,* was probably about five foot four and may have weighed three hundred pounds. "In human terms their height would not suffice for basketball, but their weight was about right for American football," wrote Simpson.

Approximately forty species of fossil penguins have been discovered. Many of the proto-penguins were larger than the biggest penguin alive today, the emperor, which can grow to four feet in height and weigh ninety pounds.

The oldest fossils belonging to the pygoscelid, or "rump-legged," genus of penguins—which includes Adélies, gentoos, and chinstraps—date back roughly 3 million years. Over countless millennia, Adélies have colonized and recolonized Antarctica as the climate naturally warmed and cooled. During glacial periods, when advancing ice caps covered the rocky coasts and nearby islands that Adélies needed for nesting, the penguins would seek refuge in more northerly climes. During warming periods, the Adélies would recolonize the Antarctic coast and islands. Radiocarbon dating of penguin bones on the Ross Sea has revealed Adélie colonies as old as 13,000 years. On the southern half of the Antarctic Peninsula, in Marguerite Bay, radiocarbon dating of bones and eggshells shows that Adélie colonies have existed in the area for at least 6,000 years. On the northwestern Antarctic Peninsula and in the Palmer Station area, no colonies older than 644 years have been found, though paleoecologists believe that penguins have been in the area far longer and that traces of their ancient colonies have either not yet been found or have been wiped away by advancing glaciers.

Over time, Adélies and other penguins evolved into superb swimming machines. Their flippers became more tapered and gradually lost the joint movement that flying birds possess, giving the penguins the stiff, powerful tools that rocket them through the water. They retained the keeled breastbones of flying birds, to which are attached the strong breast muscles that power their swimming. Their webbed feet and legs moved far back on their torsos, allowing the birds to use them—and their long tails—as rudders, and giving penguins the upright stance and walk that endears them to humans.

Their bodies also took on the sleek, football-like shape that make them supremely hydrodynamic. Their torso and wing feathers gradually shortened to the almost scalelike feathers of today, which sharply cut down on drag in the water. In addition, they developed the ability to squeeze the air out of their thick coat of feathers and subtly change shape in the water, allowing them to rocket even more efficiently through the sea.

Said Simpson, "In fact, penguins can fly. Most birds fly in the air. Many of them swim in the water, paddling with (usually) webbed feet. Penguins do neither. They fly in the water."

Today, penguins have evolved into the largest family of completely flightless birds on the planet. Yet they remain exclusively in the Southern Hemisphere. In large part this is because the strong Equatorial Countercurrent, which flows east to west, acts as a natural migratory barrier to flightless birds. It is also because penguins are ill-suited to hot equatorial waters. Even though penguins have a wider breeding range than any other order of bird—from emperors on Antarctic ice shelves at 77° S to Galápagos penguins at the equator—the order is generally adapted to cooler climes. Even the Galápagos penguin is dependent on the upwelling of the cold Humboldt Current to bring it the food it needs.

From the fifteenth to the eighteenth centuries, as European explorers moved ever deeper into the Southern Hemisphere, they were struck by the penguins' protean blend of bird and fish. In 1620, a French admiral sailing off South Africa described the jackass penguins he found there as feathered fish. Soon, however, these strange creatures came to be known as "penguins." The name was almost certainly derived from the Latin word *pinguis*, for "fat." It was originally given to auks, a northern order of seabirds with a superficial resemblance to penguins. The heavily hunted—and flightless—great auk became extinct in 1844 when the last member of its species was killed in Iceland.

BY THE END of our first day back in the field, the temperature had climbed to 40°F and the dark clouds occasionally parted to reveal a swath of blue sky. As we worked on Torgersen Island, the snorting, belching sounds of southern elephant seals (*Mirounga leonina*) on nearby Elephant Rocks reverberated across Arthur Harbor. We also discovered a charcoal-gray elephant seal pup, about four feet long, on the island's south side. Nearby was its mother, a twelve-foot beast with a large proboscis, a gray-brown hide, and enormous, bulging black eyes. As we passed her, she opened her mouth, exposing the bubble-gum-pink interior, and let fly with a guttural croak to warn us away. This cow and other large elephant seals had left wide, trough-shaped trails in the snow, which the Adélies conveniently used in their travels on Torgersen. Elephant seals are more commonly found in the subantarctic, and though small numbers had for decades visited the Palmer area in summer, they had only recently begun arriving en masse and birthing pups here—yet another sign that things were warming up.

The seals' wallows—where groups of hulking, belching, juvenile males were packed tightly together in a putrid-smelling encampment—were spreading. Many were shedding their brown skin like peeling wall-paper, prompting Jen to remark, "I just want to take a rake and scratch all that off." Walking by a wallow one day, Peter Horne shot a glance at a large elephant seal and said, "Jabba the Hutt."

As we completed our work later that week, what most struck Peter was how few Adélies remained in many of the colonies. Even this early in the season, it was clear that the collapse of Adélie populations around Palmer Station was continuing apace. A handful of the smaller colonies on Torgersen Island—each once holding several hundred pairs of Adélies—were now down to two to three dozen pairs, half the number of the previous season. On the beleaguered south side of Torgersen, Peter and Jen headed for Colony 1 to set up a repro site. Sixteen years before, the colony had been home to 166 pairs of Adélies. By 2004, that number had shrunk to 8 pairs. Now, as we snowshoed across a white expanse that had once been covered with Adélies, Horne stopped where Colony 1 should have been. Nobody was home.

"I guess we don't have to worry about that repro site," said Horne. "That's really discouraging."

Later in the day—another beautiful, placid afternoon with a vaulted blue sky and the temperature hitting 43°F—we made our way to Humble Island. As our Zodiac drew near, I saw whales spouting in a channel between Humble and neighboring Litchfield Island. Peter immediately identified them: orcas, or killer whales (*Orcinus orca*). We counted six or eight fins, the largest being the five-foot, narrow, triangular fin of a male. It soon became clear what these orcas—which actually are not a whale but, rather, the largest species of dolphin—were after: A lone leopard seal was resting on an ice floe and the orcas were attempting to dislodge it. We saw two orcas raise their upper bodies and heads out of the water, an act known as "spy-hopping" that not only enables them to scout their prey but is also believed to disorient whatever is lying on the floe, with the aim of driving it into the water.

We cruised to within a hundred yards of the orcas, cut our engine, and watched. Within a few seconds, however, the killer whales seemed to lose interest in the leopard seal. What had caught their fancy was us and our Zodiac. They began knifing through the water in our direction, at which point Peter said to Jen, who was at the tiller, "Better start the engine." Jen whipped the boat around and we headed for Humble Island, with the orcas in pursuit. As we motored toward the landing at Humble, the orcas followed, turning north out of the channel, just as we did, and then continuing to chase us as we headed northwest toward our tie-up spot on the rocks. I'd heard that there were no documented cases of orcas killing humans in Antarctica. (Later I would read of numerous cases of orcas chasing humans, dogs, and ponies on Antarctic ice floes.) I knew the orcas were just curious. But I must confess to feeling some relief when we finally made the landing at Humble.

The orcas were right behind us. They cruised past our boat, with one even spy-hopping us from fifteen feet away; I was so amazed by this performance that I cannot remember exactly what the orca looked like. All I recall is an enormous, battleship-gray form, with white patches, rising out of the water like a missile emerging from a silo. The orca family—which included a male, several females, and some young— proceeded to frolic in the two-hundred-yard channel between Humble and Norsel Point. They rolled on their backs, exposing white bellies, and several even swam under a remnant sheet of winter sea ice the length of a football field. Their spouting made a sharp hissing sound.

Soon the orcas lost interest in us and swam into Arthur Harbor. We radioed the station and the other scientific teams out on the sea that day—not out of alarm but, rather, to give them a chance to observe a pod of orcas at close range. As it turned out, one of Langdon Quetin's assistants, David Huang, was an accomplished videographer, and as the orcas swam their way he pulled out his digital video camera and shot some memorable footage. Some of the orcas swam directly under Quetin's Zodiac, their ghostly figures appearing startlingly close in the clear water. Huang captured their white saddles—unique markings by which individual orcas can be identified—as they played around his boat. One orca gracefully slipped onto its back under the Zodiac. The male paraded just in front of the boat, and Huang captured a pair of orcas as they spy-hopped next to two crabeater seals on an ice floe; he and Quetin were sure that the orcas would knock the seals from the floe and devour them, but after spy-hopping for a few seconds, the orcas moved on.

Antarctic explorers from earlier eras would no doubt have been less sanguine about the threats that orcas posed to a rubber boat full of people. It's easy to see why. Male orcas in Antarctic waters can reach thirty feet and weigh as much as twelve thousand pounds. Hunting in packs and equipped with two rows of large teeth, orcas—which are found worldwide and consist of as many as five separate subspecies—are fearsome predators. They are the only members of the cetacean family—which includes dolphins, porpoises, and whales—that regularly attack warm-blooded animals; among their favorite prey in Antarctic and subantarctic waters are seals, whales, and larger penguins, such as emperors and kings. Orcas seem to pay little attention to smaller penguins, such as Adélies, and numerous observers have reported that Adélies seem far more panicked by the appearance of a leopard seal in the water than an orca.

Scientists estimate that the Southern Ocean is home to roughly seventy thousand orcas, and these highly intelligent, social animals have been spotted in pods as large as fifty. One remarkable video, shot from a cruise ship in Antarctic waters, demonstrates the highly evolved group hunting behavior of orcas. In it, a pod of orcas works for several minutes to dislodge a lone seal from an ice floe. They finally succeed in doing so when three killer whales surge in a line up to and under the floe, creating a large wave that washes the seal from the ice and into the sea, where it is devoured.

One of the earliest accounts of an orca attack in Antarctic waters came from American explorer Charles Wilkes, who in 1840 watched as orcas killed a large whale. At one point, Wilkes wrote in his *Narrative of the United States Exploring Expedition*, the wounded whale "threw himself at full length from the water with open mouth, his pursuer still hanging to the jaw, the blood issuing from the wound and dyeing the sea to a distance around. . . . These fish attack a whale in the same way that dogs bait a bull, and worry him to death."

Early-twentieth-century adventurers had numerous close encounters with killer whales. During Shackleton's *Endurance* expedition, he and his men, marooned on the sea ice as they drifted across the Weddell Sea, saw orcas in open leads and watched as they stalked seals; the *Endurance*'s captain, Frank Worsley, came upon an eight-by-twelve-foot hole where an orca had smashed through foot-thick ice, hurling large blocks onto surrounding floes. The men's greatest fear was that orcas would mistake them for seals and attack. Photographer Frank Hurley described one encounter:

> Once I was out with one of the sailors, and we were crossing a wide lead that had just frozen over. We had not gone 50 yards when we heard whales blowing close by. Quickly I wheeled the dogs on the thin and treacherous ice and, swinging as sharply as possible, made a dash for safety. . . . The whales behind—there were three of them—broke through the thin ice as though it were tissue-paper and, I fancy, were so staggered by the strange sight that met their eyes, that for a moment they hesitated. Had they gone ahead and attacked us in front, our chances of escape would have been slim indeed; but fortunately we reached the solid ice and made for a big hummock. The killers charged the floe and poked their heads over the edge. Never in my life have I looked upon more loathsome creatures. Yet, being now in comparative safety, the one thought that came to me was, "What chances one misses in venturing out without a camera or a gun."

In 1911, as the members of Robert Falcon Scott's *Terra Nova* expedition were moving supplies across the frozen Ross Sea, a section of ice holding three men and four ponies broke away. Orcas began circling the group, and though the men managed to leap across floes to safety, three of the four ponies perished. One fell into the water when the ice split and was believed to have been eaten by the whales. Two other horses, panicked by the presence of the orcas, fell into the water, where expedition members dispatched them with ice axes before the killer whales could eat them alive.

Earlier in the expedition, a pod of eight orcas had appeared in leads around the *Terra Nova*. The photographer Herbert Ponting ran toward the edge of a floe to get a picture of the killer whales. As he did so, the whales began smashing the ice on which he and two Huskies stood. Scott described in his journal what happened next: "The next moment

the whole floe under him and the dogs heaved up and split into frag-
ments. One could hear the booming noise as the whales rose under the
ice and struck it with their backs. Whale after whale rose under the ice,
setting it rocking fiercely; luckily Ponting kept his feet and was able to
fly to security. . . . That they could display such deliberate cunning that
they were able to break ice of such thickness (at least 2 1/2 feet) and that
they could act in unison, were a revelation to us. It is clear that they are
endowed with singular intelligence, and in future we will treat that
intelligence with every respect." Ponting had no doubt that the whales
were after him. He describes how he was nearly flung into the water as the
orcas repeatedly smashed the ice from below. He recalls the fishy-smelling
blast of their breath as they spouted. He remembers seeing, from feet
away, their "little pig-like eyes" and "terrible teeth."

"I recollect distinctly thinking, if they did get me, how very unpleasant the first bite would feel," Ponting wrote in *The Great White South*,
"but that it would not matter much about the second."

AS INCUBATION CONTINUED into late November and early December, the Adélie colonies took on a rare air of tranquillity. The penguins
had built their nests, laid their eggs, and—though copulation still took
place—were largely finished with mating. For the most part, the Adélies lay quietly, about two feet apart, often facing in different directions.
They resembled black-and-white footballs, their eyes contracting to
narrow white slits as they dozed. Periodically, Adélies marched out of
the sea to relieve their mates, their wet feathers gleaming with a lac-
querlike sheen and their stomachs so packed with krill that they nearly
scraped the ground.

Returning mates waddled into the colonies and hovered over their
partners, belting out the raspy, kazoolike call that preceded the nest
exchange. Frequently, a returning mate or an aimless nonbreeding male
would stumble through alien territories, touching off a round of pecking and a flurry of protests that sounded like gobbling turkeys.

Occasionally, our birding team caused a disturbance as well. We
generally gave the Adélies a wide berth—at least ten feet—as we went
about our business. But a few times a season, the birders were obliged

to violate the penguins' territorial boundaries, an event that inevitably created a commotion. One such occasion came toward the end of November, when the birders weighed and measured twenty-five Adélies and their eggs, an exercise that gave yet another indication of the overall health of the penguins. During this exercise, I also discovered that, like humans, Adélie penguins demark a personal space inside which it is inadvisable to trespass. And as it turns out, an Adélie comfort zone is about the same as a person's—two to three feet.

On a warm, still, sunny evening, with temperatures in the lower 40s, we chose the largest colony left on Torgersen Island: Colony 14, with 600 pairs of birds. Peter and Jennifer volunteered for the unenviable task of wading into the colony and grabbing the Adélies, which first exposed them to the daggerlike jabs of numerous penguin beaks and then left them holding a squirming, enraged, and muscular spheroid that stabbed their hands until they bled. Jen, who'd trained under penguin scientist David Ainley at Cape Royds and Cape Crozier, on the Ross Sea, employed Ainley's method of penguin wrangling, which involved grabbing an Adélie by its torso, quickly tucking its head under her arm, and holding on to the bird by its legs. Peter used Fraser's technique, during which, in one lightning-like move, he seized the penguin where its flippers joined its torso. I was assigned to fetch the eggs after the penguins had been removed from the nests and to help measure the length of each Adélie's flippers and culmen, the featherless portion of a bird's bill.

Simply holding an Adélie's flipper and measuring it is sufficient to give one an understanding of the power of these birds. The penguins' might was electric, and the team measured them rapidly so as not to harm their flippers or put them under an extended period of stress. Peter and Jen then lowered the Adélies into cloth sacks to weigh them. At first the Adélies squirmed wildly, but once in the sacks and suspended from a pulley scale, they usually settled down for a few seconds.

Retrieving the eggs was not without its risks and offered insight into the pugnacious and intrepid character of the Adélies. As I tiptoed into the colony to grab the exposed eggs, the Adélies snarled at my approach and then assaulted me, even though I was four times their height. One particularly belligerent penguin bounded up to me and, before I could move out of the way, plunged its beak into the flesh below my knee. Like an awl, it penetrated my rain pants, thick fleece pants, long underwear, and skin. The jab drew blood and hurt like hell. But my knee was nothing compared to the hands and arms of Peter and Jen, which, by the end of the evening, were crisscrossed with cuts and scratches.

The Adélie's audacity has earned it the admiration of virtually everyone who has observed it for any length of time. Comparing the character of the three pygoscelid penguins, Murphy said, "The Johnny Penguin [gentoo] turns tail; the Adélie stands his ground; the Ringed Penguin [chinstrap] charges." In this instance, I would take issue with the eminent ornithologist and argue that the Adélie is even feistier than the chinstrap. (Even though Fraser and his birders greatly admire the Adélies, any occasion on which the team would have to handle a penguin or wade into a colony would leave the members muttering, "Little bastards!" Another observer—Pamela Young, the wife of a biologist— had this to say after spending a summer at an Adélie colony with her husband: "I could hardly bear the sight of the little monsters.")

The combination of cheek and curiosity displayed by the Adélies irked Robert Falcon Scott. Early in his final expedition, the penguins would inevitably approach the ship's dogs as the men were exercising them on the ice. Scott described the scene in his diary:

> Groups of these [Adélies] have been constantly leaping on to our floe. From the moment of landing on their feet their whole attitude expressed devouring curiosity and a pig-headed disrespect for their own safety. They waddle forward, poking their heads to and fro in their usual absurd way, in spite of a string of howling dogs straining to get at them . . . they come a few steps nearer. The dogs make a rush as far as their leashes or harness allow. The penguins are not daunted in the least, but their ruffs go up and they squawk with semblance of anger, for all the world as though they were rebuking a rude stranger. . . . Then the final fatal steps forward are taken and they come within reach. There is a spring, a squawk, a horrid red patch on the snow, and the incident is closed. Nothing can stop these silly birds.

On Torgersen Island, removing the Adélies from their nests—and trying to direct them back home—caused a short-lived rumpus that illustrated both their airheadedness and the intensity of the brief breeding season. On several occasions, no sooner did Peter or Jen lift an Adélie off its nest than one of its neighbors—either a nonbreeding male or a partner standing by its incubating mate—would waddle over and sit on the temporarily abandoned eggs. The brooding instinct is strong, and when an Adélie sees an egg on the ground, its inclination is to incubate it. The English penguin biologist Bernard Stonehouse reports penguins brooding empty jars, snowballs, cameras, gloves, and frozen fish.

The most nerve-racking moment of the measuring exercise came at the end, when we carried the Adélies back to their colonies, lowered them to the ground, and pointed them in the direction of their nests. Some would skitter through the colony and immediately return to their nests. Others would run wildly through the colony, dodging the pecks of their incensed neighbors and running about helter-skelter, with the jerky motions of a silent movie character, before finding their way home. Finally, there were the Adélies whose eggs had been claimed by a needy neighbor. After a period of confusion, the Adélie would eventually realize that a neighbor was squatting on its nest and would drive the penguin away with a few pecks or swats of the flipper. Then, as quickly as the colony had been stirred up by our actions, things quieted down; the tightly packed Adélies readjusted themselves on their eggs and went back to a state of détente with their neighbors.

One of the paradoxes of Adélie penguins is that they are simultaneously gregarious and irascible. They can't live without one another, yet they're often at odds with their fellow birds—not unlike humans forced to coexist in communal circumstances. A few days after we measured the Adélies, Brett Pickering and I were in a Zodiac checking water depth and clarity not far from Palmer Station. As we drifted in the boat, we watched as a lone Adélie on an ice floe spotted a group of Adélies porpoising through the sea. The Adélie on the ice began to honk out greetings to the passing penguins, then scurried to the edge of the ice floe, dove in, and began swimming after the penguins with an urgency that indicated that it did not want to miss out on the action.

Watching as the penguin caught up with the group, Pickering said, "They hate each other, but they love to be together."

Bernard Stonehouse, speaking of the sociability of penguins, said, "Lone penguins of any kind seem restless, incomplete creatures: unless molting or dying (when they prefer to be alone) their most pressing aim is to find other penguins."

WITH THE IMPROVED weather, the retreat of the sea ice, and the stepped-up tempo of life in the Antarctic, Fraser's team had little downtime in the field. So, one afternoon on Litchfield Island, it was with some relief that I greeted Peter Horne's suggestion that I sit with the boat for a while. Finding a comfortable spot where I could rest against a boulder, I removed my heavy orange float coat to use as a cushion. The coats are designed to keep your head above water in case you wind up in the Southern Ocean, though a pessimist might argue that all wearing a float coat accomplishes is prolonging the death agony in the freezing sea and making it easier for the search-and-rescue team to locate the body.

Nestling against the rock, I watched as the weather underwent a pronounced change for the better. Until midafternoon, we had been experiencing an inclement Antarctic day of leaden clouds, steady winds, and wet snow. But as I sat next to the ocean on Litchfield, shortly before five P.M., a blue hole appeared in the sky to the south and began spreading north, and I watched as the advancing cell of high pressure tugged the clouds off the mountains of the peninsular range.

The Southern Ocean teemed with life, and all I had to do was sit and let Antarctica's abundance come to me. Several Adélie penguins rode a tablet of ice past me, slowly pushed by gentle winds toward the Marr Ice Piedmont. A few hundred yards away, Adélies on Torgersen Island sent up a constant racket as they blared greetings to each other and their eggs. Antarctic terns dipped into the surface of the sea, plucking krill and issuing shrill peeps as they flew overhead. I could hear the screech of kelp gulls and the bellowing of elephant seals. Blue-eyed shags flew low overhead, and I listened to the *whump . . . whump . . . whump* of their wingbeats.

I was close to drifting off to sleep when a leopard seal cruised past me in the water, less than ten feet away. Its reptilian head poked out of the sea, but the seal glided by without paying me any attention. Closing my eyes again, I was startled a few minutes later by loud expulsions of air. I swung my head to the left just as five crabeater seals—gentle-looking creatures with silvery coats—swam past, exhaling as they surfaced. I watched as the crabeaters amused themselves by swimming under and around a slab of ice about sixty feet across. I observed the seals for several minutes before they moved on, then sat for another fifteen minutes watching the advancing blue sky and listening to the sounds of an Antarctic spring.

WHEN I SPENT a month with Fraser's birding team in January 2004, I quickly learned of his fondness for making asides about his uniquely picturesque work environment. Arriving at one of the more far-flung islands in his domain, after we'd wound our way through icebergs and gazed at the imposing beauty of the peninsular range, Fraser would tie up the Zodiac and say, "Nice commute, eh?" Or reclining against a rock as we sat in the sun eating lunch, Fraser would survey the panorama and remark, "Well, another lousy day at the office."

It was, indeed, some office. The five Adélie islands that lay within several miles of Palmer Station—Torgersen, Humble, Litchfield, Cormorant, and Christine—formed the core of his study area, and with good reason: Even traveling three miles in the icebound waters of the early season is trouble enough. Each of these islands had its own beauty, although the two easternmost—Cormorant and Christine—offered the most dramatic views of the Bismarck Strait and the Antarctic Peninsula.

But there are other penguin rookeries within fifteen miles of Palmer, and these more remote islands possess a breathtaking beauty that surpasses that of islands closer to the station. As the ice loosened its grip, we began to visit these spots to count penguins—Adélies, gentoos, and chinstraps—and study brown skua populations.

Dream Island lies eight miles to the northwest of Palmer Station, and one trip there reveals why the Englishmen who explored the area chose the name. A team from the British Naval Hydrographic Survey Unit visited the island during the 1956–57 summer season and christened it Dream, according to the United States Geological Survey, "because among the island's natural features are a cave and, in summer, a small waterfall, with mossy patches and grass." That may be part of the story. But when I first stood atop the highest point on Dream Island, just off the southwestern tip of Anvers Island, and gazed at a dazzling sea dotted to the horizon with icebergs, at several humpback whales spouting a mile away, at the scores of nearby islands in the Joubin chain, at more than a thousand penguins arrayed across the island's craggy landscape, and at Mount Français soaring above the Marr Ice Piedmont, there was no question in my mind why someone had designated this place Dream: Its beauty was so far outside the realm of human experience that it did not seem real.

The first time we traveled there during the 2005–06 season came as we were finishing up our work on Litchfield Island. Standing atop one of Litchfield's hills in early December, we looked at clearing skies, rafts of sea ice being blown offshore, and a path opening up to the west. It was then that Peter Horne suggested we should go to Dream.

The relatively late hour meant nothing; the sun would not set until close to midnight. And so, around four-thirty P.M., we traveled in two Zodiacs to Dream Island under bright blue skies. Our route paralleled the southern coast of Anvers, and we sped by an impressive collection of icebergs, many four to five stories high, and weaved in and out of rafts of brash ice. Arriving at the island, we tied up in an inlet, where our presence aroused about two dozen Antarctic terns nesting on a nearby ridge. The birds buzzed us, alternating their piercing calls with clucking sounds as they warned us away from their nests.

Dream is a rugged, hilly island about two-thirds of a mile long and nearly bisected by a narrow inlet. It is composed of gray rock, much of it basalt, that has been shattered into countless pieces by eons of harsh Antarctic weather. Orange and black lichens coat many of the crumbling heaps of stone. As we walked across the island, counting penguins, the shards of rock clinked underfoot. Adélie penguin colonies once blanketed most of the island, but now they're concentrated along a few ridgelines and in a broad, windswept area in the center of Dream.

Much of the island was still covered by snow in early December, but as the snow melted, the vestiges of abandoned Adélie colonies became manifest—large, confederate gray swaths of nesting pebbles, set against the darker gray of the rock outcroppings.

Two recently arrived members of Fraser's team, Brett Pickering and Kristen Gorman, had finally joined us after the aborted effort to reach Palmer on the *Laurence M. Gould*. Brett is a powerfully built man in his mid-thirties with chestnut-colored hair and a matching beard. He had worked with Fraser for five seasons, was handy with engines and other things mechanical, and possessed a calm, genial disposition. Like many at Palmer, Brett was gripped by wanderlust, and he and his brother had outfitted a Mercedes truck called a Unimog into a high-tech camper that they planned to drive through South America. A graduate of the University of New Mexico, Brett had a deep scientific bent and, next to Fraser, knew more about the natural history of the region than any other member of our team. But he never lorded his seniority or experience over the team and, when the time came to make a decision, he was fond of saying, "Your call." Pickering was someone you'd want at your side in a crisis.

Kristen Gorman, a congenial woman in her twenties with blond hair and an adventurous spirit, had worked on numerous ornithological field teams in the United States and Canada. She had a master's degree from Simon Fraser University in Canada and was working in Antarctica for the first time. Gorman would go on, under Fraser's tutelage, to work on a Ph.D. about the causes behind the region's disappearing Adélie populations.

Like other penguin rookeries throughout the region, Dream—once the largest Adélie rookery near Palmer, with an estimated 10,000 to 12,000 nesting pairs in 1970—had experienced an 80 percent drop in Adélie numbers. Meanwhile, the population of chinstraps—a penguin distinguished by the trim black line running from ear to ear under their chins and a penchant for warmer climates—had slowly increased. Chinstraps possess a memorable, braying call that resembles the sound of someone trying to turn over a jalopy's engine. The two species cohabitate peacefully on Dream, though there is little question in Fraser's mind which one will ultimately prevail in this warming environment, and it isn't the Adélies.

As we walked the island and did our work—including identifying, by leg bands, the nesting pairs of brown skuas—the hour grew late and the sun bathed the land and sea in a crystalline light. To the west, a tabular iceberg, many blocks long, had run aground. Less than two miles to the northwest was Cape Monaco, a thick ice promontory on the Marr Ice Piedmont. The cape, named by Jean-Baptiste Charcot in honor of Prince Albert of Monaco, a patron of Charcot's expedition, is identifiable from miles away by its nunatak, a small, black rock ridge that protrudes through the glacier.

From Dream's ridges, we could clearly see the most far-flung birding-team destination in Palmer's environs: the Joubins, a collection of more than 150 rocky islands flung across the sea at a point where giant, flat-topped icebergs drift up the western Antarctic Peninsula and run aground. The Joubins lie roughly fifteen miles west of Palmer Station, but from Dream, the closest of the islets lie just six or seven miles distant. Fraser visits the Joubins—home to small populations of Adélies, chinstraps, and gentoos—only when the *Laurence M. Gould* is near the station and the weather is good; fifteen miles across the Southern Ocean in a little rubber boat is about as far as he likes to push his luck. When you're standing on a ridge in the Joubins and looking west, there's nothing between you and New Zealand but thousands of miles of Southern and Pacific Ocean.

We left Dream at ten P.M., heading for Palmer. The ride back was mesmerizing as the lowering sun turned the Marr Ice Piedmont, the peninsular range, and the countless icebergs a radiant gold. We traveled in silence, for there was nothing to say about such beauty. That night, around midnight, the setting sun limned scattered high clouds in shades of burnt orange, copper, and rose.

For weeks, our route to another breathtaking Adélie colony, Biscoe Point, had been blocked by ice. We tried again in early December, but were stopped several miles from Biscoe by rafts of brash ice too thick to penetrate with our Zodiacs. In need of coffee to banish the damp chill, we turned off our engines and drifted near the edge of the ice in Biscoe Bay, sipping from our thermoses. Two miles in front of us, the triangular face of Mount William rose out of the Marr Ice Piedmont. We listened as the glacier cracked and rumbled, occasionally shedding a section of its face; first we saw a puff of ice and snow spilling off the glacier's face, soon followed by a deep booming that carried for miles. As we sat, a raft of several dozen gentoo penguins surfaced next to our Zodiacs, issuing clipped, barklike calls as they regrouped before continuing their swim to their feeding grounds. Nearby was a five-story tabular iceberg, its whitish-blue face close enough for us to distinguish with binoculars the striations representing annual layers of accumulated ice and snow.

It was a spectacular year for icebergs at Palmer Station. Farther offshore, larger tabular icebergs had been carved into saddle-shaped forms by waves washing over their sagging middle sections. Nearer to shore, we'd once boated past a small, grounded berg that was virtually transparent, a cottage-sized piece of glacial-blue crystal. Its surface was dimpled with indentations like those on a golf ball, and sunlight streamed through it as if bathing a glass cathedral. Nearby was another pale blue iceberg in whose surface wave action had bored several large holes, giving it the appearance of a sculpture by Henry Moore. Its base was visible under the limpid water, emanating a vivid turquoise color. On a clear day, cruising past these sculpted masses of ice was magical, but in gloomy weather—when much of the color had drained out of the bergs—the great rafts of ice took on a forbidding look. Making his way through a sea of icebergs more than two centuries before, Georg Forster, Captain Cook's naturalist, wrote, "The whole scene looked like the wrecks of a shattered world."

ONE EVENING, AS we were iced in, the team sat in the birders' tent and spoke by phone with Fraser, who was surprised that the ice had returned but surmised correctly that the juxtaposition of a stalled high-pressure system over the Weddell Sea to the north and a stationary low-pressure system to the south kept packing ice against the coast. The long periods of windless weather kept the ice locked in place. "I don't know," said Fraser. "This season it's just so incredibly difficult to get a feel for what's going on. It's truly bizarre. In most years this ice moves off the coast and is dispersed, but this year it's like the ice is anchored there."

As December advanced, the number of Adélies of all descriptions—successful breeding pairs, unsuccessful breeders, immature birds that had not yet bred, and successful breeding pairs that had lost their eggs due to skua depredation or other causes—neared the season's peak. With the increase in population, the tranquillity of the earlier days of incubation was often shattered. Our team witnessed some epic brawls, one of which began on Torgersen Island when a large Adélie, apparently a male, attempted to drive another penguin off a two-egg nest. It was impossible to tell which was the aggrieved party or how the dispute began. But for five minutes, the larger Adélie mercilessly pounded its opponent with rapid-fire flipper blows. At times the flipper assault was so intense that it sounded like a person sticking his finger into the blades of a fan. The large penguin pursued the smaller one through the colony, smashing it against rocks and slamming the bird into other penguins and nests. Soon, much of the southern section of the colony was embroiled in the fight, whose escalation brought to mind a bench-clearing brawl at a baseball game. Tufts of down drifted through the air. Miraculously, given the pandemonium in that part of the colony, no eggs seemed to have been crushed.

The brute penguin eventually drove its opponent out of the colony, where the vanquished bird stood in stunned silence. It was a bedraggled-looking creature, its feathers ruffled and its eyes winking shut in pain and exhaustion. Just after the fight ended, the penguin did something I had seen many Adélies do when pummeled in a scuffle or startled by the intrusion of a human or elephant seal: It vigorously shook its head from side to side, a gesture that reminded me of nothing so much as my own golden retriever, Charlie, who, when hurt or alarmed by a loud noise, shakes his head in the same fashion.

CHAPTER 6

PREDATORS

Nature is an uncompromising nurse.
—APSLEY CHERRY-GARRARD,
Terra Nova expedition, 1910–13

ONE GLANCE AT THE ANTARCTIC LANDSCAPE—A CONTINENT'S worth of ice pushing to the sea, leaving only the occasional strip of rocky beach by the shore—tells you all you need to know about the seabirds and marine mammals that breed there. Few environments are more inhospitable. Spend any time in Antarctica, though, and the unforgiving nature of the place is cast in even starker relief. The Adélie penguin not only has to survive in a world of ice, but at all stages of life—egg, chick, and adult—it must evade other creatures bent on devouring it. On land, the Adélie faces the skua. At sea, the Adélie encounters the leopard seal. But as many scientists and explorers have observed, these predators perform a vital function of culling the unfit and weak from the penguin gene pool. After watching a South Polar skua dispatch an Adélie chick, Apsley Cherry-Garrard addressed the issue of the survival of the fittest, Antarctic style.

"There is a great deal to be said for this kind of treatment," he wrote in _The Worst Journey in the World_. "The Adélie penguin has a hard life; the Emperor penguin a horrible one. Why not kill off the unfit right away, before they have come to breed, almost before they have had time to eat? Life is a stern business in any case: why pretend that it is anything else?"

SHORTLY BEFORE THANKSGIVING, I watched as a pair of brown skuas on Torgersen Island—a male, leg band No. 8378, and a female, leg band No. 8598—chose Adélie Colony 15 as their dining spot. Loitering near the colony, the two skuas walked nonchalantly up to a peripheral Adélie nest and began their assault. The male stood at the head of the Adélie penguin, which lay tightly on the nest. The female skua stationed herself at the rear. Then they took turns lunging at the penguin, forcing it to whip its head back and forth in an effort to protect its eggs. Brown skuas will never directly attack healthy adult Adélie penguins, which weigh twice as much as skuas and can poke out a skua's eye with one well-aimed stab of the beak. The pair's goal was simply to force the Adélie off its nest for an instant, so that one of the skuas could grab an egg. (Forty years ago at Palmer Station, a pair of researchers observed a brown skua pulling on the tails of Adélies in order to expose their eggs, then snatching them.)

But this particular Adélie—apparently a more experienced breeder—fended off the skuas. So after a few minutes, the pair simply moved to a neighboring nest and began harrying another Adélie, which evidently wasn't a veteran breeder. Thrusting repeatedly at the penguin from two sides, the skuas quickly flustered the bird and, within twenty seconds, had its last egg. The skuas walked just a few feet away, where they cracked open the egg and ate it.

The Adélie might have been able to save its egg had it given chase. But once an Adélie's egg or chick is dragged more than a few feet away, the penguin doesn't seem to connect the mayhem taking place nearby with its own offspring. "The adult penguins," Robert Cushman Murphy wrote in recounting an attack on a chick right in front of a colony, "ceased to have any comprehension of what was taking place before their eyes."

James Murray, a biologist on Ernest Shackleton's 1907–09 *Nimrod* expedition, came to the following conclusion: "As in the human race, their gathering in colonies does not show any true social instinct. They are merely gregarious; each penguin is in the rookery for his own ends, there is no thought of the general good. You might exterminate an Adélie rookery with the exception of one bird, and he would be in no way concerned so long as you left him alone."

As I observed time and again at Palmer Station, a pair of brown skuas, working in tandem, was a formidable predatory machine. The attacks by brown skuas were particularly devastating in the roughly one-month period between the laying of Adélie eggs, in early to mid-November, and the appearance of brown skua eggs, in December. During that period, both members of a brown skua pair were free to double-team a lone Adélie penguin trying to protect it eggs. And from what I saw, if brown skuas are hungry they always succeed in snatching penguin eggs or small chicks. Like most humans observing a predator stalking its prey, my instinct was to root for the hunted. But to watch the persistence and skill of brown skuas snagging Adélie offspring is to develop respect and affection for these raptorlike creatures, which Murphy once called "the berserkers among birds." That said, seeing brown skuas pilfering an Adélie penguin egg was a great deal easier than watching them assault a fluffy penguin chick—an occurrence that would become commonplace a little later in the season.

Brown skuas own the skies above Adélie penguin rookeries, utterly dominating the other skua species found in the region, the South Polar skua. Of the two main skua species in Antarctica, the brown skua is the larger and is found at lower latitudes, including the northern Antarctic Peninsula, the subantarctic islands, and as far north as South Georgia and the Falklands. The South Polar skua—*Catharacta maccormicki*—is more numerous and is found at higher latitudes, such as the Ross Sea, where it is the chief predator of Adélie penguins. In the northern Antarctic Peninsula, the two species' breeding ranges overlap, and the Palmer Station area is home to far more breeding pairs of South Polar skuas than brown skuas. But the larger browns—with a wingspan of four to five feet and weighing up to five and a half pounds—rule.

Like an organized crime cartel, the brown skuas use intimidation and bodily harm to keep South Polar skuas and competing brown skuas away from their chief source of sustenance in summer: Adélie penguins. A common site on islands such as Torgersen is a dominant pair of brown skuas defending their feeding territory, a process that begins with piercing calls and a display of spread wings. But should an intruder fly too low over a penguin colony or land near it, the dominant brown skuas will attack and drive off the trespasser. Throughout the Adélie breeding season, skuas streaked overhead in aerial combat, with dominant birds driving interloping birds off Torgersen and other penguin islands. As the skuas flew past, the passage of the wind through their wing feathers sounded like a kite yanked at high speed through the sky. Occasionally, the two birds would collide in midair, twisting and tumbling in a blur of wings and feet before decoupling. In the mid-1970s, on Litchfield Island, one of Fraser's fellow University of Minnesota graduate students saw an especially fearsome pair of brown skuas kill several intruding South Polar skuas.

As Adélie penguin populations steadily declined in recent years and dwindled toward zero on Litchfield Island, several brown skua pairs from Litchfield muscled their way into Adélie colonies on Torgersen Island. During my season at Palmer, only one brown skua pair actually nested on Torgersen. The other brown skua marauders came from Litchfield. Indeed, it was a pair of brown skuas from Litchfield that wreaked the most havoc on Torgersen that spring and summer—a male, leg band No. 8518, and a female, leg band No. 9771. In a matter of weeks, this pair managed to decimate Adélie Colony 23, a small outpost on Torgersen's southwest side.

About twenty-five feet in diameter, the colony sat on a small knoll ringed on one side by jagged, foot-high rocks protruding from the ground. On November 18, 61 Adélies, occupying 33 nests, sat and stood in a small semicircle of gray pebbles surrounded by snow. Two days later, the skuas had reduced the number of nests to 24, and penguin eggshells littered the ground nearby. Ten days later, on November 30, Peter Horne and I approached the colony in a heavy snow that was driven sideways by 25-mile-per-hour winds. Patrolling the edges of the colony was the pair of skuas, whose continued depredations had knocked the number of nests down to 13. The remaining Adélies, hunkered low in the snowstorm, looked forlorn against the curtain of snow and the slate-gray sea.

On December 7, I was on Torgersen Island with Brett Pickering. We were doing snow transects, and I was winding up my tape measure and walking north across the island when Brett, who had been holding the other end of the tape, approached me. The sunlight bouncing off the snow was blinding, and I was paying scant attention to my surroundings.

"What the hell!" exclaimed Brett. "Is Colony 23 gone?"

Twenty feet to my left was a circle of gray pebbles. Not a penguin was in sight. And thus ended Adélie penguin life at Colony 23 on Torgersen Island, a spot where penguins had nested for hundreds of years. It was an incongruous event on such a lovely, warm day, and Brett and I stood for a minute, staring at the uninhabited gray spot, framed by the Antarctic Peninsula's ice-draped mountains. Later I counted 37 empty Adélie eggs strewn around the colony.

The extirpation of Colony 23 has been repeated at dozens of other colonies in the Palmer region in recent years and is a sign of an Adélie population in deep trouble. When nature is in balance, the annual toll skuas exact on a penguin rookery—frequently devouring a third of eggs and chicks—is significant but not catastrophic. Yet when outside forces, such as the rapid warming of the Antarctic Peninsula, intervene and begin sharply reducing Adélie penguin populations, the impact of brown skua predation becomes wildly disproportionate. This is precisely what is happening at Palmer Station: The increasingly inhospitable climate of the northwest Antarctic Peninsula pushes Adélie colonies to the edge of oblivion, and the brown skuas shove them over.

Three decades ago, Torgersen teemed with 9,000 breeding pairs of Adélie penguins. Over the years, this mass of nesting penguins has been whittled away to isolated Adélie colonies. Some colonies, such as 14 and 16, still hold a respectable number of penguin pairs—600 and 400 breeding pairs, respectively. But nearly all of the remaining colonies have shrunk drastically, containing only 30 to 60 pairs. For brown skuas, this new state of affairs makes the hunt for Adélie eggs and chicks far easier. Dropping into the middle of a large, densely packed penguin colony is risky business for a brown skua, exposing it to attacks from all sides. But as Adélie colonies contract to a few dozen nests, there really are no longer any central nests. All the nests are either on or next to the perimeter, where a patient pair of skuas can pick off egg after egg, chick after chick, until the colony is no more. During my season at Palmer I saw this scenario repeated again and again.

"These colonies get down below a certain size and the skuas just wipe them out," said Fraser. "When the total number of breeding pairs drops below fifty, the skuas just start to hit them. Any colony that drops below forty pairs is doomed."

The brown skuas controlled their domain with a regal detachment common to top-of-the-food-chain predators. A few days after the demise of Colony 23, I came across the male brown skua mainly responsible for the mayhem there. He was standing atop a rock at eye level, and I slowly walked over to him, advancing to within about six feet. His hooked beak was black, his brown plumage stippled with flecks of ash-colored feathers. Thin, straw-colored feathers gilded the brown plumage on his head and mantle. As he swiveled his head from side to side, the skua looked fierce and unperturbed, his dark eyes alertly surveying me and the penguins in the distance.

THESE BIRDS HAD no greater admirer than Robert Cushman Murphy, who studied brown skuas during an extended visit to South Georgia Island in 1912–13. He described them in his *Oceanic Birds of South America*:

> I became extremely well acquainted with the Brown Skua, which has left, I believe, a more vivid impression in my memory than any other bird I have ever met. The skuas look and act like miniature eagles. They fear nothing, never seek to avoid being conspicuous, and, by every token of behavior, they are lords of the far south. In effect, they are gulls which have turned into hawks. Not only are they the enemies of every creature they can master, living almost entirely by ravin and slaughter . . . they are tremendously strong, heavy and vital birds. . . . Energy is apparent in every movement of

the skua—in its rapacity, in the quantity of food it can ingest
within a few moments, and in the volume and continuous-
ness of the screams that issue from its throat.

Murphy's admiration for the audacity and skill of the brown skua,
both as predator and scavenger, steadily grew over the several months
he spent doing bird studies on South Georgia. Once, as Murphy and
members of his party shot teal, petrels, and terns for his collection, the
brown skuas quickly learned to associate the report of the gun with
meat and often grabbed the dead bird and flew off with it before the
men could retrieve it. When the men on Murphy's whaling brig, *Daisy,*
tossed scraps of food overboard, the brown skuas inevitably outcom-
peted every other scavenger. They grabbed seal blubber and entrails out
of the bills of southern giant petrels and albatrosses, and if a piece of
food was dropped by another seabird the skuas would snatch it before
it hit the water. As members of the brig's crew were cutting up elephant
seal blubber, one brown skua landed on the mincing table and was
induced to eat blubber off the edge of a knife, even allowing itself to be
petted. Other skuas would land on the carcass of an elephant seal as it
was being skinned, jumping back a few feet only when the sailors
shooed them away.

As Murphy skinned king penguins, brown skuas would gather and
eat meat from his hands. When he tossed pebbles at the brown skuas to
drive them away, the birds merely looked at him. Once he discharged
his shotgun directly over their heads to see their reaction; none flew
away, though several did stop clucking and briefly fell silent. Murphy
described brown skuas issuing the territorial display—wings outspread,
head held high emitting a loud call—as "the apotheosis of defiance,"
noting that "they fairly split the air with their shrill cries."

On South Georgia, the young ornithologist soon learned that the
neatest and most efficient way to skin king penguins—nearly as large
as emperors—was to remove the bird's skin, then turn it inside out and
let the skuas strip it of all fat and meat. The skuas, Murphy recalled,
"would pick off the blubber as cleanly as it could have been done with a
scraper, and in much less time."

"When they deign to notice me at all," Murphy wrote in his diary, "they glance up with bright, fearless, unsuspicious, brown eyes, accept from my fingers any food I offer them. . . . They are as close to wholly intrepid as any birds can possibly be."

My fellow birding team member Kristen Gorman summed up brown skuas this way: "The skuas make me feel like I'm in a *Harry Potter* episode or *Lord of the Rings*. Very medieval."

The merciless predation of skuas upon penguin chicks has struck visitors to Antarctica from the early days of exploration. This is largely because everything that occurs in a penguin colony takes place in plain sight, and since neither skuas nor penguins are alarmed by the presence of humans, the skuas go about their business brazenly. The attacks are also disturbing because a skua cannot take on an adult Adélie penguin or even a large chick, which means that they prey on smaller chicks. And watching a skua peck out the eyes of a still-living chick, or disembowel one and begin eating the krill from its stomach while it is alive, will move even the hardest heart.

Fraser once encountered a brown skua that had blinded a half dozen chicks and then cached the immobilized penguins in a small group until it was ready to eat them. "You looked at these creatures," he recalled, "and you said, 'They don't have a prayer. They're just meat.'"

Euan Young, a zoologist who conducted a five-year study of South Polar skuas on the Ross Sea in the 1960s, said skuas were often viewed by explorers and visitors as "the hyenas of the Antarctic paradise." One reason skua attacks are especially drawn out is that the web-footed skuas do not have the sharp talons raptors use to attack and hold their prey. "Skuas do not possess an effective killing weapon," he wrote in *Skua and Penguin: Predator and Prey*. "They win in the end because they are tougher."

Adult Adélies do sometimes fight back to defend their chicks. Young once saw an adult Adélie grab a skua by the neck with its beak and beat it with its flippers for thirty seconds. The Adélie tossed the skua out of the penguin colony and it rolled down a slope, unable to stand or move.

Watching skuas maraud through penguin colonies has prompted some members of Antarctic expeditions to take vengeance. Exploration parties threw lit cigarettes, which the skuas would swallow. Others laced meat with chili powder and watched as skua after skua ate it and threw it back up. Levick reports seeing men kill skuas with ice axes or rocks. Others shot the predators.

Around Palmer Station, brown skuas return in late October or early November after spending the winter in more northerly parts of the Southern Hemisphere, from Argentina to New Zealand. Females generally lay their eggs in early December, having already been feeding on Adélie penguin eggs for roughly two weeks. The brown skua chicks hatch around the New Year, making their entry at a time when abundant Adélie chicks provide food for the adult skuas to feed their rapidly growing offspring.

Today, with the climate changing and Adélies in sharp decline, there are signs that brown skuas are suffering as well. Thirty years ago, more than 15 pairs of brown skuas nested on the five penguin islands nearest Palmer Station, feasting on roughly 15,000 pairs of Adélie penguins. Now, however, with only about 2,000 pairs of Adélie penguins remaining on those five islands, the skuas are struggling. Researchers have estimated that the optimal feeding territory of a brown skua pair contains 750 to 2,000 pairs of Adélies, meaning the five islands near Palmer have enough penguins to sustain up to three pairs of brown skuas. Today, 13 brown skua pairs regularly nest on those islands, but their reproductive success is declining markedly. The old pairs of these long-lived birds keep coming back, but now many of them often fail to successfully raise a single chick because there simply aren't enough penguin eggs and chicks to feed skua offspring during the crucial first few weeks of their lives.

A striking example of this has occurred on Cormorant Island, which had close to 900 breeding pairs of Adélies in 1974 but is now home to only 92. Two brown skua pairs used to nest on Cormorant Island. Today, only one pair remains, and that couple hasn't successfully raised a chick in years. Fraser thinks it's only a matter of time before the number of breeding pairs of brown skuas around Palmer Station is sharply reduced. "The future for the brown skuas," said Fraser, "isn't any brighter than it is for the Adélies."

For years, scientists believed that brown skuas did not migrate to the Northern Hemisphere, but a team of Scottish researchers recently reported that DNA testing of two skuas found in the British Isles suggests they were migratory brown skuas. No skua species, however, can match the epic migrations of the South Polar skua, which has been known to travel nearly from pole to pole. South Polar skuas, which range farther south than any other bird species, migrate from Antarctica to Greenland, Siberia, Japan, Canada, Alaska, Mexico, and Brazil. They move quickly; Parmelee's team banded a South Polar skua that left the Palmer area in mid-April and was recovered in Oregon on July 9. In January 1975, his group banded a South Polar skua on Shortcut Island, near Palmer Station. The skua is believed to have left the area and headed north in early April of that year. On July 31, 1975, an Inuit hunter at Godthabsfjorden, in Greenland, shot the skua and gave its leg band to authorities. The bird had covered nearly nine thousand miles in just over three months.

LATER IN THE season, on Torgersen Island, I had an opportunity to witness the Adélies' other main predator—the leopard seal—display its hunting prowess. On a blustery December day—with winds gusting to 30 miles per hour and bands of low, dark clouds, their undersides a menacing shade of purple-blue, spreading over the region from the northwest—I walked to the south shore of Torgersen. This rocky beach is a major staging area for foraging Adélies, and I stood and watched the penguins coming in and out of the sea. Offshore, set against the dark sky, scores of icebergs glowed a vivid white or glacial blue.

Several dozen Adélies, fresh from the Southern Ocean, lay on one of the island's remaining snowfields, resting after their foraging trips. Farther on, roughly two hundred Adélie penguins, many smeared with guano, stood on the lead-gray rocks by the water's edge, waiting to plunge in. As I approached the shoreline, my eyes were drawn to something in the water; no more than sixty feet offshore, an enormous leopard seal cruised up and down the beach, its sleek dark head knifing through the sea. Its thick back and its length—the seal looked to be a dozen feet long—convinced me that the creature was the same gargantuan female that had swum under our boat in late October and that we had seen from time to time since then near Torgersen and Litchfield islands.

The seal—a "lep" in Palmer parlance—was so close to the shore that the Adélies must have spotted her. Adélie penguins are notoriously skittish about going into the water, since it is the sole environment where an adult Adélie is vulnerable to predation. The group of two hundred was strung along the shoreline, nervously communicating to one another with honks. Two dozen Adélies were perched on large boulders right at the waterline when a wave rolled in, sweeping the penguins into the sea; they fell like bowling pins, and some were dashed against the rocks. But as the water washed back out, the two dozen Adélies rode the surge out to sea and called to one another. That prompted many of the remaining Adélies to dive in, as if signaled by a starter's pistol. The penguins swam underwater for about ten seconds and then surfaced, roiling the dark sea off Torgersen with the explosions of their porpoising torsos.

The leopard seal was nowhere in sight, and as the Adélies raced through the water, swimming toward foraging grounds to the south, I found myself simultaneously hoping that they would make it, yet also wanting to see a leopard seal catch a penguin—something I had not witnessed before.

About a hundred yards offshore, amid the bursts of porpoising Adélies, I glimpsed a large splash. A few seconds later, there was a thrashing on the surface. Raising binoculars to my eyes, I saw the dark, serpentine form of the leopard seal emerge from the water. She had the penguin in her mouth and, with terrific violence, began flaying the water with its body, whipping it left and right. Once, as the predator briefly released the penguin, I saw one of its flippers move. The seal seized the penguin again and smacked it on the surface several more times, until much of the skin separated from the carcass. Five minutes after the attack began, the seal began to eat the skinned penguin. The water was red with blood.

In a matter of minutes, skuas, kelp gulls, and Wilson's storm petrels showed up to scavenge debris from the surface of the sea. No seabird dared alight on the surface so close to the seal, and so they darted in to retrieve bits of flesh off the water. A skua flew directly over me, a fist-sized chunk of penguin skin in its mouth.

That evening, our team returned to work on Torgersen. Standing on the island's southwestern shore, looking across a channel to Litchfield

Island, I saw the large female leopard seal again cruising back and forth. Not far away, a second seal was hunting. As I watched, a group of Adélies from Humble Island porpoised through the channel. The female seal disappeared and then reappeared a few seconds later, her charcoal-gray back surging through the sea as she chased a penguin. The escaping Adélies rocketed out of the water in a fan-shaped array. One penguin, apparently the seal's target, leapt high out of the sea as it frantically tried to escape the pursuing lep. (Adélies have been clocked at 10 miles per hour, and biologists believe they can swim even faster when chased.) I watched and waited, expecting to see the seal surface at any second with the penguin in its mouth. But as the Adélies kept streaking south, the seal came up empty.

The next afternoon, under blue skies, I sat on a rock on the south shore of Torgersen Island and watched the female polish off four Adélies in less than three hours. Her size entitled her to claim this prime water, through which several thousand penguins had to pass to get from the island to their feeding grounds. Lazily patrolling the shore, and sometimes coming within a few yards of land as she eyed Adélies standing on rocks, the female seal often hid behind passing ice floes. At one point, I watched through binoculars as dozens of Adélies porpoised through the Bellingshausen Sea, heading straight for the southern coast of Torgersen and the leopard seal. As they neared the shore, the seal dove. Soon, I saw the penguins bursting out of the sea like minnows chased by a striped bass. The seal's back arced powerfully out of the water, and she surfaced with an Adélie in her mouth. This seal, like many others, seemed almost to play with the Adélie, flinging it around on the surface of the sea before finally killing it by chomping down on its head. The lep would then begin the brutal thrashing that would separate the carcass from the skin. One writer described a leopard seal off South Georgia Island grabbing a gentoo penguin and "shaking it like a dog with a rat."

The penguins that made it safely past the seal sped into the shallows, frantically zigzagging before launching themselves out of the water and onto boulders on the cobble beach. Roger Tory Peterson, in his book *Penguins*, described Adélies popping out of the sea like "jack-in-the-boxes or as my wife put it, 'like slippery watermelon seeds.'"

The presence of a leopard seal patrolling the sea near a rookery leaves the Adélies onshore in an agitated state. Even when no seal is lurking nearby, Adélie penguins think long and hard before plunging in. When a lep shows up, the dithering reaches epic proportions, with the Adélies jostling each other and shifting nervously as they gaze into the depths, waiting for a leader to take the plunge. "The object of every bird in the party seemed to be to get one of the others to enter the water first," wrote Levick. "The appearance of a sea-leopard in their midst was the one thing that caused them any panic."

THEIR FEAR IS well-founded. The leopard seal, *Hydrurga leptonyx*— which translates as "small-clawed water worker"—is a first-rate predator that got its names because of leopard-like black spots on its silvery fur. Females can grow to thirteen feet in length and weigh as much as eleven hundred pounds; both sexes possess strong jaws, a huge gape, and long canine teeth backed up by extremely sharp postcanine teeth. Leopard seals have a unique windpipe that opens only when they breathe, making room for a very large gullet that enables the seals to swallow penguins nearly whole. The leopard seal is, in the words of biologists, an "obligate" of the pack ice; these solitary animals spend their time either in the water or on ice floes. Little is still known about their habits, and scientists estimate their numbers at 100,000 to 400,000, all in the Southern Ocean.

Although best known as penguin killers, leopard seals primarily eat krill. One study found that 50 percent of the leopard seal's diet is composed of krill, 20 percent of penguins, 14 percent of other seals, and 15 percent of fish or cephalopods. Still, they are the only seals that regularly attack and eat warm-blooded animals. Evidence of their carnivorous ways can be seen on countless crabeater seals in Antarctica. Crabeater pups are one of the leopard seal's favorite targets, and by some estimates 80 percent of adult crabeater seals bear the scars of a close encounter with a leopard seal. Crabeaters often escape the jaws of leopard seals by twisting their bodies, which accounts for the corkscrew-shaped marks on their skin.

When penguins are readily available around rookeries in the

summer, the seals display a prodigious appetite, devouring penguin after penguin until they are so full that they must repair to an ice floe to digest scores of pounds of flesh, bone, organs, and feathers. Levick and his party shot a leopard seal and upon cutting it open found "eighteen penguins in various stages of digestion, the beast's intestines literally stuffed with the feathers remaining from the disintegration of many more." In Prydz Bay, Antarctica, a leopard seal consumed nine penguins in 110 minutes. Opening up one leopard seal, Robert Cushman Murphy found the remains of four king penguins in its stomach—about 140 pounds of food before being digested.

Various studies suggest that leopard seals kill from 1 percent to 5 percent of penguins at any given rookery. The highest toll reportedly came one year at Cape Crozier, when a researcher extrapolated from the kills he had witnessed and concluded that four leopard seals ate fifteen thousand Adélies there in a fifteen-week period, roughly 5 percent of the breeding population. Chicks are especially vulnerable as they fledge, but as Ainley has pointed out, so many chicks often enter the water at the same time that the seals—focused on killing one penguin at a time—do not take a heavy toll on the fledglings. Swift, agile, and, in the words of Murphy, "graceful beyond any other Antarctic seal," the lep is even more effective as a predator when the sea is filled with brash ice or ice floes, behind which the leopard seals can conceal themselves. When swimming among floes that can easily crush a penguin to death, Adélies must slow down, and this makes them an easier target. Several scientists have seen a combination of ice floes, high swells, and leopard seals exact a steep price from Adélies. In January 1966, a researcher at Cape Crozier documented 32 dead and injured Adélies on a 650-foot stretch of beach in twenty-four hours: 5 died from ruptured stomachs, 14 had broken legs, 11 had seal bites on their necks, and 2 had deep seal wounds on their stomachs.

Adélies can survive terrible injuries. One year, Fraser came across a grievously wounded female Adélie in a colony. "The seal had grabbed her by the head and ripped her breastbone [open] right at the neck and you could look down into her stomach cavity," said Fraser. "You could actually see her lungs working in there. But she spent a few days recouping, hunched over, and I'll be damned if in less than a week she wasn't back in the water, feeding her chicks. She and her mate even pulled a brood off."

Explorers and scientists have understandably given leopard seals a wide berth, although until recently there were no documented cases of leopard seals killing a human being. On numerous occasions, leopard seals appeared to be attacking people on ice floes or in small boats, but what looked to a terrified individual like an assault might have been a leopard seal merely investigating this new creature in its realm. One indisputable attack occurred as Shackleton and his men drifted on the ice across the Weddell Sea. Crew member Thomas Orde-Lees was skiing back from a hunting trip across melting sea ice when a leopard seal burst out of a lead between floes and lunged at him. Orde-Lees yelled to Frank Wild, Shackleton's second-in-command and the best shot among the crew, to get his rifle. The large leopard seal then slithered onto the floe and began chasing Orde-Lees. Soon, it dove back into the water and swam under Orde-Lees, following his shadow. As Orde-Lees reached the end of the floe, the seal poked its head out of the water, slithered onto the floe, and began chasing him once more. Just then Wild arrived from the *Endurance* with his gun; he shot the seal when it had closed to within thirty feet of Orde-Lees. Afterward, the hungry men cut open the seal's stomach, found undigested fish, and fried them.

A half century later, in the early 1960s, Richard Penney—on two separate occasions—was standing on an ice edge when leopard seals lunged at him, their mouths wide open. In 1972, two men from Palmer Station were crossing Arthur Harbor in a small, motorized whaleboat when an Adélie penguin, fleeing from an attacking leopard seal, jumped out of the water and into the boat. The Adélie, with several bloody puncture wounds in its breast, stood in the boat while the seal surfaced, circled the boat, and then raised itself out of the water and gazed over the gunwale, apparently looking for the penguin. The men sped off. That same year, also in Arthur Harbor, a leopard seal slammed into a diver's oxygen tanks, spinning him around in the water.

In 1974, Fraser's first year at Palmer, two scuba divers were harassed by a large leopard seal in Arthur Harbor. The seal watched the men at a distance and then became increasingly aggressive as they swam up a cliff face in an effort to get out of the water. The divers were worried enough to pick up a pair of yard-long iron bars left from earlier construction, which they used to fend off the seal. When they rose to sixteen feet, the seal trapped them in a rock alcove for thirty minutes, making threat displays by shaking its head, blowing bubbles, and repeatedly striking the iron bars with snakelike lunges. After forty-five minutes, the Zodiac driver was able to distract the leopard seal, enabling the divers to swim to shore.

In the ensuing years, leopard seals bit into numerous Zodiacs at Palmer Station. On one occasion, Fraser and his birding team had tied up their boat at Humble Island to work in the penguin colonies. Returning to the craft, they found that a leopard seal had bitten into the rubber boat and sunk it, engine and all. Today, all Zodiacs at Palmer are outfitted with hard, bite-proof cones that slip over the pair of pointed ends at the stern.

One of the most remarkable encounters between a leopard seal and a person was chronicled, in words and pictures, by the underwater photographer Paul Nicklen in *National Geographic* magazine. Working not far from Palmer Station, Nicklen began photographing a twelve-foot female that became fascinated with his presence and interacted with him for two days. The seal was alternately playful and threatening. After grabbing a penguin chick, she swam up to Nicklen and dropped the still-living chick on his camera. "Then," recounts Nicklen in the article, "she opened her mouth and engulfed the camera—and most of my head." The underwater picture he snapped of the seal, from only inches away, is a classic: a penguin foot dangles in front of the lens and the seal's head is so close to Nicklen's camera that you can count the hairs on her silver fur and see the tiny ridges on her pink tongue. After making more threats toward Nicklen for forty-five minutes, she ate the penguin. "The next day, as if wanting an audience, she came looking for me," wrote Nicklen.

On another occasion, the female leopard seal grabbed and released a penguin chick for more than an hour, continually offering it to Nicklen. "When I ignored her, she blew a stream of bubbles from her nose in a threat display and tried again," wrote Nicklen. "More frightening than the canines of the large female was the jackhammer sound she let loose that rattled through my chest. She was warning off another leopard seal that had snuck behind me. It worked—the visitor moved on."

Nicklen photographed leopard seals for three weeks, spending hour after hour in the frigid water in the presence of this great predator. His courage is all the more striking when you consider that he was familiar with the story of Kirsty M. Brown, a twenty-eight-year-old British marine biologist working at the United Kingdom's Rothera Station, 250 miles south of Palmer Station. As Brown and a partner were snorkeling at a study site in a bay next to Rothera on July 22, 2003, a leopard seal locked onto her and pulled her deep underwater. A two-person shore team accompanying the divers immediately rode to the site in a rescue boat. After the seal released Brown and she floated to the surface, the team performed cardiopulmonary resuscitation (CPR) as the boat raced back to the base, run by the British Antarctic Survey. But despite more than an hour of CPR performed by the spotter team and the station doctor, Brown died. It is the only documented instance in which a leopard seal has killed a person. Whether the seal meant to kill Brown or was merely toying with her is unclear.

The Swedish filmmaker Göran Ehlmé, who has spent years in Antarctica photographing leopard seals, says that the line between attacking and playing is a fine one. "These seals, they are mostly curious," Ehlmé told *National Geographic*. "I tell other divers, 'If you get scared, just close your eyes. Then open them. The seal won't bite you, but it will be very close . . .' It's not strange that the seal has the reputation it has. The first time I saw one, I got scared. The big head. The large mouth. The sinister eyes. The icy water added to the fear. I had to rethink things through a bottle of whiskey and a long sleep."

CHAPTER 7

FRASER

Isolation among the fastnesses of nature does not bring loneliness: that can perhaps be only felt in its full extreme among the busy haunts of men.

—WILLIAM S. BRUCE, Scottish National
Antarctic Expedition, 1902–04

ON DECEMBER 21, THE ANTARCTIC SUMMER SOLSTICE, I stepped out of a Zodiac onto Torgersen Island, postholed through a snow bank, and soon heard a sound I had never heard before: the faint, insistent peeping of newly hatched Adélie chicks begging for food. Moving closer, I caught my first glimpse of downy-gray chicks, just a few inches long, tucked under their parents' brood patches. Some Adélies had two chicks, some one chick and one egg, and others a single chick or egg. Several of the eggs were pipped, and I could see the chicks working their way out of the shells with their egg tooth, a short, sharp point on the bill used to punch a hole through the shell during hatching.

One chick, its down still wet, was half in its shell. At this emergent stage, the newly hatched chick, with its frail body and tiny flippers, seemed barely able to lift its head to beg for food. Yet, trembling from the effort, it struggled to raise itself up and eat. Thanks to instinctual behavior embedded in its genes, the chick knew to beg for food by rapidly tapping its bill against its parent's. This action triggered a parental response to regurgitate small amounts of krill into the mouth of the chick; arching its head and neck toward the ground, the parent opened its mouth, into which disappeared the head of the chick. After the food was exchanged, glistening strands of half-digested krill connected adult to offspring.

On the more snow-free north side of the island, under abundant sunshine, hatching was further advanced and many of the nests contained two chicks. They had apparently been hatched four to five days earlier, and were generally larger than the chicks on the south side. The bodies of the chicks were a smoky gray color, and their heads were black or charcoal gray. Some were six inches tall and starting to develop the sagging belly and pear-shaped form of Adélie chicks.

For roughly two weeks after hatching, the chicks are unable to maintain their own body temperature—a function known as thermoregulation—in the cold climate and need to be at least partially brooded by their parents. But on this warm, still day, there was little need to transfer body heat from adult to chick. Indeed, it was so warm—by Antarctic standards—that some adult Adélies stood with their mouths open, panting rhythmically. While newly hatched chicks burrowed under their parents, the bigger Adélie chicks flopped on the ground, largely exposed to the elements. Some lay with their heads under the adults, presenting their derrieres to the world, while others faced outward, basking in the heat that radiated off the stones. After feeding the chicks, the parents would often lie down, completely covering their progeny. One wondered how the chicks breathed and why they weren't crushed, but when the parents eventually stood up, the chicks still lay there, alive and well, if looking a bit flattened.

I watched as one small chick, which would have easily fit in the palm of my hand, incessantly begged its parent for food. The adult disgorged small amounts of krill, but the chick continued to peep and tap the parent's bill. Finally, the adult regurgitated a two-inch blob of krill. The chick grabbed it, but the morsel was too heavy, and it dragged the chick's head to the ground.

The sound of peeping chicks could be heard all across Torgersen

Island's north side, and Adélies marched to and from the sea as they relieved their mates on the nest. In a corner of one colony, roughly twenty Adélies performed the ecstatic display, with heads pointing heavenward, flippers flapping up and down, and staccato honking issuing from their mouths. Brown skuas regularly patrolled the skies over the colonies, causing the adult Adélies to rise up in alarm and squawk as one.

THERE WAS A time, just a few days before, when I'd wondered if I would ever get a chance to lay my eyes on the newly arrived chicks. In mid-December, the sea ice had blown back in, relegating us to the station once again. Indeed, on the solstice, a thick and jumbled field of sea ice filled the waters of Arthur Harbor. But a bizarre series of circumstances had forced us to figure out a way to get to Torgersen Island, despite the ice.

Roughly a week before the solstice, on a day of light sea ice, the birding team had traveled to Torgersen to place two telemetric penguin eggs under a couple of Adélies. The artificial eggs, affixed to a small plywood base, would measure the temperature and heart rate of the penguins, data that would reveal whether the presence of tourists on half the island unduly agitated the Adélies. (The answer? If kept ten to fifteen feet away and well monitored, tourists do not seem to have an impact on Adélie populations.) As one member of our team lifted the penguin off the nest, another grabbed the real eggs and placed them in a portable incubator. A third team member then covered the base of the telemetric egg with stones, after which the penguin was returned to the nest so it could incubate the telemetric egg.

We carted the real eggs back to the station in the incubator, planning to return them to the parents in a day or two, when the tests of the telemetric eggs were completed. Then the ice blew back in, blocking our way to Torgersen. A day went by, then two, then three, and soon Peter Horne figured he'd better call the boss, since the chicks could hatch anytime. Sitting in the birders' tent, the team spoke with Fraser at his home in Montana to discuss the unprecedented situation of possibly having to raise a pair of penguin chicks at the station until the ice cleared.

"We're trying to figure out what kind of krill puree to make here to feed them," said Brett Pickering, only half-joking.

"Well," Fraser replied over the speakerphone, "Kristen and Brett, you're just going to have to put on black-and-white suits and start the incubation shift."

By December 19, Peter Horne and Brett Pickering had had enough. Consulting with Fraser, they devised a scheme for the two of them and Jen Blum to dress in immersion suits—head-to-toe survival outfits that keep out the frigid water—and return the incubating eggs to their rightful nest on Torgersen Island. The trio climbed into a tougher-skinned Zodiac that was less likely to be punctured by the ice and proceeded to blaze a trail to Torgersen. They revved the outboard engine and nudged their way through the floes, and when they encountered a particularly large slab they would hop out of the boat and drag it across the ice. Occasionally they used oars to pole the Zodiac through the tightly packed floes. Gradually, their orange forms receded, and in just under an hour they had covered the half mile to Torgersen. After removing the two telemetric eggs and replacing them with the real eggs, the trio headed back to the station.

The big news was that chicks had started to hatch. And now, at least, the birding team had a way to get to the three closest islands—Torgersen, Litchfield, and Humble.

Two days later, on the solstice, we donned survival suits, loaded tents, sleeping bags, and food into the Zodiacs—just in case we were marooned on one of the nearby islands—and made our way through the ice to Torgersen. The weather remained warm and windless. I was in the lead Zodiac with Brett and Jen, and as we leapt out of the boat to drag it across floes, or sat on the bow kicking slabs of ice out of the way, I began to sweat heavily in the immersion suit. The heat of the sun was swiftly melting the snowy surface of the disintegrating remains of winter sea ice, and it was clear that, no matter what direction the wind blew, ice was not going to confine us to the station much longer. As we nudged our way through the floes, we released brown clouds of diatoms embedded in the ice.

Four days later, the sea ice was gone for good. On that day, we rode full-throttle to Dream Island, our passage unimpeded by ice. No longer dampened by a covering of sea ice, widely spaced swells rolled in from the Southern Ocean, and our Zodiac rose and fell in an exhilarating rhythm as we streaked across the water. I realized that even though I had been at Palmer Station for two months, living and working by the sea, I had rarely felt the ocean's presence because of the heavy cover of ice. But on a late-December day, as I breathed in the salt air and savored its scent, I was, at last, acutely aware of the sea.

Weeks of warm weather and recent rains had transformed the islands. The dark, rocky circles where the penguins were nesting were expanding rapidly outward as the winter's snow and ice melted.

As the new year approached, with Fraser's arrival imminent, the five-person birding team moved into the heart of the reproductive season, a seven-week period during which we would watch the Adélies grow, fledge, and slip into the sea. We also stepped up our work with skuas and southern giant petrels. The most exhausting work came in late December and early January, with the team visiting numerous nearby islands and many ice-free points of land as we participated in a worldwide survey of southern giant petrels.

This magnificent bird, with a six-foot wingspan, appears to be in decline across much of its range because it is frequently hooked and drowned as it dives for bait on the countless longlines laid out by fishing fleets. Estimates place the species' population at 46,000 pairs worldwide. One of the few places where the population of southern giant petrels is either stable or increasing slightly is in Antarctica, where fishing is generally prohibited within the Antarctic Convergence.

Roughly 500 pairs of southern giant petrels nest in the vicinity of Palmer Station, and counting them kept us in the field for twelve or thirteen hours a day. On Litchfield, an irregularly shaped island about three-quarters of a mile long and a half mile wide, we scrambled to the top of a half dozen hills where giant petrels made their nests. The way up took us through steep ravines with waist-high snow, and then up forty-five-degree slopes where we ascended slowly, careful not to damage the island's unique moss beds. Litchfield Island has one of the most extensive collections of the Antarctic moss *Warnstorfia laculosa* on the peninsula. At the base of the island's hills, the thick cushions of moss that existed several decades ago have been destroyed by the ever-increasing population of Antarctic fur seals, whose numbers are climbing around Palmer as rising temperatures lure these creatures from more temperate regions to the north. But extensive pillows of moss, often a foot deep, remain on the island's summits and in its gorges, clinging to the rocks amid the snow and ice.

Struggling to the top, we were greeted by southern giant petrels sitting on nests made of moss, grass, and limpet shells. The nests were situated among rocks and boulders splotchy with pale green, black, and cream-colored lichens, and the petrels—with their mottled, light-gray plumage—blended so well with the rocks that I nearly stepped on one. Giant petrels choose these summits—some rising 150 feet above the sea—as nesting sites because they can take a few running steps and then soar off the cliffs into the air. Lifting off on flat ground at sea level requires far more time, runway, and effort.

The giant petrel survey took us to islands where our Zodiacs rose and fell three to five feet in the swells, forcing us to time our leaps onto rock ledges with the apogee of the boat's ascent. The survey also led us to Norsel Point, where waves smashed against the rocks with a hollow thud. The swells propelled rafts of brash ice against the rock ramparts, filling the air with a whooshing clatter. Norsel Point, about a mile and a half northwest of the station, was once connected to the Marr Ice Piedmont, but the melting and collapse of a large section of the glacier recently severed the point from the Marr.

On western Norsel Point, we hiked in bright sun up and down slopes covered in jagged rocks, censusing and banding giant petrels. Ever-increasing numbers of subantarctic elephant seals are moving into the Palmer area, and they have fouled large areas of Norsel Point, destroying moss beds on the ledges. Encountered on Norsel's rocky shelves in groups of a dozen or more, the brown elephant seals—almost all juvenile males—were repulsive. A white crust covered their noses, and a creamy orange excrescence oozed from their anuses. They released a copper-red urine, and near their wallows, pools of melted snow, urine, and feces accumulated. Later in the season on Norsel Point, one particularly foul pool turned Pepto-Bismol pink. Although adult males can weigh up to eight thousand pounds, the juveniles probably weighed roughly one thousand apiece.

When he visited Norsel in January, Fraser recalled its lush moss beds and said, "It was a Garden of Eden at one time."

One evening, with the shadows lengthening, I stood on one of the highest points on Norsel and could see all the area's seabirds either nesting or in flight, from the tiny Wilson's storm petrel, to blue-eyed shags, to Antarctic terns, skuas, and, of course, penguins. Widely scattered clouds passed overhead, subtly transforming the panorama of mountains, glaciers, icebergs, and ocean. It was almost the New Year, I had been at Palmer Station for two months, and gradually I was coming to realize why this place, and this work, exerted such a pull on Bill Fraser. The magnificent landscape and seascape changed by the minute. You spent your days working with wild birds in terrain virtually untouched by man. No day in the field was ever the same, and each left you with a pleasant feeling of exhaustion. Where else, in the modern world, was such a life possible?

BY THE END of December, many of the Adélie chicks were ten days old and growing at an exponential rate. At hatching, Adélie penguin chicks weigh about three ounces. By day 5, they often weigh 12 ounces. Give the chick three to four more days and, if well fed, it will double its weight to 25 ounces. And by the time they reach two weeks, the chicks can weigh two and a half pounds. This astronomical weight gain occurs thanks to a krill pipeline that runs from the Southern Ocean to the chicks' gullets, with the parents—ceaselessly shuttling to and from the sea—as the conduit. The chicks gain weight like sumo wrestlers, with one observer describing them as "miniature Buddhas." From an evolutionary point of view, however, this rapid accretion of body fat is a necessity in a bird that has about fifty days to grow to adult size, jettison its adolescent plumage, and head into the sea.

Shortly after Christmas, on Torgersen Island, I saw chicks nine inches tall lying down, working their legs as they sought shelter under their parents. The chicks' webbed feet, protruding from their rounded torsos as they lay facedown, seemed enormous. By this time, if the second egg in a nest had not yet hatched, the large, ungainly chick would inevitably shove it out of the nest, where it would be picked up in short order by patrolling brown skuas.

While most of the chicks thrived, others struggled to survive. Walking among the colonies on Torgersen and Humble islands, I saw numerous nests where smaller Adélies—hatched several days after the first chick—were fighting to get their share of krill as their larger, older siblings nudged them aside. Studies have shown that second chicks experience higher mortality than first chicks.

And then there were the chicks that had been abandoned by their parents; the only question about the fate of these Adélies was whether they would perish first from exposure and starvation or whether a brown skua would swoop in and eat them. They were a pitiful sight, hunched over and far smaller than other chicks, their down matted with guano. Most were barely able to open their eyes.

Penguins are usually abandoned when a parent dies at sea, frequently by being devoured by a leopard seal. The remaining parent will disgorge the contents of its stomach to the chicks and then wait for its partner, expecting it, as usual, to show up within a few days. Newly hatched Adélie chicks can survive for nearly a week because their yolk sacks, which are inside their bodies, can be slowly absorbed and provide nutrition. But older chicks need to be fed every day or two. At some point, with the chicks and the surviving parent growing hungry, the adult will head into the Southern Ocean. By the time it returns, chances are good that its chicks will be dead.

Adult Adélies rarely feed other chicks, identifying their own by voice. In one study, the penguin biologist William Sladen observed 71 pairs of Adélies, and only twice did he see an adult Adélie feed a strange chick. One day, in a cold rain, I saw an emaciated chick trying desperately to force its way under the brood patch of an adult Adélie with two chicks of its own. The abandoned chick finally managed to find a place in between the two larger chicks. But the chances that it was able to remain in that warm spot, and persuade a strange parent to feed it, were small. Two days later when I returned to the nest site, the orphaned chick was gone. Later, in a different colony, I did see an adult with three chicks lined up under it in descending size, like stacking dolls. The adult seemed to care for this troika for several days before the chicks began to form crèches; as far as I could tell this was a rare instance of an Adélie being adopted by a strange parent.

Spending hours a day observing the chicks during the first two to three weeks of their lives left me amazed that, throughout Antarctica, about 75 percent of chicks survive to fledging. On January 4, on Humble Island, Jen and I walked up to Colony 3 to check on five of her closely monitored repro nests. The area where the nests had been was now occupied by a belching mob of three dozen elephant seals. While the adults likely escaped as the elephant seals rumbled into the colony, the chicks—scarcely able to move at so young an age—had no doubt been crushed. One of the dead chicks was visible among the seals.

Then there are the skuas. Around the New Year, with many of the chicks ten to fourteen days old, predation by brown skuas reaches its peak. The first three weeks of a chick's life are known as the "guard stage," when they are protected by their parents before forming crèches. During the first half of the guard stage, the chicks are covered by their parents and generally hidden from marauding skuas. But after day 10, the clueless chicks begin to wander away from their parents, and the skuas are ready. On Torgersen Island, I watched as a pair of skuas calmly stood a foot from an Adélie with two small chicks in a peripheral nest. The skuas darted in and out, and within a few seconds one of them snatched a chick by the tail, dragged the peeping creature six feet away, and delivered several quick blows from its beak to the chick's brain, killing it. The pair each grabbed an end of the chick and tugged. First its head came off, and one skua ate part of that. Then the skuas yanked off the legs and ate those. Then they pulled some more and each wound up with a piece of the torso. At one point, as they gobbled up the chick's innards, the skuas each snatched opposite ends of a piece of intestine and pulled at it like two people tugging on a strand of spaghetti. Within a couple of minutes, about the only trace of the chick was a spot of blood on the snow.

Later, I saw a skua fly over a colony, slow down, and, with a rapid backpedaling of its wings, dip quickly and grab a seven-inch chick. Holding the chick by the tail, the skua flew off, passing over Brett

Jen Blum, left, and Peter Horne snowshoe toward a penguin colony on Cormorant Island. In the background is Mt. William, on Anvers Island.

The remaining members of a once-sizeable Adélie penguin colony on Cormorant Island. Anvers Island and the Marr Ice Piedmont are in the background.

OCTOBER

Adélie penguins on Torgersen Island wait to nest.

An Adélie pair mating, with the male standing on the female. Their beaks tap against each other and their genitalia touch in the "cloacal kiss."

On Torgersen Island, Adélie penguins struggle to save eggs flooded by snowmelt. Increasing snow and snowmelt are one reason Adélie penguin populations are in steep decline around Palmer Station.

A female elephant seal and her pup on Torgersen Island. Elephant seals, sub-Antarctic mammals that have moved down the Antarctic Peninsula as it has rapidly warmed, have only recently started to breed in the Palmer Station area.

An Adélie parent regurgitates krill to its chick.

Bill Fraser prepares to grab an Adélie so his team can place a radio transmitter on its back to time the duration of the penguin's foraging trips.

Juvenile Adélies, smeared with guano, take on a moth-eaten look as they grow their first set of adult feathers and lose their down.

Bill Fraser on Humble Island, in front of the last two chicks on the island. During the 2005–2006 season, the Adélie population on Humble Island, which once may have numbered in the thousands, disappeared.

A South Polar skua, one of two skua species—along with the brown skua—that prey on Adélie eggs and chicks in Antarctica.

Gentoo penguins on Biscoe Island. As the climate around Palmer Station has warmed, greater numbers of gentoo penguins, a sub-Antarctic specie, have moved in.

An iceberg aground near Palmer Station.

A southern giant petrel and its chick on Humble Island.

Fledged juvenile Adélies are held for a few minutes in the "pengy prison" as they wait to be weighed and measured by Fraser's team.

Fledged juvenile Adélie penguins huddle together before making the plunge into the Southern Ocean, where they will have to fend for themselves.

Pickering, who said he could hear the upside-down chick peeping as the skua flew by.

Not long afterward, I watched as an Adélie penguin, fresh from the sea, walked up to the nest from which its chick—the sole surviving off-spring of this pair—had just been snatched by a brown skua. The adult Adélie, its belly bulging with krill, bowed to its mate, and the pair engaged in the loud mutual display, with bobbing heads and a succession of raspy calls. After a minute or two, the Adélie on the nest relinquished the territory to the newly arrived mate, which stood ready to feed the chick. But with no one to feed, the couple restlessly moved around the nest, occasionally bowing to each other and silently weaving their heads back and forth.

As the New Year arrived, the weather was often brilliantly clear and the sun shone nearly around the clock, setting around twelve-fifteen A.M. and rising two hours later. We enjoyed perpetual light and seemingly endless sunsets that turned into equally drawn-out sunrises. Around this time, scientists and staff at the station were fond of gathering on the balcony off the bar late at night to debate whether we were witnessing an optical phenomenon known as the "green flash." A classic green flash is a burst of vivid green light that briefly appears just above the sun as it is setting, a result of higher-frequency green-blue light being visible longer than lower-frequency red-orange rays.

The clarity of the Antarctic atmosphere and our unobstructed view of the setting sun across the sea persuaded some at Palmer Station that green flashes were a regular occurrence on clear evenings. But what left some oohing and aahing looked to me like a short-lived band of verdant light that was no more extraordinary than any other of the sublime shades of the spectrum on view during so many Antarctic sunsets. What I saw certainly didn't match what crew members of the U.S. Coast Guard icebreaker *North Wind* observed on New Year's Eve 1946 in Antarctica. "On the southern horizon appeared a green shore; close-mown lawns, bordered by hedges, sloped gently upward into eider-down clouds," wrote Thomas R. Henry in *The White Continent*. "The effect was like a Chinese landscape painting, fifty miles long and ten miles high, suspended over the horizon."

One rainy, overcast evening, we were on Humble Island checking on giant petrels when the wind swung sharply around from the north-northeast. We took note of the change because after a day of light, chilly winds from the south, the northern breeze brought with it a pronounced warmth. Then, around eight forty-five P.M., not long after we had returned to station, a fierce wind exploded out of the north, rising pre-cipitously from 10 miles an hour to sustained winds of 45 miles per hour and gusts of 55 miles per hour. By one A.M., gusts reached 68 miles per hour. The surface of Arthur Harbor was roiled by whitecaps, and waves smashed into the rocks around the station, sending sheets of sea spray hurtling through the air. Wilson's storm petrels, skuas, and kelp gulls struggled to make forward progress in the face of the gale. Walk-ing down the boardwalk from the galley to my dorm, my windbreaker flapping madly, was an exhilarating experience that involved bending sharply at the waist and working my legs as if they were underwater.

The north wind brought warmth from the South Atlantic. That night, the temperature climbed to nearly 50°F. The sudden arrival of balmy temperatures was instructive, as it vividly illustrated one of the key forces heating up the Antarctic Peninsula: an increase in warm winds streaming into the region from hotter temperate zones.

BILL FRASER FINALLY arrived at Palmer Station aboard the *Laurence M. Gould* on January 5, shortly after eight A.M. Although the birding team had been in frequent touch with Fraser by phone, Peter and the other members were relieved that Fraser was finally on the scene. His unobtrusive manner, breadth of knowledge, and devotion to his team members had cemented the affection of the birders. When Fraser arrived, I assumed that he would take over as team leader from Peter Horne, but that never happened; Horne remained the leader until we all left in mid-March, consulting with Fraser but deciding on a daily basis which islands we would visit and what work we would do.

In Fraser's absence, we could count the penguins, measure the snow, and perform the other tasks integral to the fieldwork, but Fraser saw things we didn't see, drew conclusions none of us was capable of drawing, and had an intuitive ability to survey the state of the seabird species, the marine mammals, the sea ice, and the weather to fathom how the season was unfolding.

This sixth sense was hard earned. To spend most of one's professional life at a single field station, returning nearly every year, decade after decade, often for four to five months at a time, is to come to know an environment and the living things that inhabit it as well as a person can know any given piece of the planet. Accompanying Fraser in the first few days after his arrival as he reacquainted himself with the penguins, seabirds, and seals was like watching a finely tuned organism return to its native terrain after some time away.

Although fog soon rolled in on the day he arrived, by early afternoon Fraser was out in the field, where he would work, with only a day or two off, for the next two and a half months. That first day, on Shortcut Island—located two miles east of Palmer Station—Fraser was pleased to see that after three years of complete reproductive failure, nearly all of the closely monitored South Polar skua breeding pairs had produced one or two eggs. He walked across the gentle terrain among the gray, lichen-covered rocks, checking the roughly sixty nest sites along eight low ridgelines, which the birding team referred to by the letters A through H. Had it not been for the skuas, walking Shortcut would have been a pleasure, for the island is one of the most verdant in the Palmer area ("verdant" being a relative term in Antarctia), with patches of moss and grass sprouting everywhere. But it is not for nothing that the map of Shortcut in our field notebooks was labeled "Monster Island." Although some of the South Polar skuas—referred to as "Spolars" by Fraser and his group—have become habituated to humans, the majority have not and attack the birding team with fury. However, all the aggravation, both for the South Polar skuas and the people who study them, has paid off. Fraser's research has yielded a rich database of information, much of which indicates that these birds are struggling to reproduce as the climate changes and the ice-dependent silverfish— once a key part of Spolar diets—disappears.

As he and the team progressed across the island—three members covering one side, three the other—the South Polar skuas objected strenuously. Their shrieks, as we moved from territory to territory reminded me of a series of car alarms going off down a city block. "They guard their territories so closely they might as well put up a white picket fence," Fraser remarked at one point.

The habituated South Polar skuas allowed Fraser to slide his hand under them as they sat on the nest, whereupon he pulled out the olive-green or sage-colored eggs, speckled black and brown and a little larger than a chicken egg. We weighed the eggs in green mesh bags, measured their length, and wrote on them with a Sharpie marker: C-8, for example, to identify the ridge and nest number, and E-1 and E-2 to identify the sequence the eggs had appeared in the nest. (In addition to giving a nesting pair a number, the team for several years identified one particularly aggressive pair of South Polar skuas by writing "Ass-holes" on their wooden nest stake.) The nests, resting on bare ground, were constructed of long plugs of moss, golden green at the top and straw-colored at the bottom.

The unhabituated and more aggressive South Polar skuas dove at us, striking the notebooks we held over our heads. On one occasion, as I sat on a rock taking a break, unaware that I was near a skua territory, one of the birds zoomed in and hit me so hard with its banded leg that my hat flew off my head, my face stung as if I had been slapped, and my ears rang. Often, as Fraser and the team handled the eggs, the skuas stood next to us, opening their white-banded wings in a display of aggression, unleashing deafening cries, and sometimes tugging on our sleeves or pants. The South Polars were lighter-colored than the brown skuas, with taupe or walnut-colored heads, necks, and breasts.

As I stood over Fraser, protecting him from attacking skuas, one of the birds jumped on my hunched back and began tearing at my wind-breaker and oilcloth hat. I shooed him away, and after Fraser finished weighing and measuring the eggs, he recounted how a South Polar skua had once landed on the back of one of his team members and sliced a large gash in his ear with its beak.

"If anything makes sure you don't make it home this year, it's these guys," said Fraser, who years ago on Shortcut Island had been hit so hard in the head by a South Polar skua that he momentarily blacked out and nearly rolled off a ledge into the sea, twenty feet below.

That first afternoon, when the two halves of the team met back at the landing on Shortcut, Fraser said, "It looks great. There are a lot of new breeders, a lot of new eggs. They're starting strong. But they started strong the last few seasons, too, and by the end of January there was total failure."

As he spoke, Fraser dabbed a cut on his wrist with a handkerchief—a wound inflicted while he was reading the leg band of a giant petrel on Shortcut.

In the tent that first night, Peter Horne and the team brought Fraser up-to-date, answering his questions about how various brown skua pairs were faring on the islands, how many satellite tags had been placed on giant petrels, how much Adélie diet sampling Peter and Kristen would do when they cruised south to Marguerite Bay on the *Gould*, and how Adélie penguin reproductive success looked that year.

Then Fraser asked about the Adélie numbers, which, from our preliminary figures, looked like they had fallen 20 percent from the previous year. "We're supposed to have ten thousand pairs of Adélies," said Fraser. "Does that look right?"

"I don't know," replied Pickering. "It looks more like eight thousand."

"Man," Fraser said, shaking his head. "It's not a good time to be an Adélie down here. . . . How about gentoos?"

"They're up fifty percent," replied Horne.

"Yeah, in our little cruise down here through the Neumayer and on Petermann Island there were a ton of gentoos," said Fraser. "When this area started to open up with less sea ice, the gentoos started moving along the coast. Now they're becoming the dominant species."

During his first week back at Palmer, Fraser visited as many islands as possible, taking the pulse of an ecosystem he had not seen in two years. Arriving at Humble Island, he had not even stepped off the Zodiac when he remarked that considerably more Antarctic terns were nesting near the landing than in previous years. Within seconds of striding to the center of the island, he commented on the sharp increase in elephant seals and their encroachment on the penguin colonies. Fraser didn't particularly like these massive, stinking beasts—not because of their repulsive habits and appearance but because they tended to wallow right next to the Adélies. "The elephant seals have all this space on these islands," he said as he gazed at dozens of the massive creatures, "yet they have to go right up against the penguin colonies."

MOST OF ALL, during his first few days back at Palmer Station, Fraser was dismayed at the continuing, rapid disappearance of Adélie penguins. On Humble—an island about a third of a mile long, with Adélie colonies concentrated on low rises on the eastern side—Fraser was struck by the large gaps that had opened up between the colonies as the number of breeding pairs had plunged to 925, down from 2,716 three decades before.

He and I traveled by Zodiac to Cormorant Island, a hilly outcropping three miles east of Palmer Station. The temperature hovered around freezing, and a low, thick ceiling of clouds periodically unleashed a snow shower. We were there to do what is known as the "one-chick, two-chick" count, a survey of the number of Adélie chicks in each nest. It's a valuable exercise, as healthy penguins with abundant supplies of krill or fish generally rear more two-chick broods than one-chick broods. Fraser and I did the one-chick, two-chick survey on several islands, including Torgersen, and by the end of the day one thing was clear: The smaller colonies, which were far more vulnerable to skua predation, had considerably more one-chick nests than the larger colonies, where the skuas could not easily nab eggs or chicks from interior nests.

Where the penguin colonies were small, the one-chick, two-chick exercise was simple, but on Torgersen, with its relatively large colonies, the count took intense concentration, especially on Fraser's part. He was known as an accurate and fast counter of penguins, a skill he had honed over several decades but one that I found especially difficult to master, especially as the chicks grew larger and—in the big colonies— you were confronted with a mass of penguins in constant motion. Fraser's technique was to hold his left arm straight out, notebook in hand, and use the notebook as a divider to break the colonies into more manageable segments. During one-chick, two-chick, I stood with a mechanical counter in each hand and stared at the ground, which improved my concentration, as Fraser called out, "one-two-two-two-one-two-one-two-two-two-one-one-one-two . . ." If there was one chick in a nest, I clicked the counter in my left hand; two chicks, and I clicked the counter in the right hand.

Before beginning the one-chick, two-chick count on Cormorant, Fraser and I scrambled up the island's steep hills to make sure that all Cormorant's giant petrels had been banded during the worldwide giant petrel survey. After checking the petrels, Fraser walked to a ledge overlooking the three remaining Adélie colonies, located on cobble beaches about seventy feet below. "Holy shit!" he exclaimed, gazing at the 166 remaining penguin nests in the widely spaced colonies. Three decades before, there had been 892 nesting pairs on the island. (By the 2008–09 season, the number of Adélies on Cormorant had dropped to 88 pairs—a decline of nearly 90 percent since Fraser first set foot on the island.)

As we did the chick counts that day, Fraser remarked that we were getting to them just in time. Many of the chicks were ten inches tall and seemed nearly as wide from their steady diet of krill. The chicks were approaching three weeks of age and were beginning to drift a foot or two from their parents. In just a few days, the chicks would start banding together in the juvenile clusters known as crèches. At that point, the nesting order breaks down, making it impossible to tell how many chicks individual pairs have produced.

Before leaving Cormorant Island, we visited its sole remaining brown skua nest. Fraser was surprised that the pair was still able to reproduce, given how few penguins remained on the island. As one member of the skua pair harried us, Fraser weighed and measured the nest's sole egg. Turning it over in his hand, Fraser remarked that its color was not the customary deep olive green but a paler shade, possibly because of the skua's poor diet. "I don't think this chick is going to make it," said Fraser, a prediction that proved to be correct. That season, the brown skua pair on Cormorant Island produced no chicks to the fledging stage.

Visiting Christine Island—where the number of breeding pairs had dropped from 1,972 pairs to 329 pairs in the past thirty years—Fraser was chagrined to see that three of the island's nine remaining Adélie colonies had disappeared since he'd been there two years earlier. Several of the remaining colonies were so small that he pronounced them a "total wreck."

One evening as we wrapped up our work on Torgersen, Fraser looked at groups of a dozen or two Adélies walking past us on their way from the sea to their colonies. As the overcast skies grew imperceptibly darker, the penguins' white breasts gleamed against the gray cobble, the clinking of their pink feet on the stones reminiscent of wind chimes.

"There used to be so many Adélies here," recalled Fraser, "that in the evening when they were returning from the sea, all you could see was this wall of white breasts coming up from the beach."

And then there was Litchfield, where the Adélie population was on the verge of disappearing. On Fraser's first visit to Litchfield since his return, he walked from the landing to the other side of the island, traversing a broad expanse of small pebbles once used by Adélies to construct their nests.

"Everywhere you see these rocks, there used to be penguins," said Fraser as he slowed briefly to survey the island. "All these areas used to be colonies—here, there, over there. Until about 1990, the decline wasn't extreme. But it has just dropped steadily after that."

Some of the stones were burnished to a fine patina from centuries of Adélies walking over their surface and buffing them with a unique Antarctic polishing agent: The diatoms consumed by the krill contain silica that the Adélies, after eating the krill, excrete onto the rocks. "Over hundreds of years, the diatoms help grind and polish these stones," said Fraser, rubbing his fingers over one of the shiny stones. "If you grab some fresh guano and rub it between your fingers, it feels like sand."

The last Adélie redoubt on Litchfield Island was Colony 8, an oval-shaped patch of stones fifteen feet across at its widest point and surrounded by a ring of worn, pale gray rocks. The colony sat just a few feet away from an inlet on Litchfield's southern side. As Fraser and I neared the colony—the last of the ten that had existed when he'd first arrived, in 1974—he stopped and stared at 11 adult Adélies loitering around 5 nests containing 7 chicks. At the start of the season, the struggling colony had had 15 breeding pairs, but the group's unfettered exposure to skua predation had cut that tiny number by two-thirds.

Litchfield Island's penguin rookery numbered 900 breeding pairs when Fraser first came to Palmer. The University of North Carolina paleoecologist and ornithologist Steven Emslie, who has excavated Adélie colonies on Litchfield Island, estimates that they date back to the sixteenth century.

Fraser said a smattering of adults, some possibly as old as twenty years, kept returning to their ancestral breeding grounds, but that chicks were not surviving the winter. "When this colony goes," he noted, "it will be the first time in at least five hundred years that there will be no Adélies on this island."

Since Fraser first arrived at Palmer Station, the Adélie penguin populations have plummeted by more than 80 percent. The number of Adélie breeding pairs on the five islands in his core study area—Torgersen, Humble, Litchfield, Cormorant, and Christine—has dropped from 15,202 pairs to 2,646 pairs. If you add Adélies from the two more distant islands Fraser has studied—Dream and Biscoe—the number of breeding pairs on all seven islands has fallen from roughly 30,000 to 5,600. (Fraser knows that the penguins have not simply been moving south; he placed thousands of flipper bands on Adélies in the 1990s and almost none showed up in other colonies along the peninsula.) Meanwhile, the Adélie's cousin from warmer climes—the gentoo penguin—is arriving in force, following the heat as it moves down the Antarctic Peninsula. In 1993, there were no gentoo penguins in Fraser's study area. Today there are 2,400 pairs. As Fraser is fond of saying, "There goes the neighborhood."

UNRAVELING THE MYSTERY of why Palmer Station's Adélie penguins are disappearing has been a decades-long investigation involving many scientists, with Bill Fraser at its center. His path to prominence in this important global-warming story has been long, circuitous, and, by traditional academic standards, unconventional. Fraser's success has also involved serendipity: By chance, he happened to find himself working in a region warming more rapidly than almost anyplace else on earth. But Fraser's accomplishments have been shaped by a great deal more than luck.

Years spent hiking every inch of the islands around Palmer Station, learning the contours of every penguin colony, and becoming familiar with scores of individual skuas and giant petrels have led to important insights. Had the climate in the northwestern Antarctic Peninsula not been changing so swiftly, Fraser would still have carried out a classic ecological study of one of the earth's most important wild places. But as he painstakingly assembled a picture of this icebound environment and the seabirds and other creatures that inhabited it, the climate was being transformed, with the sea ice contracting, glaciers retreating, weather and snow patterns shifting, and seabirds and mammals responding to these cascading changes. Finding himself at the heart of this ecological upheaval, Fraser did his best to make sense of it. By general agreement of his colleagues, he has done a first-rate job, although in keeping with his unconventional streak, he has published considerably fewer scientific papers than colleagues such as David Ainley. In Fraser's mind, he is merely waiting until he has amassed a comprehensive set of data, until trends become more evident, or until he has new and important things to say.

After returning in 1976 from his long stay in the Antarctic, Fraser began writing his dissertation on kelp gulls in the Palmer Station region. Having married his high school sweetheart in 1970, he helped support his wife and young daughters as a house painter while he plugged away on his Ph.D. In 1978, forward progress on his dissertation—along with any prospect of returning soon to Antarctica—came to an abrupt halt when he was diagnosed with testicular cancer. Fraser underwent a major surgical procedure known as a retroperitoneal lymph node dissection, which involved opening up his abdominal cavity from stem to stern and removing numerous lymph nodes.

It took Fraser months to recover from the surgery and its complications, at which point doctors discovered a small spot of cancer in each lobe of his lungs. He then came under the care of a renowned University of Minnesota oncologist, B. J. Kennedy, who prescribed a brutal six-month regimen of chemotherapy. "I was sitting across from him and he was shoveling soup into his mouth and he said, 'If you survive my chemotherapy, you'll live,'" recalled Fraser.

He was horribly ill during much of the chemotherapy protocol, but in the end the Kennedy cure worked. Fraser came away deeply impressed with Kennedy's command of oncology and his mastery of the latest research.

"I had recently come back from doing research at Palmer, but I still didn't have this deep appreciation of what good science can do," recalled Fraser. "He showed me the power of research done well."

Fraser's battle with cancer sidetracked him for nearly two years. Because some of his treatments were experimental and not covered by health insurance, he wound up owing more than $100,000 in medical bills. So, as he gradually resumed writing his dissertation in the early 1980s, Fraser—who had worked in construction during summers in high school and college—also started a construction company to pay those bills and help support his family.

In 1983, David Ainley asked Fraser to join him on the first of three scientific cruises to the Weddell Sea and the western Antarctic Peninsula. Funded by the U.S. government, these expeditions were designed so that researchers could study penguins, seabirds, and other marine life on and around the region's sea ice in different seasons. The research was conducted under the auspices of a program known as AMERIEZ: Antarctic Marine Ecosystem Research at the Ice Edge Zone. Fraser was keen to join the cruises, for it had been seven years since he had last seen the continent and he was afflicted by a phenomenon shared by many who spend time in Antarctica.

"Once you have been to the white unknown," wrote Frank Wild, Shackleton's second-in-command on the *Endurance*, "you can never escape the call of the little voices."

For Fraser, a cruise to the northern edge of the Weddell Sea in the austral winter of 1988 was a turning point in his emerging understanding of how climate change had the potential to reshape the Antarctic Peninsula. At the time, scientists were just beginning to grasp the impact on the natural world of rising temperatures caused by man-made greenhouse-gas emissions. Fraser had such a "Eureka!" moment on the 1988 cruise, when he was struck by the central role sea ice played along the Antarctic Peninsula, particularly in the life history of Adélie penguins.

The cruises took place aboard two vessels, with one—a U.S. Coast Guard icebreaker—operating inside the pack ice and another ship outside. Fraser, Ainley, and their colleagues censused penguins and other seabirds as the ships cruised along grid lines in the ice-covered Weddell Sea and the largely ice-free Scotia Sea, to the north. During the 1988 winter cruise, conducted from June to August, Fraser was aboard the icebreaker, whose grid extended from the edge of the Weddell Sea ice to seventy-five miles inside the pack.

As the cruise unfolded in bitterly cold conditions, with temperatures sometimes plunging to −40°F, what quickly struck Fraser was the complete predominance of Adélie penguins on the pack ice and the absence of chinstrap penguins. Some chinstraps rested on the ice within a mile of open water, but once the icebreaker sliced through the pack to a depth of ten to twenty miles, Fraser found only tens of thousands of wintering Adélie penguins, along with smaller numbers of ice-dependent emperor penguins. Working with binoculars from the bridge, Fraser made rough counts of more than 10,000 Adélies per square mile in some places. They were resting on recently formed gray ice, which is only several inches thick and not as solid as the white ice deeper inside the pack. The Adélies—most likely from Paulet Island, Signy Island, and other large colonies at the northern edge of the Antarctic Peninsula—preferred the gray ice because leads would frequently open up, giving them access to krill and fish in the Weddell Sea.

"You would be on the bridge at dawn, which was about ten in the morning, and you would see these single-file lines of Adélies—thousands of birds—trekking along, looking for where the ice had broken up the night before," Fraser recalled. "And the minute they would find these leads they would just vanish through them. That's where the krill were, right below the ice."

The location of the gray ice changed frequently, with its extent expanding swiftly as winter set in. The northern Weddell Sea—protected from more moderate South Pacific weather by the imposing barrier of the Antarctic Peninsula range and subjected to frigid winds roaring off the polar plateau and the enormous Filchner-Ronne Ice Shelf—is a far colder environment than the peninsula's northwestern coast. Fraser remembers going to bed as a severe cold snap set in and waking up the next morning to find that the ice edge had spread outward by several miles. On the rare occasions when the sun was out and up—for about two hours around noon—and temperatures were plummeting, Fraser could stand on the bridge and literally watch the sea ice form before his eyes.

"Suddenly you'd see what looks like grease on the water, and then that would stop moving," said Fraser. "And before you knew it, the sea was turning gray, gray, gray, and finally you would see an inch or so of ice just appear."

Rarely in sight of land, and subjected to brutal storms, Fraser acquired an appreciation of just how profoundly inhospitable Antarctica can be. "There's nothing good for a person here—except for the soul," Fraser told me later.

Aboard the second vessel, in the ice-free Scotia Sea, Ainley discovered an entirely different picture: an abundance of chinstraps in the open water and on icebergs, and a near-complete absence of Adélies. The 1988 cruise produced other revelations as well, including convincing evidence that juvenile krill survive the winter by inhabiting the underside of the sea ice, where they eat life-sustaining phytoplankton embedded in the frozen ocean.

By the time of the 1988 Weddell Sea cruise, scientists had documented a sharp increase in chinstrap penguins in the northern Antarctic Peninsula, as well as a huge jump in fur seal populations, particularly at South Georgia Island. Some Adélie penguin populations in the northern Antarctic Peninsula were actually starting to show a slight decline. The widely accepted explanation for the increase in chinstrap penguin and fur seal populations was the decimation of baleen whales in the Southern Ocean by commercial whaling operations, which continued into the 1980s. The thinking went that with these voracious krill consumers largely removed from the sea, krill populations had rebounded sharply, sparking a resurgence in populations of creatures that ate the crustacean, including fur seals and chinstrap penguins.

But as the Weddell Sea cruise ended, Fraser began to wonder if the theory that whale depletion leads to krill rebound was off the mark. If that hypothesis was true, then how to explain that even as chinstrap populations were growing robustly, krill-eating Adélie populations were beginning to falter? He also was struck by the vivid contrast that the cruise had revealed, with Adélies flocking to the pack ice in winter and chinstraps living at sea, on icebergs, and at the edge of the pack.

Not long after the cruise, he attended a conference in Hobart, Australia, during which a number of papers discussed growing evidence of global warming.

"And that," said Fraser, "is when I sort of put these stories together. It reeked of habitat change due to a warming climate."

The sea ice seemed to be decreasing. Ice-loving species like Adélies were starting to decline. Ice-avoiding species like chinstraps and fur seals were increasing. He began to believe that these changes had little to do with krill abundance and a lot to do with a warming winter habitat and less sea ice. "It was like a light bulb going off," said Fraser.

In 1989, just as he was finally receiving his PhD, Fraser began working on a paper suggesting that global warming and decreasing sea ice were the major reason behind shifting populations of penguins along the Antarctic Peninsula. He was out in front on this issue, and many colleagues greeted his hypothesis with skepticism. Fraser spoke with scientists at NASA, which had been using satellites to monitor the extent of sea ice along the peninsula for about a decade. NASA researchers told him, however, that there were no discernible trends in sea ice, up or down. But Fraser—joined by Ainley and the Trivelpieces— examined temperature trends since midcentury from four stations on the northern Antarctic Peninsula. The temperature record showed a steady decrease in the frequency of the cold years that led to extensive sea ice formation along the northwestern peninsula, which occurs when mean annual air temperatures fall below 24°F. At midcentury, roughly four out of five years saw mean air temperatures below 24°F. But by the 1970s and 1980s, the frequency of such cold winters had fallen to one or two out of every five years, meaning—in Fraser's mind—that sea ice extent or duration must also have decreased. That NASA satellites had not yet detected the trend did not deter Fraser. Indeed, by 1996, NASA satellites began picking up the declining sea ice along the Antarctic Peninsula. Today, the well-documented loss of the peninsula's sea ice is striking.

In 1991, with Fraser as lead author, he, Ainley, and the Trivelpieces wrote a paper arguing that it was primarily shrinking sea ice—not an increase in krill due to the cessation of whaling—that was leading to the growth of chinstrap populations and the decline of Adélies. The prestigious journals *Science* and *Nature* rejected the paper, but in 1992 it was published in *Polar Biology*. A prominent scientist with the British Antarctic Survey, John Croxall, published a paper questioning Fraser's thesis, saying that it was "certainly premature" to conclude that changing environmental factors, such as shrinking sea ice, were the reason behind shifting penguin populations. (Croxall now says that, given the accumulated evidence of the last two decades, there is "no doubt" that declining sea ice has been a crucial factor affecting penguin populations.)

Fraser's article was one of the first scientific papers to suggest that global warming was beginning to nibble at the edges of the world's coldest continent, and it planted the notion in Fraser's mind that in the years to come, climate change was likely to dwarf all other factors affecting Adélie penguins on the northwestern Antarctic Peninsula.

CHAPTER 8

HIGH SUMMER

We were now reveling in the indescribable freshness of the Antarctic that seems to permeate one's being, and which must be responsible for that longing to go again which assails each returned explorer from polar regions.
—ERNEST SHACKLETON, *Nimrod* expedition, 1907–09

BY THE SECOND WEEK OF JANUARY, THE RIGID ORDER OF THE Adélie colonies—the nests generally constructed two feet apart, from center to center, the penguins maintaining their personal space as assiduously as Tokyo subway commuters—began to break down. As is sometimes the case in human communities, adolescents were behind the spreading disarray. The young Adélies—many entering their fourth week—were gaining two ounces a day as their parents shuttled single-mindedly to and from the sea to forage for krill. Until January 8, one parent remained with the chicks while the other was in the Southern Ocean, but on that day we watched as the first crèches began to form. Three or four chicks started to band together, their rotund bellies so stuffed with krill that they brushed against the chicks' pink feet. The young penguins' thick, charcoal-colored down had not yet taken on the moth-eaten look that would soon signal the start of the molt.

The formation of crèches—the word means crib, or day nursery—signified a number of things. First, that the appetites of the young Adélies had become so insatiable that both parents were forced to simultaneously forage at sea. (Anyone familiar with the eating habits of teenage boys can appreciate the imperative of Adélie parents doubling up on the feeding run.) Second, that the guard stage—with chicks under the watchful eye of their parents—was ending, because the chicks could now easily maintain their own body temperatures and were just entering the period where the brawniest could fend off skua attacks. Third, and finally, that the chicks were beginning to test their independence, taking their initial, halting steps outside the secure perimeter of the nest space to hang around with fellow juvenile penguins.

With the chicks' demand for krill reaching its peak, Fraser wanted to get a sense of the abundance of the crustacean in the surrounding waters that January. One way was to affix satellite transmitters—rectangular instruments not much bigger than a matchbox—to the backs of Adélies and track their movements over time. If the penguins stayed many hours at sea and foraged far away, it meant the krill were scarce. In years of krill abundance, however, the Adélies often swam no more than ten to fifteen miles, returning within half a day with ample food for their chicks. The location of the Adélies' feeding grounds near Palmer Station was no secret. Indeed, if you stood on the beaches of the penguin rookeries and watched, the Adélies themselves showed the way as they porpoised through the water almost due south. They usually traveled a dozen miles, to the mouth of the Palmer Deep—an undersea canyon more than three thousand feet below the surface that funneled nutrient-rich bottom currents upward, attracting large swarms of krill. That a krill hot spot was near Anvers Island's Adélie colonies was no coincidence. Penguin rookeries along the Antarctic Peninsula had become established in areas that offered two essential elements: snow-free nesting beaches and nearby foraging grounds.

A second, less-expensive way Fraser gauged the state of krill abundance was by attaching smaller radio tags to the backs of Adélies on Humble Island. Palmer Station's support staff had built a plywood shed on a Humble Island ridge and placed a radio receiver inside. When the Adélies were on the island, the receiver detected their radio signals.

When the seabirds plunged into the Southern Ocean in search of krill or fish, the receiver stopped picking up the signal—enabling Fraser and his team to know exactly how long the Adélies were away on foraging trips.

On January 10, on Humble Island, Fraser extracted 20 birds from Colony 2, which held more than 600 breeding pairs arrayed along a gently sloping ridge of Confederate-gray rocks. Recent rains had turned the ground under the penguins' feet into a tacky guano bog, its hue ranging from brick red to liver-colored. Radiating out from some of the nests like spokes of a wheel were white streaks of guano produced by Adélies that had managed to catch fish, which produces chalk-colored excrement. Many of the adults, just in from the sea, had sparkling white breasts, but the downy chicks—which had spent more than three weeks lying and standing in seabird excreta—were smeared head to foot with guano.

Approaching the edge of the colony, Fraser dropped a green hand towel a few feet outside the perimeter in order to mark the location where he would snatch an Adélie. Crouching and leaning forward on one leg, he slowly reached into the colony, his arm insinuating itself toward an adult with two chicks. With one swift motion, Fraser grabbed an Adélie by the flipper and handed it alternately to me or one of the other team members. When it was my turn, I held the penguin with both hands where the flippers joined the torso and walked the bird—the resistance of its powerful body sending jolts into my arms—toward another group of colleagues. I then handed the penguin to Brett Pickering, who steadied the animal on his lap by holding its legs together and placing a firm hand on its back. All but the feistiest Adélies calmed down as Peter Horne or Jennifer Blum attached the radio transmitter—a device about the size of a double-A battery, with an eight-inch antennae—to the penguins' feathers, using heavy-duty, waterproof tape and plastic ties.

After all the radio tags were attached—ten on females, ten on males—I walked to the nearby beach where Humble Island's Adélies departed and returned from their foraging trips. Along the way, I passed a colony where more than a dozen wallowing elephant seals were encroaching on penguin nests. The day before, I'd watched an Adélie from that colony march up to one of the seals that had moved too close to the penguin's chicks and jab the seal in the mouth. The seal had retreated, slithering back several feet as it opened its mouth wide in a display of aggression. Watching a ten-pound penguin rout a thousand-pound seal had reaffirmed my admiration for these birds.

The Adélies' cobble beach on Humble was about 125 feet wide, flanked on both sides by crumbling rock walls roughly twenty feet high. The water was shallow and placid, protected from the Bismarck Strait by Litchfield Island to the southwest. Plankton were not blooming in the nearby sea, and on this overcast day the water was absolutely clear and tinted faintly green, the rocks on the bottom plainly visible to a depth of many feet. Incoming Adélies zigzagged through the sea and shot up through the shallows until their stomachs nearly scraped bottom. Landing on both feet as they leapt out of the water, the penguins walked gingerly over the rocks, occasionally hopping over a larger stone. They gave a wide berth to four hulking juvenile male elephant seals with drab brown backs and undersides the color of tarnished brass. Some of the Adélies stood just a few feet from the water's edge and preened themselves, distributing oil from a gland in the tail to their feathers, their necks arching gracefully as they ran their beaks down their backs. Others preened nearby on several wide snow ledges stained pink with guano.

Outgoing birds walked with deliberation to the beach and slipped into the shallows, where many luxuriated in the sea, seeming to take genuine pleasure in washing off the grime of the colony. They splashed with their flippers, dipped their heads under the water, took short warm-up swims near the beach before heading to sea, and called to one another as they surfaced. Standing on a ledge and watching the penguins, I realized how utterly in their element the Adélies were, exhibiting a grace and fluidity they lacked on land.

Nearly a century before, after witnessing a similar scene on the Ross Sea, G. Murray Levick wrote, "So extraordinary was this whole scene, that . . . it seemed to us almost impossible that the little creatures, whose antics we were watching were actually birds and not human beings. Seemingly reluctant as they had been to enter the water, when once there they evinced every sign of enjoyment, and would stay in for hours at a time."

After a minute or two of swimming near the beach on Humble Island, the penguins then turned south and began porpoising toward the Palmer Deep, passing through the channel between Litchfield and Torgersen islands. They made their way to the foraging grounds at roughly 3 to 5 miles per hour—a typical traveling speed in water.

When foraging, Adélie penguins dart to and fro in the water, picking off krill or fish one by one with their beaks, "going just about as fast as a barnyard fowl feeds on grain thrown on the floor," in the words of Australian explorer Douglas Mawson. Outfitted with tags that measure depth, time, and speed, Adélies have been recorded diving as deep as 558 feet and have remained underwater for nearly six minutes, though most dives are less than 150 feet and last two to three minutes. (The largest and deepest-diving penguin, the emperor, has been measured diving to 1,755 feet—500 feet deeper than the Empire State Building is tall—and staying underwater for eighteen minutes.) In order to remain underwater for so long, the Adélies not only use the air in their lungs but also metabolize oxygen from their breast-muscle tissue.

While gathering food for their chicks, Adélies undergo a physical transformation: Their stomachs thin and become more elastic, which enables them to pack in far more krill than at other times of the year. In winter, Adélies might fill their stomachs with seven ounces of food. But at the height of summer, when the chicks are growing most rapidly, an Adélie on a single foraging trip can stuff two pounds of krill into its stomach.

The bounty of the Southern Ocean is essential for the survival of Adélie populations, for it enables them to often successfully raise two chicks in a clutch—an important evolutionary advantage in an environment where mortality is high, especially among young penguins. From 1986 to 1998, Fraser and his colleagues banded hundreds of Adélie penguin chicks and adults annually. What he found was that only about 15 percent of the chicks lived to age five, which is when most Adélies begin to breed successfully. Were there fewer prey available and Adélie pairs could support only one chick, the grim mortality statistics—attributable, in part, to the hardships of surviving an Antarctic winter on sea ice and at sea—would make it difficult for populations to maintain themselves.

During my season at Palmer, krill seemed to be in shorter supply, as the satellite tags showed the Adélies sometimes traveling forty-five miles from Anvers Island to forage and staying out for twenty-four to ninety-six hours. Fraser also noticed that we had seen few humpback whales—baleen whales that eat krill—feeding in the surrounding waters, further convincing him that krill were scarcer that summer.

ON JANUARY 14, as the summer neared its peak, Fraser took advantage of a particularly fine day to visit the wildest spot within reasonable Zodiac range of Palmer Station: the Joubin Islands. Plainly visible from Palmer Station, the scores of islands in the Joubin archipelago range in size from a half-mile long to just a few dozen yards; beyond them lies the unimpeded expanse of the Southern and Pacific oceans. With temperatures in the mid-30s, the skies largely clear, and the winds light, we set out from Palmer Station at around nine-thirty A.M. Fraser and I were in one Zodiac and Brett Pickering and Jen Blum in the other. The remaining members of our team—Peter Horne and Kristen Gorman—were spending the month on the *Laurence M. Gould* as it cruised down the Antarctic Peninsula as part of the Long Term Ecological Research annual survey to study the effects of climate change on the region. Peter and Kristen worked most of the time aboard the *Gould,* counting seabirds. But for a week they lived in a remote field camp on Avian Island, in Marguerite Bay, where Fraser was conducting a study of a large Adélie penguin rookery still thriving—at least for the moment—in a far colder environment that resembled Palmer Station's more frigid climate a half century earlier.

As our Zodiacs left the shelter of Litchfield Island and sped at full throttle to the southwest, we began to feel widely spaced swells. The sky was a brilliant blue and the Bellingshausen Sea a deep sapphire. Along the way we passed several reefs—some barely submerged, others just protruding above the surface—upon which waves crashed and foamed. After forty-five minutes, we reached the outer ring of the Joubins, cut our speed, and cruised into the tranquil interior of the archipelago. Surrounding us, drenched in sunlight, were groups of low-lying islands strung along placid channels whose clear, turquoise waters were more reminiscent of the Caribbean than the Antarctic. The archipelago was encircled by the remains of dozens of sheer-sided, tabular icebergs that had run aground as they drifted north, their sides sculpted by wave action.

Most of the islands of the Joubins remain nameless, but five do have numbers, bestowed by Fraser because they harbor penguin colonies. We stopped first at island No. 8, its crumbling, weathered rocks ranging in color from light smoke to lead gray. The island is one of the few places in Antarctica where all three species of the *Pygoscelis* genus of penguins—Adélies, chinstraps, and gentoos—nest side by side. Spread along ridges that often were just fifteen feet above sea level, the penguins tended to segregate by species, but in several places Adélies nested amid chinstrap colonies, and gentoos among Adélies. Hardwired to breed early because they mate in the coldest regions and their reproductive season is shortest, the Adélies were the most advanced nesters, with some chicks a foot tall and already shedding their down and growing adult feathers. The chinstraps were slightly behind the Adélies, their chicks—covered in pale gray down—standing eight to ten inches tall. Finally there were the gentoos, which breed two to three weeks after the Adélies in the Palmer region. Some of their chicks looked just a few days old, and many were still tucked under their parents' brood pouches, baring their fuzzy hind ends to the world.

The demographic story playing out closer to Palmer—Adélie populations collapsing, chinstrap numbers increasing slightly, and gentoos going through the roof—was repeated on island No. 8 and all the penguin rookeries on the Joubins. Walking across the island counting the different species, Fraser and Pickering kept up a running commentary as they approached Adélie colonies that had disappeared in the past two years and gentoo colonies that had sprung up in their place.

"These gentoos aren't supposed to be there," said Pickering, looking at a crude map of the island's rookeries, which needed to be updated to reflect a new gentoo colony.

Glancing at the gentoos, Fraser replied, "The future."

Farther on, in yet another empty Adélie colony, a lone gentoo penguin stood amid the unused nesting pebbles and performed his species' version of the ecstatic display, arching his head skyward and emitting a jackass-like bray. Fraser stopped and eyed the penguin warily, leaving little doubt that he viewed the spreading gentoo populations as a botanist would the kudzu vine's takeover of the American South.

"Look," Fraser said to Pickering, "there's a gentoo displaying here. There's going to be a gentoo colony here soon."

The Joubins were a magical and restful place. As we strolled across the islands, I gazed at a tableau of icebergs, glaciated mountains, and jade-colored waters in the nearby shallows. Patches of tangerine-colored lichen covered large boulders. Moss sprouted among shattered columns of basalt. The penguin colonies also possessed a large number of pewter-colored rocks worn smooth by the passage of penguin feet over thousands of years, some of the larger stones as slick as a buffed flagstone floor. Penguin colonies have likely existed on the Joubins for far longer than on the islands near Palmer Station, for a simple reason: During the last glacial maximum in Antarctica, more than thirteen thousand years ago, glaciers are believed to have spilled off the Antarctic Peninsula and Anvers Island, entombing the nearby islands in ice. The Joubins—located farther offshore—have in all likelihood been ice-free for considerably longer, opening up breeding beaches for penguins.

One of the final rookeries we visited was on an island where the remains of a whaling ship, believed to have sunk nearby in the 1920s, were strewn across a broad expanse of cobble. Pieces of sun-bleached wood lay among several whale ribs more than ten feet long, their pitted, pale-gray surface stained by green algae. This wreckage only added to the mystery of the Joubins, which, in the remote world of the Antarctic Peninsula, had an even more pronounced end-of-the-earth feel than any other spot we visited.

Farther down the beach, we encountered our first Antarctic fur seal of the season, a stout, whiskered, dark gray creature resting by the sea on some well-polished rocks. Unlike the other seals around Palmer Station, the Antarctic fur seal is an eared seal of the Otariidae family; the species thus has more in common with sea lions, also in that family, than with the so-called true seals that inhabit the Antarctic. Among its sea lion–like characteristics are powerful foreflippers and a capacity to ambulate on all fours, which means that—unlike the slow-moving true seals—the fur seal can drag itself across a rocky beach as fast as a person can run. Fur seals also have a nasty bite; considering that and their speed, we gave them a wide berth.

Fur seals have made a remarkable comeback in recent decades, their numbers estimated at more than two million in the Southern Ocean; most of these breed on South Georgia. Because of this rebound, they have been migrating to the Palmer Station region in greater numbers over the past two decades. Fraser believes that the region's warming climate has also attracted these subantarctic creatures. During his first year at Palmer, Fraser and David Parmelee's other students saw no fur seals. Their numbers slowly grew over the next two decades, and in the 1993–94 season Fraser and his team tallied nearly 900 fur seals. He estimates that roughly 4,000 fur seals now inhabit the Palmer area in summer.

Returning to Palmer Station, we streaked down the face of swells, bottoming out in troughs so deep that we sometimes lost sight of the Marr Ice Piedmont. About halfway to the station, the slow rollers gave way to a confused sea. Fraser scarcely eased back on the Zodiac's throttle, and as we bounced across the choppy ocean the boat almost went airborne on several occasions, smacking back down on the water with a spine-jarring jolt. Soaked with sea spray, I clutched the ropes on the Zodiac's gunwales and held on as the line of mountains and glaciers in front of me bounced wildly on the horizon. I have rarely experienced a sense of exhilaration as heady as the one that came over me on that ride home.

NOT LONG AFTERWARD, on another brilliantly sunny day that defined the high-summer season at Palmer Station, we returned to Dream Island to perform a task that the team had put off until Fraser's arrival: banding a pair of utterly unhabituated brown skuas. As it had been on many days that season, the wind was scarcely strong enough to ripple the water's surface as we traveled to Dream. We sped across Wylie Bay, which lies between Palmer Station and Dream Island, under an azure sky, arriving on Dream at ten A.M. As Brett and Jen counted penguins on the island's east side, Fraser and I made the steep climb up the island's tallest hill—about 120 feet above the sea—over fractured rocks.

The pair of brown skua adults Fraser planned to band had begun nesting atop the high ridge two years before. He also intended to weigh and measure several of that season's brown skua chicks. Six reproducing brown skua pairs remained on Dream Island, down from a peak of 9 in the 1970s, when the island harbored roughly 12,000 pairs of Adélie penguins. By the 2005–06 season, only 3,535 Adélie pairs remained on Dream. (By the 2008–09 season, the number of breeding pairs had plummeted to 2,207 pairs.)

"Once the threshold of one thousand pairs of Adélies per skua pair is crossed, we start to see this effect reproductive success," Fraser said as we stood atop the ridge on a balmy day and gazed at the deep blue of the sea and sky. "If you start at Biscoe and head north and west here to Dream, you see the collapse of brown skuas. It's an ecological cascade, a beautiful example of a predator-prey system that is tracking environmental changes. The brown skuas are more or less decreasing at the same rate as the Adélies."

Near the first skua nest, Fraser scanned the landscape of moss and rocks for thirty seconds before spotting the skua chick, which had scurried about twenty feet from its home territory. Walking over to the young bird, he scooped it up and measured the length of its beak and the primary feathers on its wings. The skua, about half the size of a chicken, was a gangly creature with wispy, taupe-colored feathers. Its primary feathers, which would soon give it the ability to fly, were just beginning to emerge from their tubular sheaths. The bird's parents, a relatively relaxed pair, stood five to ten feet from us and emitted shrill cries but never attacked.

That was not the case with the next pair, which Fraser was intent on banding so that he could follow their breeding success—or lack thereof—in the coming years, as the Dream Island Adélie populations continued to crash. No sooner had we entered the unbanded birds' territory, close to the ridge's summit, than the pair began swooping low over our heads. I surveyed the craggy landscape and saw nothing, but Fraser quickly spied their chick as it fled from us, its long legs stumbling over the rocks. Fraser retrieved the chick and we swiftly measured its bill and primaries, then placed it in a mesh bag and weighed it.

Intent on using the chick as a lure to capture and band the parents, Fraser instructed me to hold on to the young bird. Kneeling on the ground, I grabbed the chick with both hands and placed it between my legs. Its body was fragile and warm, and I could feel its heart pounding so rapidly that the beats were impossible to count. Occasionally the bird would struggle to break free, but I held it firmly, and in time the chick settled down slightly, its head swiveling back and forth, exquisitely alert to every sound and movement. Fraser knelt next to me as the parents stood nearby and screeched.

I was beginning to wonder how he intended to snare the parents, for he had no net. I was still pondering that question when one of the adults, unable to tolerate our holding its chick any longer, took off and flew for our heads at high speed. Crouching low, I kept my eye on Fraser, and as the bird streaked overhead Fraser's right hand shot up and grabbed the skua by one leg. The bird's wings flapped wildly, stirring the air and making a sound like an umbrella being opened and closed rapidly. Within several seconds Fraser had folded the bird's wings against its body; then, holding the skua to his windbreaker, he gathered together the bird's feet and wing tips with one hand. All the while, the skua was biting Fraser, opening up cuts on his hands and wrists. Still clutching the bird, Fraser turned the creature around and asked me to hold its feet and wing tips, which I did. We let the chick go, and it fled downslope. Then, as I clutched the skua's legs and held its beak shut, Fraser used his free hand to fish around the pocket of his windbreaker and extract a half-inch-wide aluminum leg band and a pair of banding pliers. Tucking the bird under his arm, Fraser then attached the band to the skua's left leg. Throughout this exercise, the skua was, for the most part, pacified, although from time to time it would struggle and expel gusts of breath through its nostrils.

Rising slowly and holding the skua's wings tightly against its body, Fraser walked to the edge of a ridge and released the bird, which flew fifteen feet away, landed, and screeched at us as it spread its wings in a territorial display.

Meanwhile, Fraser retrieved the chick, which had scurried twenty-five feet downhill, and brought it back to me. Once again, as I held the chick and we both knelt, Fraser waited for the second parent to buzz us in defense of its offspring. The skua swooped low overhead once or twice before Fraser snagged it by the legs in a single fluid motion. Within a minute, as I grabbed the bird by its legs and held its beak closed, Fraser banded this bird, as well. I loosened my grip on the bird's beak so Fraser could take the skua and release it, and as I did the bird bit down on my gloved finger with such force that it felt like a man squeezing the digit with a pair of pliers.

After releasing the second skua, Fraser once again pursued the chick, which he returned to its territory. As we quickly walked away, Fraser's hands and wrists were bleeding, a price he paid because he couldn't effectively snatch the birds out of the air with gloves on. He refused to use a net because it could damage the skua's flight feathers.

After working in the Adélie colonies, we piled into our Zodiac at around six in the evening and rode to Biscoe Point, sixteen miles to the southeast. The seas remained placid and the skies clear, save for scattered high clouds moving in from the south and the west. The sun was slowly dropping, casting a soothing light on the water and the peninsular range. Cruising through the Bismarck Strait, we saw, to our south, a long, tabular iceberg into whose sides had been carved three arches, giving the slab of ice the appearance of a Roman aqueduct. We had not seen any appreciable sea ice in weeks, but as we came within a mile of Biscoe Point, which jutted out from the Marr Ice Piedmont in front of the sheer, triangular-shaped face of Mount William, we ran into a thick field of brash ice that had broken off from the glacier. With the ice scraping against the Zodiac and knocking into our propeller, we slowly made our way to the landing at Biscoe, passing a half dozen crabeater seals and two leopard seals lounging on floes.

Situated near the southeastern tip of Anvers Island, Biscoe Point is a finger of battleship-gray rocks that juts out from the Marr Ice Piedmont and sits in the shadow of Mount William. The point is generally covered in far less snow than other penguin rookeries because it is subjected to strong katabatic winds that flow off the the ice-covered mountains and sweep away the snow. ("Katabatic" comes from the Greek word *katabatikos,* which means "going downhill." In Antarctica, these winds are created when cool, dense air roars off the polar ice cap onto the coast; in colder regions of Antarctica, katabatic winds often reach hurricane force.)

Biscoe Point—which commands a breathtaking panorama of the peninsular range—is in need of a rechristening. As recently as twenty years ago, the Marr Ice Piedmont covered part of the point. But the retreat of the glacier has revealed that what once looked like a peninsula is actually an island, now separated from the glacier by fifty feet of open water. The warmer weather has brought other changes to Biscoe, as well, mainly in the form of gentoo penguins.

The Adélies occupy the lower ground nearer the sea, and the gentoos—slightly larger penguins distinguished by orange bills and wedge-shaped white spots over their eyes—colonize the higher ridges. Fraser had not been to Biscoe in two years, and as we puttered to our landing site he looked over the rapidly expanding gentoo penguin colonies, which had spread across a series of terraces all the way to the highest ridge. "Is that a gentoo colony way the hell up there?" he asked. "This is just amazing. I am absolutely floored." The 761 nesting pairs of Adélies—down from the 3,000 pairs in 1986—were relegated to a few ridges close to the sea.

Indeed, for the first time, more gentoos—902 pairs—than Adélies were nesting on Biscoe. As we ranged across the terraces where the gentoos had built their round, high-sided nests, the invading penguins filled the air with their braying, which sounded like scores of bulb-shaped bicycle horns being squeezed simultaneously. Gentoos are renowned for being the most laid-back of the pygoscelid penguins, and as they wandered past us, utterly unconcerned by our presence, Fraser chuckled and said, "They are oblivious. They're in their own zone."

A layer of clouds covered most of the sky, save for a few patches of blue above Mount William. The sea, now lead gray, was streaked white with rafts of brash ice that meandered through grounded icebergs toward the Antarctic Peninsula. Mount William loomed above us to the north, its ridges coated in ice. The snow plastered to its nearly vertical front was etched with fine lines where pieces of ice had rolled down.

Fraser was in for another surprise as we walked to the end of the point, next to the terminus of the Marr Ice Piedmont. For two hundred yards, we traversed a gradually sloping terrain of smoke-colored stone and shattered rocks, some neatly fractured by frost into thin slices. When Fraser had first come to Palmer Station, the area we were walking across had been buried under more than one hundred feet of ice. During his last season at Palmer, in 2003 and 2004, the remnants of that ice dome had covered an area about the size of a football field. Now, the ice patch was half that size and only ten to twenty feet thick. On its surface, small, fist-sized rocks had been heated by the sun and had bored holes in the ice. We dipped our hands into these little wells, scooping out and drinking water that was thousands of years old. Beneath the rapidly disappearing plate of ice I could hear the trickling of meltwater flowing to the sea.

Where the Marr Ice Piedmont had withdrawn, patches of Antarctica's two vascular plants—a hair grass, *Deschampsia antarctica,* and a pearlwort, or cushion plant, *Colobanthus quitensis*—were colonizing new territory amid the glacial till.

"If someone had taken you here ten or twenty years ago and said, 'This will all disappear in ten years,' you would have said, 'You're fucking crazy,'" Fraser told me. "The ice cap on Biscoe has been here for thousands of years, and now it's almost gone. I am in awe that it has taken such a short time to happen. What you're seeing here is what you would have seen if you had been standing in Wisconsin fifteen thousand years ago as the glaciers retreated. This is what these landscapes must have looked like as the ice melted. It's the sheer power of the earth—ice and rock. You see a glacier pull back and the ground exposed and plants and birds come along and colonize. You see these ancient cycles happening right here."

We sat on rocks and gazed at the glacier's face, which was several stories high. Its luminous, light blue front was honeycombed and much of it slumped forward, looking like melted wax. This flowing river of ice was very much alive, even more so now that rapid warming was accelerating its slide to the sea. The noise coming from the glacier was constant—sharp cracks, deep rumbles like the sound of furniture being moved across a floor, and from time to time the showering of ice inside a hidden crevasse. The snapping sounds intensified and then, just in front of us, a fifteen-foot chunk of the glacier calved into the narrow channel separating the Marr and Biscoe. The cascading pieces of the glacier sent waves lapping against nearby rocks. Thousands of ice shards from this and previous calvings hissed as they were buffeted by the waves. Then, things quieted down and we listened to the tinkling of pieces of brash ice knocking against one another. The newly exposed face of the glacier was a heavenly shade of blue, attained over thousands of years as the large air bubbles in the ice had been compressed by the accumulated weight of compacted snow.

AS JANUARY PROGRESSED, the team twice traveled in the evening to Torgersen Island to do Adélie diet sampling. This entailed grabbing several penguins, pumping water into their stomachs through plastic tubing until they regurgitated, and then collecting their stomach contents in a white plastic bucket. This important exercise gave Fraser a good idea of what the Adélies were eating. Indeed, it was through diet sampling that Fraser had begun to notice that krill of a certain age and size tended to be present in Adélie diets in different seasons; this had led him to the conclusion that heavy ice years tended to produce large numbers of juvenile krill, which would then be widespread as adults several years later in the sea around Palmer. But diet sampling was an intrusive procedure, and occasionally the sampling would puncture a penguin's stomach, leading to its death. And with Adélie populations in free fall at Palmer Station, Fraser was increasingly loath to be responsible for the death of even a single penguin.

"I think it affects me more than it affects the rest of the field team just because I know that it's very likely that the bird we're diet sampling is probably an old animal because recruitment is so poor now," said Fraser. "It's not inconceivable that that bird is in its teens. And it really bothers me that here's a bird that's survived thick and thin and gone through hell and it's an old bird and I come along and it dies because of me. And the thing is, if you kill one bird you're killing at least one chick, probably two."

We successfully sampled one adult, whose stomach was filled with a smaller species of krill. Brett Pickering then pumped water into the stomach of a second Adélie, which soon regurgitated a small amount of krill.

"Is that blood?" Pickering asked.

Drops of blood spattered into the bucket as the Adélie regurgitated some more krill. We watched intently, hoping the bleeding would stop. Pickering released the penguin. It stood for a few seconds, then lay down on the pebbles. The penguin shook its head, spraying a combination of water, krill, and blood. Everyone, especially Pickering, looked stricken. The bird rose and tried to walk, but couldn't. Bloodstained bubbles poured from its mouth. Just as I was thinking that someone should put the Adélie out of its misery, Fraser silently picked up the penguin, walked twenty-five feet away, knelt down, placed the Adélie between his legs, grabbed a rock, and ended its life with a swift blow to the head.

Jen Blum looked away, her face flushed and tears in her eyes. Others of us were on the verge of crying, as well. Fraser returned to the group and said, "It's over. This diet sampling has to end."

We walked in silence back to the boat landing. In the slanting evening light, Adélies padded back to their colonies, stomachs bulging with krill. We all knew that the loss of one penguin would have no bearing on the fate of the Torgersen Island rookery, but the death of this Adélie—at our own hands—seemed horrible nevertheless.

Finally, as we neared the Zodiac, a distraught Fraser spoke up.

"Something has changed," he said. "I don't know what it is, but something has changed, and I want to find out what it is. We have done hundreds of these diet samples for years with no problems, and now in the last few years some birds have started dying."

For the rest of the season, the team never took another diet sample.

CHAPTER 9

THE CRÈCHE

They are extraordinarily like children, these little people
of the Antarctic world, either like children, or like old
men, full of their own importance and late for dinner, in
their black tail-coats and white shirt-fronts—and rather
portly withal.

—Apsley Cherry-Garrard,
Terra Nova expedition, 1910–13

The crèching juvenile Adélies took over the penguin islands, reminding me of nothing so much as a pack of adolescents yearning to be grown-up but having scant idea of how to care for themselves. In the third week of January, the charcoal-gray chicks clustered in ever-larger groups, flattening individual nests as adults darted into the colonies to perform their minimal parental duties—regurgitating krill into the mouths of their offspring—before quickly fleeing the ceaseless begging of their progeny.

Around the middle of the month, I witnessed the first of what would become an uncountable number of feeding chases, during which hungry chicks ran after their parents begging for food. It was a comic sight, with the unsteady young penguins—flippers back and bulbous torsos angled forward—tripping and falling as they pursued their parents with frantic, staccato steps. The parent, usually just in from the sea, would customarily turn and feed the chick, but if a pair of young penguins were especially relentless in their supplication, the parent would frequently wheel on its offspring and peck them fiercely. As Ernest Shackleton observed, "The chicks are both imperative and wheedling."

After hundreds of hours of observing crèches and feeding chases, William Sladen concluded that the chases serve several purposes: They enable parents to disgorge a meal to their chicks away from other clamoring young penguins. They keep the chicks fit and give them confidence to venture outside the colony. They also make the chicks more aware of skuas and other predators.

None of that seemed to matter much to the Adélie parents, which looked increasingly hassled as January progressed. When they weren't at sea, most chose to lie on pebbles or snowbanks near the water, pulling themselves together after a stressful feeding session or upon returning from a foraging trip. Although the adults were often resting no more than twenty to thirty yards away, the chicks made no effort to find their parents, and for good reason: The colony was where dinner had always been served, so why go looking for a meal elsewhere?

The crèche stage lasts a month or so, starting when the chicks are about twenty days old and continuing until they acquire adult plumage and head into the sea roughly thirty to thirty-five days later, in the first half of February. Crèching has developed, in part, because both parents are forced to forage simultaneously to nourish a pair of rapidly growing chicks, prompting the chicks to band together. The crèche serves as a defense against skuas and other predators, since there is safety in numbers, and a huddle of chicks provides some measure of group insulation—a benefit that is more important in far colder Adélie breeding grounds than Palmer, such as on the shores of the Ross Sea.

Some early students of Adélie penguins also believed that crèches represented a type of communal feeding system, with adults providing nourishment to chicks in the crèche other than their own. Even as astute an observer as G. Murray Levick wrote that "it seems hardly possible for the adults to recognize the individuals of so large a gathering and to detect a stranger should one turn up." But, indeed, it is possible for adults to recognize their chicks, and they do so by the physical characteristic that is most individualized in penguins: their voices.

This ability was on display throughout the crèching period. Toward the end of January, on Humble Island, I spent several hours watching adult penguins returning from the sea to nourish their chicks, an exercise that involved sophisticated discrimination between a peguin's own progeny and those of other Adélies. Some parents would wade into colonies bustling with large chicks and immediately be set upon by hungry youngsters. Stopping in front of a pleading chick, the adult would swing its head back and forth, issue a trumpeting call—a form of the loud mutual display—and wait for the response. Some of the chicks would answer with a peep, and others would respond with a croaky call, the penguin version of an adolescent boy's cracking voice. The adult Adélie was, in effect, querying the chicks, and if the chick was the adult's offspring and responded with a recognizable voice, the adult would feed it. If the chick did not belong to the adult, the Adélie would ignore the return call and either keep marching or peck the impostor until it backed away. As the number of returning parents peaked in the evening, the scene at the Humble Island rookery was boisterous, with scores of greeting calls splitting the air and dozens of chicks in hot pursuit of their parents at any given time.

A leading expert on penguin voice recognition, Pierre Jouventin of the Center for Functional Ecology and Evolution, in France, says penguins are able to recognize one another because they have two voice boxes, which produce unique amplitudes and frequencies that add up to individual vocal signatures. The penguin calls are so idiosyncratic that chicks can often recognize a parent after only a few syllables; the trumpeting is so powerful that the sound can penetrate a tightly packed cluster of emperor penguin chicks huddled against the cold. Having a unique voice is vital to all penguin species, but it is especially important for emperor and king penguins, which do not construct nests and have no defined territories; instead, they incubate their single egg while it rests on their feet.

TOWARD THE END of the month, the comically sloven look of the chicks—sagging bellies, slouching posture, down and feathers smeared with guano—reached new lows. As they lost their down and gained adult feathers during the molt, they took on a scruffy air, with patches of dirty fluff contrasting with sleek, blue-black feathers to create absurd designs. Some chicks had a checkerboard of down and feathers running across their bodies. Others had down across the upper halves of their backs, resembling a mink stole, while many retained a stripe of down on their heads, giving them a Mohawk hairstyle. Still others had patches of down on their heads that resembled an English barrister's wig or an Edwardian gentleman's muttonchop sideburns. The permutations of these down designs were endless, but all left the chicks looking ridiculous. The French explorer Jean-Baptiste Charcot described the chicks as resembling "stuffed birds in a badly maintained collection, where the exhibits had suffered from the attacks of moths or rats."

Occasional rains in the second half of January did little to improve the penguins' appearance, as the colonies became stinking guano swamps. On the morning of January 22, a twenty-four-hour blow exploded from the north. With it came warm breezes, and by one P.M. the temperature at Palmer Station hit 51.1°F—the high temperature for the season and just below the station record of 51.4°F, set on December 11, 2000. That evening, the wind speeds hit nearly 60 miles per hour. Early the next morning, around four A.M., the wind reached hurricane force, with gusts of 80 miles per hour. The station cook had to grip the railings of the boardwalk as she struggled to get from the dorm to the galley to prepare breakfast. Two shipping containers, half the standard size, were stacked by the dock; the force of the wind blew the top one over. I lay in my warm bed that night listening to rain and wet snow pelt my window as the wind howled.

In midmorning, the winds ceased as abruptly as they had begun, dropping to 15 miles per hour. I stood on the boardwalk and stared at a section of the Marr Ice Piedmont that, with the collapse of a one-hundred-yard ice bridge separating Arthur Harbor and neighboring Loudwater Cove, was now cut off from the replenishing ice river of the larger glacier. Several days of wind and rain, following the summer's warm temperatures, had stripped the snow cover from the long, truncated finger of ice on Norsel Point, exposing the decaying glacier below. Instead of the vibrant, bluish-white hue of a living glacier, this shrinking wedge of ice had a dingy appearance, with gray glacial till visible on its surface and the pitted facade slumping as the glacier melted and retreated. Cutting off a section of a glacier from its source of ice is akin to depriving a plant of water, with the same results.

Counting chicks in the sodden colonies was a decidedly unpleasant experience, forcing us to slosh through inches of guano and breathe in the choking stench of penguin excreta. When I first came to Palmer in January 2004 and nearly gagged as I stood next to a wet penguin colony in high season, I looked at Fraser and—stating the unnecessary—said, "Man, what a smell!" To which Fraser responded, "Smells like life!"

Like 95 percent of all seabirds, Adélies—and almost all species of penguins—are colonial nesters. They cluster together because colonies facilitate socializing and breeding, enable the birds to learn the location of feeding grounds by following their more experienced neighbors, and provide protection against predators. In the Antarctic and parts of the high Arctic, seabirds and penguins also evolved as colonial nesters because there was so little ice-free land along the coast on which to breed.

A seabird colony is, in the words of Roger Tory Peterson, an "ancient mortuary" where the skeletons of dead birds are deposited in strata dating back centuries, even millennia. It is also the repository of generations of guano, sometimes piled so deeply that in places, such as Peru, the guano of Humboldt penguins and other seabirds is commercially harvested for fertilizer. The result, especially in wet weather, is a stench that can be detected miles offshore. When men from Captain Fabian von Bellingshausen's expedition discovered Zavodovski Island, in the South Sandwich chain, in 1819, they were forced to return to their vessel because the stink from the largest penguin colony in Antarctica—now numbering an estimated one million pairs of chinstraps—was so overpowering. In 1902, aboard the *Discovery* with Robert Falcon Scott, the physician and naturalist Edward Wilson claimed he could smell the Cape Crozier colony, with more than 100,000 breeding pairs of Adélies, from thirty miles downwind. As the *Discovery* approached Antarctica's largest Adélie colony, at Cape Adare—then probably home to more than 200,000 Adélie breeding pairs—Wilson was confronted with an astounding scene.

"They covered the plain which was nearly 200 acres in extent, and they covered the slopes of Cape Adare above the plain, to the very top, and they were [over 1,000 feet] up from the plain," Wilson wrote in his diary. "The place was the colour of anchovy paste from the excreta of the young penguins. It simply stunk like hell, and the noise was deafening. . . . From a distance it is like a whistling roar, and when, from the cliffs of Cape Adare, we looked down upon the 200 acres swarming with shouting penguins and their whistling, piping chicks, one was reminded of nothing so much as a rink with a thousand chattering skaters."

TORGERSEN ISLAND'S PENGUIN colonies were orders of magnitude smaller than the teeming Ross Sea rookeries described by Wilson. But on a late-January evening, with hundreds of adult Adélies commuting to and from the sea to feed several thousand chicks, the island was bustling. While on the march, the Adélies had a determined, almost preoccupied air that has repeatedly struck observers as quite human. Watching Adélies on the shores of the Ross Sea, Scott remarked, "Their businesslike air was intensely ludicrous; one could imagine them saying in the fussiest manner, 'Can't stop to talk now, much too busy.'" The French Antarctic explorer Mario Marret described Adélies marching back into their colonies with the "self-satisfied air of landed proprietors . . . retaking possession of what belonged to them."

It is, of course, their upright bearing that above all gives penguins their human appearance. That many penguin species, and particularly Adélies, look like gentlemen dressed in tuxedo and tails makes us anthropomorphize them even more. From the moment men came to Antarctica, they developed an affection for penguins customarily reserved for canine companions. During the first summer of fur seal hunting in the South Shetland Islands, in 1820–21, Captain Robert Fildes, from Liverpool, wrecked his ship, the *Cora*, forcing him and his men to live in a tent on the shores of Desolation Island. The men made bunks out of casks from the wreck, and their cat took up residence in an old barrel. She was soon joined by some indigenous wildlife.

"Two penguins . . . came up out of the water and took their station alongside of her in the cask, they neither minding the people in the tent or the Cat, nor the Cat them, poor shipwrecked puss used to sit purring with their company," Fildes wrote in his journal. "These penguins used to go to sea for hours and as soon as they landed again would make direct for the tent and get into the cask."

The penguins were so determined to join the cat and the men in the tent that, even if one of the crew members tightly shut the flap, the penguins found a way to wiggle under the canvas and get inside.

During the ordeal of the *Endurance* expedition, Shackleton and his men were amused and comforted—and nourished—by Adélie and emperor penguins on the icebound Weddell Sea. At the start of their journey, as they were entering the sea ice, three Adélies walked across the floes to investigate the ship. One of his men pulled out a banjo and began playing "It's a Long Way to Tipperary," which, as Shackleton recounts in *South*, "the solemn-looking little birds appeared to appreciate." The bagpipe, however, was another story, and when a Scottish member of the expedition began to play the national instrument, the Adélies "fled in terror and plunged back into the sea," according to the expedition's photographer, Frank Hurley.

Shackleton's men were especially fascinated with the four-foot-high emperor penguins, which appeared from time to time through leads in the pack ice. Once, as the *Endurance* was locked in the ice in the winter of 1915, three emperors burst through a veneer of new ice to follow some of Shackleton's men who were waddling away, "penguin style," to lure the emperors. The emperors followed, at one point bowing ceremoniously to the men, before trying to flee. They were captured, with one calmly being led away by the flipper while the other two struggled. Later in the day, five more emperors appeared, with one of them knocking down a crew member and stomping on his chest as the men tried to subdue the penguin. All were destined for the pot.

Months later, as the pressure of the Weddell Sea's ice floes was crushing the *Endurance*'s wooden hull, emperor penguins revisited the sinking vessel.

"A strange occurrence was the sudden appearance of eight emperor penguins from a crack 100 yards away at the moment when the pressure upon the ship was at its climax," Shackleton wrote. "They walked a little way toward us, halted, and after a few ordinary calls proceeded to utter weird cries that sounded like a dirge for the ship."

Mainly, for these early explorers, the emperors and Adélies were a heartening presence and a source of fascination amid the grand, yet often bleak, Antarctic landscape. Frank Debenham, a geologist on Scott's *Terra Nova* expedition, watched raptly as an Adélie approached a three-inch crack in the sea ice and studied it with the circumspection of a "gentleman about to jump a 3-foot ditch."

Levick enjoyed watching a spectacle that convinced him penguins were playful creatures. In the rookeries, Levick never saw Adélies engaged in what could be interpreted as play. But he repeatedly watched Adélies amusing themselves in the water and on the ice. The tide flowed past the Cape Adare rookery at about 6 to 7 miles per hour, and Levick observed Adélies launching themselves out of the sea onto passing ice floes, riding them for half a mile past a long ice ledge on shore, diving back into the sea, and then swimming back against the tide to make the same ride again. Penguins, as Apsley Cherry-Garrard noted, are "an object of endless pleasure and amusement."

IN THE LAST week of January, amid another run of warm, placid days, a noticeable shift took place in the penguin colonies, signaling the beginning of the end of the reproductive season. Adults became increasingly scarce, and groups of fifty or more chicks—some of them almost fully fledged—formed in the larger colonies, untended by grown-ups. Ever-larger groups of adults rested by the sea, and Fraser said that some of the fully fledged penguins might have been abandoned by their parents and were past their peak chick weights. The Mafia-like domination of the colonies by brown skuas began to break down as kelp gulls, South Polar skuas, and giant petrels showed up in the rookeries, picking spilled krill off the ground and scavenging the many carcasses of Adélie chicks left behind by the brown skuas. You could still stand on an island like Torgersen and watch brown skuas flashing through the sky in hot pursuit of interloping South Polar skuas. But the brown skuas had plainly begun to let down their guard, ushering in a period of creeping anarchy.

As January came to an end, another change was brought into sharp relief: the large number of colonies in which not a single chick had successfully been reared to fledging. The season began with breeding pairs occupying 41 colonies on the five islands closest to Palmer Station, slightly more than half of the 75 colonies that had existed thirty years before. But by the end of January, 10 of those 41 colonies were empty. The number of nests in the vanishing colonies had simply grown so small that the brown skuas were easily able to wipe out the 10, 20, or 30 eggs and chicks that had been produced earlier in the season.

In late January, the birding team stopped at Litchfield to weigh and measure brown skua chicks and check on the last Adélies in Colony 8. All that remained was an adult standing next to two chicks in an oval of nesting pebbles ringed by larger, pale gray rocks. The pair of chicks looked healthy, but they had not yet begun to fledge and were only eight to nine inches tall.

Gazing at the scene before turning and leaving, Fraser said, "As soon as that parent leaves to feed, those chicks will be picked off by skuas in an hour."

Five days later, on January 29, several of us returned to Litchfield, anxious to find out if the chicks had managed to survive. Leaving the landing and walking across the many abandoned colonies, I strained to see the pair, but as we neared the other side of Litchfield it was clear they were gone—eaten, as Fraser had predicted, by skuas. At least five hundred years of Adélie occupation of Litchfield, with close to 900 breeding pairs when Fraser first came to Palmer, had come to an end.

"Litchfield," said Brett Pickering, "is officially over."

The lone adult stood staidly in the colony, flippers at its sides, scarcely noticing us. It was a gorgeous evening, warm and still, with a soft blue sky streaked with scattered high clouds. The late-summer sun turned the Bismarck Strait a shade of deep indigo. Except for the gentle slosh of the surf and the occasional cry of a brown skua, the island was silent.

On Torgersen Island, 5 of the 21 colonies that began the season with breeding Adélie penguins failed to produce fledged chicks. These 5 colonies had been reduced to remnant numbers of 33 breeding pairs or less, and all were driven into oblivion by skua predation. The south side of the island, once home to 1,200 breeding pairs of Adélies, was nearly devoid of penguins.

On a cool, overcast evening, I stood on Torgersen Island and witnessed the demise of Colony 12, which had had more than 200 breeding pairs when Fraser had arrived at Palmer Station in 1974. Located in the center of the island, Colony 12 was about thirty feet long. In late November, it had contained 27 active nests, most with two eggs. By late January, a lone adult and a small chick were all that were left. The two penguins stood side by side, although it was unclear if the adult was the chick's parent. As I watched, the adult turned and toddled toward the sea, leaving the chick on its own. The adult was fifty yards away when a brown skua glided low over the chick, and I thought to myself, *I am about to watch the last chick in this colony be devoured.* The skua kept on going, however. A minute or two passed, and then the chick—perhaps instinctually processing the warning that the skua had represented—began walking slowly toward Colony 14, a large assemblage of penguins about sixty feet away. I cheered it on, relieved that it would not remain exposed in the abandoned colony. At the same time, I harbored doubts that the stunted chick would survive, especially if one of its parents returned to the empty colony and could not find the chick for its feeding.

AT THE END of January, I spent two nights on Torgersen Island, hoping to get a sense of the nighttime rhythm of an Adélie rookery. On January 29, after wrapping up work on Torgersen around eight-fifteen P.M., Brett Pickering and Jen Blum helped me pitch a tent near Colony 13, another of the colonies that had failed to produce a fledged chick that season. Once again, the weather was superb—largely clear skies, almost no wind, and the temperature hovering around 40°F. By nine P.M. the sun had cast long shadows across the island. Near Torgersen's center, the outcropping of jagged basalt columns was brilliantly lit, the lichen on the rock faces radiating a vivid orange against the white of the Marr Ice Piedmont.

I spent much of my time watching penguins amble in from the sea to feed their chicks. The adults moved gingerly across the terrain, walking almost as if the stones hurt their feet. As I observed ceaseless feeding chases—with some adults backpedaling furiously, stopping occasionally to regurgitate krill into the mouths of their chicks—the sun slowly set, lingering above the horizon before finally dropping into the Bismarck Strait around ten forty-five in a burst of orange and gold. Over the land, the sun's last rays cast magenta hues on the white dome of the Marr Ice Piedmont and lit up the summits of Mount Français and Mount William in an ethereal shade of pink. As darkness gathered, Torgersen's rocks were cloaked in a midnight blue, and a chrome sheen covered the nearby waters.

I was observing some Adélies in the deepening twilight when I was startled by the sound of wildly flapping wings and the shrieking of a skua. Turning toward the sea, I saw, about fifteen feet away, a brown skua battering a foot-tall Adélie chick. Using its wings and its body, the skua drove the Adélie against a boulder and began relentlessly pecking it in the head. Peeping wildly, the penguin hunkered down, at one point managing to stumble a few feet away before the skua—half-flying—caught up with it. The skua sat on the chick's back, delivering violent blows with its beak to the chick's head. The mugging went on for two to three more minutes, and then the chick's peeping ceased. I assumed that the chick was dead, yet somehow it managed to rise. Dazed, bleeding from its head and an eye, it weaved and stumbled toward a nearby colony. I waited for the skua to jump the chick again, but it did not, enabling the young penguin to stagger safely to the edge of a crèche, where it stood motionless.

Shortly after midnight, the sky grew sufficiently dark that I could see stars to the northeast, a sighting that would have been impossible only a few weeks before, at the height of the Antarctic summer. I walked to a snowbank next to the rocky beach on the southern end of Torgersen. There, more than 300 Adélies had assembled on a snow shelf about fifty yards long, some lying down, some nibbling snow, some standing and preening. It was quiet, save for the breaking of small waves on the beach and the occasional rumble of a chunk of the Marr Ice Piedmont calving into the sea.

I slept fitfully that night, awakened by the peeping of penguins chasing their parents, the screeching of skuas, and the sound of a skua walking across the top of my tent. At three-thirty A.M., when I got up to relieve myself in the intertidal zone, the sun was rising to the southeast as Adélies commuted between their colonies and the sea. I emerged the next morning to find a giant petrel eating a penguin chick twenty feet from my tent. A half dozen kelp gulls were in view, scrounging krill spilled during the frantic penguin feedings of the night before.

Two days later, on another sparkling night, I again slept on Torgersen Island. With the evening sunlight streaming across the landscape, I ate dinner on a rock near the now-extirpated Colony 23 and watched the procession of penguins returning from their foraging trips. My meal consisted of a sandwich, beef jerky, and a few ounces of bourbon, which I sipped from a plastic cup. Soon I was joined by the brown skua that had wiped out Colony 23. It sat on a rock no more than ten feet away, its elegant head swiveling constantly, cocking first in my direction, then tilting slightly as it followed the passing parade of penguins. The skua—the gold in its feathers highlighted by the sun—was alert to every subtle change nearby, its gaze sizing up what was, or was not, a feeding opportunity.

I sipped the bourbon and looked at the scene to the southeast, where the black rock faces and pristine ice caps of the peninsular range were veiled in a light haze and a few wispy clouds. I have always had trouble sitting still for very long and am not given to frequent feelings of peace and contentment, but as I sat on the rock and absorbed the scene—the mountains, the icebergs, the passing penguins, the skua—I experienced an overpowering sense of tranquillity and joy.

Walking around the island later that evening, I saw something I had not seen that season: a pair of chicks chasing their parent all the way to the beach. When the parent stopped by the shore, the chicks hung out nearby and gazed with an air of incomprehension at the sea. After ten minutes, apparently sensing that they did not yet belong so close to the medium that would define the next chapter of their lives, the chicks returned to their colony.

Shortly after eleven P.M., I followed an Adélie parent to the apron of snow on Torgersen's south side. As I neared the snowbank, the noise of peeping chicks and trumpeting Adélies faded, replaced by the sound of waves gently breaking against rocks. I watched as the penguin gracefully preened itself and ate some snow. Dozens of Adélies slept nearby, still as statues in the fading light. Others stood on the snow—some preparing to go into the sea, some just emerging from it—and shook their heads, swished their tails, and puffed up their feathers. They went silently about their business, their poses dignified and stoic as they prepared to continue, at considerable cost to themselves, the feeding of their large and hungry chicks.

To the southwest, several tabular icebergs were silhouetted against a golden band of sky. The icy facades of Mount William and Mount Moberly were brushed with a pink light. The dark forms of nearby islands—DeLaca, Janus, the Outcasts—loomed on the horizon. Engrossed in the scene, I failed to notice that two penguins had silently walked to within ten feet of me, one to my left, one to my rear. They had lain down on the cobbles and seemed to be asleep, their eyes gently opening and closing. Turning around to look at the rookery, I saw scores of penguins walking toward me, heading to the sea, their breasts faintly glowing white in the last of the light.

CHAPTER 10

INTO THE SEA

They had mated at last, built their nests, procreated their species, and, in short, met the severest tests that Nature can inflict upon mind and body, and at the end of it, though in many cases blood-stained and in all caked and bedraggled with mire, they were as active and brave as ever.

—G. MURRAY LEVICK,
Terra Nova expedition, 1910–13

ALMOST OVERNIGHT, THE ADÉLIE PENGUIN CHICKS BEGAN TO move en masse to the beaches. One day they were loitering in their colonies, shedding down at a rapid rate and pestering their parents for food. Then, not long afterwards—as if by genetically embedded signal—the chicks decided it was time to leave. Some got to the cobble beaches by chasing a parent to the water's edge. Others stumbled down to the shore in packs of five to ten. Still others, sensing that the colonies were rapidly emptying out, wandered down to the sea on their own. But no matter how they got there, the chicks were in no hurry to take their first plunge into the Southern Ocean. Nearly all of them spent many hours, and often days, milling in large groups by the water, from time to time flapping their flippers rapidly, as if warming up for the swim. Many stared at this new medium with what—to human eyes, at least—seemed like a grave comprehension that this next step in their lives was a very big one indeed.

In the first few days of February, only one or two fledged chicks meandered to the beaches. Then, on February 5, fifty chicks—some of them not fully fledged—showed up on the main penguin beach on Humble Island. Appraising the fitness of the young Adélies, Fraser noticed the presence of green stains on some of their white breasts.

"They're starting to get ready to go," he said. "You see these chicks with the bile on their breasts? That means they haven't been fed in a long time."

That day, we spotted our first molting adults. Several stood quietly on a snowbank near the Humble Adélie colonies, their bodies fluffed up from blood engorging the replacement feathers as they grew a new coat. The nearby colonies were largely quiet. Adults were scarce. Few feeding chases were taking place.

Two days later, we returned to Humble to find seventy-five chicks, nearly half of them fully fledged, standing and lying on the beach. Nine chicks had gotten up the nerve to hop out to boulders in the water, moving restlessly from rock to rock as they waited for someone to take the first dip. But after a few minutes, all nine retreated to the safety of the beach, squawking as they went.

Shortly afterward, two chicks—both with remnant patches of down on their heads—frantically pursued a parent out of the colony and down to the sea. Without hesitation, the parent leaned forward and slipped into the ocean. I expected the chicks to jam on the brakes, but they seamlessly followed the adult into the water, surfacing a few feet offshore to shake their heads and flap their flippers. The parent, swimming underwater, was long gone, but after dallying for fifteen seconds, the chicks followed, diving from time to time and occasionally calling to each other as they surfaced.

The team began to weigh about a third of the chicks on the Humble Island beach and measure their flippers and culmens (the exposed part of their beaks). This exercise was inherently unruly, and Fraser always recruited two volunteers from the station to help corral the chicks and place them in the "pengy prison"—a four-foot-high plywood box with an open top and airholes in the sides.

"What we're going to do is catch these penguins and put them in the prison, ten at a time," Fraser told us. "When we start to do that they're going to want to go home and you're going to help us keep them from doing that. You ever see a border collie work? I wish I could bring our border collie here."

Armed with ten-foot bamboo poles topped by red flags, the volunteers and I surrounded the cluster of chicks on three sides—the only open side being the water, where the chicks decidedly did not want to go. Brandishing a fishing net on an aluminum pole, Fraser caught one or two chicks at a time, extracted them by their flippers, then placed them inside the prison. The commotion caused by the netting drove the penguin chicks in all directions, with many of them attempting to flee up the guano-slick boulders that covered a slope next to the beach. It had been raining on and off for a week, and hopping around the rocks, lunging with a bamboo pole in an effort to hem in several dozen frantic penguin chicks, was akin to jogging on large stones coated in motor oil. I slipped repeatedly, barking my shins and banging my knees, but managed to keep the number of escapees to a minimum.

The fledged chicks incarcerated in the pengy prison initially made quite a racket, their flippers drumming against the plywood sides. They soon settled down, however, staring up with smoky-gray eyes at their captors and squawking as Brett or Jen hauled them out one by one to be weighed in a nylon bag. Their newly fledged feathers were shiny black and, unlike the adults', their throats were white. As they shifted nervously in the box, their pink feet, with long dark toenails, looked as ludicrously outsized as a pair of clown's shoes. After the chicks had been weighed and measured, one of the team members swiped the Adélies on the chest with a green marker so they wouldn't be netted again, then let them go.

On that and ensuing days, our team weighed hundreds of chicks on Humble, Cormorant, and Christine islands, all in an effort to gauge their health and to see if chicks in snowy colonies were being launched into the unforgiving Southern Ocean with less meat on their bones than chicks in snow-free colonies. After weighing and banding 3,500 chicks and following their progress over the years, Fraser had determined that 2,850 grams, or 6.3 pounds, was an important threshold: Chicks weighing less than that rarely survived. One reason light chicks perish, said Fraser, is that they are too buoyant and have a difficult time diving for krill.

On Torgersen Island, chicks were straggling out of the colonies and piling up on the beaches. One afternoon, I watched as a dozen chicks formed a group in Colony 16 and then meandered halfway across the island, apparently looking for a suitable beach. As the group moved across Torgersen, it picked up new chicks from different colonies, finally turning into a conga line of more than twenty-five chicks that eventually made its way to the shore on the northeast side of the island.

The north side of Torgersen, which still had two remaining large colonies, was a deserted, forlorn-looking place, with the carcasses of Adélie chicks sprawled in and around the rain-soaked colonies. Fledged chicks that were not quite ready to move to the water's edge neverthe-less deserted the stinking colonies and stood or lay many feet away on cleaner stretches of cobble. Two dozen skuas, most of them South Polars, flew overhead, and fifteen to twenty more were on the ground, tugging at bloody Adélie penguin remains. One of the brown skuas that had tightly controlled Torgersen nearly all season stood on the high ridge that bisects the island and observed the *Mad Max* carnage with the exhausted air of a merchant who could do little more than watch as looters sacked his store.

Standing on Torgersen late one evening, I thought back to the start of the season, in late October, when the land and sea were locked in snow and ice, and the penguins rested quietly amid this white world as they prepared to mate. Now, away from the beaches, I was confronted by a dark scene of oozing excrement and death. The dreary weather, turning cold once more after a temperate January, added to the fune-real tableau. A feeling of sadness swept over me as the realization sank in that the end of the Adélie season also signaled the beginning of the end of my extraordinary stay in the most beautiful place I had ever been. I was also taken aback by how quickly the Adélie chicks were abandoning their colonies and moving to the sea, though I shouldn't have been surprised: Everything about the Adélies' reproductive sea-son in Antarctica was fast-paced and compressed. One moment the chicks were hatched. The next moment they were rotund and chasing their parents for food. And the next thing I knew, they had lost their down and were filing to the beaches to be swallowed up by the Southern Ocean.

I wasn't the only member of our team feeling bereft that the Adélies were disappearing. One afternoon on Torgersen Island, Peter Horne stopped and looked around at the deserted wreckage of the Adélie colonies.

"Quiet," he said.

"I know," said Kristen Gorman. "I'm feeling this sense of abandonment, kind of like how parents must feel when their kids go to college."

In my memory, those middle days of February are cast in a dreary light for another reason. We spent several days amid rain and wind digging out traps we had placed in the colonies at the beginning of the season. These "shit traps," as the team called them, were wooden frames with a fine-mesh screen bottom. On Torgersen, Litchfield, Biscoe, and Dream, we waded ankle-deep into the guano and, using trowels and plastering knives, scraped up several inches of guano from the bottom of the three-foot-long traps. The smell was sickly sweet and overpowering, and even though I scarcely drew a breath while shoveling the shit into white plastic buckets, I was often on the verge of gagging. A previous member of Bill's team actually fainted while cleaning out shit traps, an occurrence that Fraser—a committed carnivore—attributes as much to the woman's vegetarianism as to the overpowering stench of the work.

After cleaning the traps, we hauled heavy plastic buckets of guano and rocks to the sea, where we washed off the stones and filtered the guano until we were left with what Peter Horne and Fraser called "the love"—several inches of muck that contained squid beaks and fish otoliths (ear bones) that would tell Fraser what the penguins were eating in addition to krill. We then loaded the buckets into the Zodiacs and drove them to the station, where we spent hours sifting and filtering "the love" until all that remained was a thin layer of sediment, which was eventually shipped back to the States for analysis.

The stony shorelines of Torgersen, Humble, and other islands offered a more uplifting picture than the nearly deserted colonies. Hundreds of penguin chicks were gathered on the cobble beaches, summoning the courage to plunge into the Southern Ocean. One evening, I watched a group of a dozen young Adélies scramble into the water. After a minute or two of hesitation, several began surging through the sea in what looked like a first attempt at porpoising. Within a few minutes, this raft of chicks was hundreds of yards offshore.

"When the right time comes, which they seem to know perfectly, they dive into the sea," wrote James Murray, a biologist on Shackleton's 1907–09 *Nimrod* expedition. "It is marvelous how fully instinct makes these birds independent. The parents do not take them to the water and teach them to swim. . . . Though they have spent their lives on land, and only know that food is something found in an old bird's throat, when the time comes they leave the land and plunge boldly into the sea."

Not all Adélie chicks embraced marine life so enthusiastically. Once, on Torgersen Island, I saw a young Adélie struggle through three-foot waves and then, as it cleared the surf, scramble onto a passing ice floe in a desperate attempt to find some semblance of terra firma. The chick then floated away, its little ice platform rocking in the swells. Its chances of making it were slim, as the western Antarctic Peninsula—always a harsh proving ground for young Adélies—had recently become an even more inhospitable place for ice-loving penguins.

BILL FRASER'S EFFORT to unravel the mystery of the disappearing Adélie penguins began in earnest in the late 1980s. He had occasionally visited Palmer Station in the mid- to late 1980s while taking part in scientific cruises along the peninsula. But in 1989, with his dissertation finally in hand, he decided to return exclusively to Palmer and pick up the mantle of David Parmelee's work from the early 1970s. He also shifted the focus of his research from kelp gulls to penguins and climate change. The transition to penguin work was natural for several reasons. Penguins had been a key part of his research on the three ice cruises in the 1980s. Even more importantly, however, various international scientific programs—realizing the interlinking importance of krill, sea ice, and top krill predators such as penguins and seals—were keen to fund field studies on penguins.

Fraser also realized that by returning to Palmer Station, he would be able to mine the invaluable lode of information that Parmelee and his University of Minnesota graduate students had amassed in the 1970s. Those penguin and seabird censuses represented a snapshot of an ecosystem in the early stages of rapid climate change, and Fraser sensed, correctly, that Parmelee's data would be a touchstone in the years to come. It also felt right to Fraser to return to the place where he had first fallen under Antarctica's spell.

"The intellectual decisions to return to Palmer Station were made in the 1980s," said Fraser, "but the emotional ones were established that first winter of 1975–76."

Fraser had also decided that rather than doing fieldwork in a variety of locales, he wanted to bore into one place and understand it intimately. He later told me: "It always seemed intuitive to me that the only way to really understand something is to live in it. What became really apparent to me was that the system on the Antarctic Peninsula was so incredibly variable that the only way to get a handle on understanding how that ecosystem was operating was to spend a tremendous amount of time in the field, collecting the same data year after year. Some of the best ideas I've had in my career have come because I have spent so much time here. You develop a sense for what the rhythms *should* be, the flow of things. And that's what has allowed me to pick up things that don't make sense, the anomalies. You've got normality and all of a sudden something happens that seems out of place, and those are where the windows suddenly open up. It's the anomalous years that really cue you in as to how this system is operating, and if you don't spend a lot of time there, then how would you recognize the anomalous years?"

In the early 1990s, as his research took off at Palmer, the many months Fraser was spending in the field paid off in a series of insights as to how a changing climate was the likely culprit leading to the steady decline in Adélie penguin populations.

Once, during a season of unusually heavy spring snows, he walked to the top of the low, rocky ridge that bisects Torgersen Island and looked around. This is what he saw:

"I looked to my right, where most of the Adéliés are, and that area was almost snow-free and there were thousands of birds there. Then I looked to my left—the south side—and it was under a meter of snow, with a thousand Adélies sitting on the snow, having a hell of a time try-ing to breed. In fact, there was very little habitat exposed in some of those areas on the south side. Again, that was one of those moments where you go, 'Wait a minute, this is so obvious!'"

What was obvious to Fraser was that the state of Adélies on the south side—where populations were declining far more rapidly than on the north side of the island—was related to the abundant snow. As he stood on the ridge and contemplated this piece of information, it also became clear to him that he was, in fact, standing on the reason why the south side was snowier than the north: This relatively modest crest of crum-bling, lichen-colored rock was still high enough to create a wind barrier that prevented the prevailing northerly winds from blowing the snow off the south side. The north side of Torgersen, exposed to the frequent strong winds, had largely been swept clean, and penguins there were busy incubating eggs on open, dry ground. On the south side, the Adé-lies were either still waiting for nesting pebbles to be exposed or were struggling to build nests on several scattered territories where the snow had partially melted. Meltwater ponds in the colonies were a major prob-lem, particularly in heavy snow years, as eggs quickly became addled if covered in frigid water.

Not long afterward, Fraser was rummaging around in a drawer in the birders' hut when he came across an aerial photograph. It had been taken from a helicopter by a photographer for the conservation group Greenpeace, who had given it to Fraser. He hadn't paid much attention to the photo when he'd received it, but now, after the revelation on the Torgersen ridge, Fraser was struck by what he saw. The photograph showed Litchfield Island in the foreground, most of its territory deep in snow because it lay in the lee of high hills. In the background was the circular form of Torgersen Island. Its northern half was black—virtually snow-free. It southern half was white, with most of the territory blan-keted in snow.

"All of a sudden a light bulb went off and I said, 'Holy shit! This is a very real thing. It's not my imagination at work.'"

Fraser began looking at censuses of Adélie colonies on the five penguin islands closest to Palmer, and a pattern became evident: Adélies nesting in the lee of promontories were faring worse than colonies on open, windswept ground, such as Humble Island and the northern half of Torgersen Island. Clearly, snow that lingered on nesting grounds well into spring made it more difficult for Adélies to successfully rear chicks, in part because of the hazards of meltwater. But Fraser wanted to know more: Was the region experiencing heavier snowfall than in earlier decades and, if so, why? And what, exactly, was the mechanism by which increased snow on nesting grounds was leading to the steady decline of Adélies?

One possible answer to the second question came to him during the 1995–96 reproductive season, which began during one of the snowiest years on record at Palmer Station. In February 1996, with the fledged chicks gathered on Humble's small beach as they prepared to go to sea, Fraser and his team were in the midst of weighing the chicks when an insight came to him.

"I was handling the chicks," he recalled, "and it suddenly dawned on me that nearly all the chicks were light. They were all runts. We had experienced a heavy snow year, and it immediately crystallized that if the snow leads to light chicks, they're not going to survive the winter. They don't have a chance. Whether a population increases or decreases is based on whether recruitment of young compensates for mortality. So if chicks are light, they aren't surviving that first winter, and aren't being recruited back into the population."

Examining his data, Fraser discovered that heavy snow years—especially years of heavy spring snows—led to lighter chicks throughout the Palmer area. And when he compared data among islands for the same years, he found that fledged chicks on Humble Island, which is relatively snow-free by spring, often weighed a half pound to a pound more than chicks on Cormorant and Christine islands, many of whose colonies are in the lee of high ridges. From 1986 to 1998, Fraser and other scientists attached flipper bands to, and weighed, 13,500 chicks in the Palmer area. (He stopped banding in 1998, when studies showed that the drag created by the bands made it more difficult for penguins to forage and could potentially increase mortality.) What the banding revealed was that a difference of only a few ounces—say, between a chick that weighed 6 pounds, 3 ounces and one that weighed 6 pounds, 8 ounces—often determined whether a chick survived the winter.

"When we weighed the banded chicks, we found that the ones that returned were often just a hundred grams [3.5 ounces] heavier than the ones that didn't return," said Fraser.

As Fraser ruminated on this issue, and discussed with colleagues why snowier Adélie colonies and delayed breeding would lead to lighter chicks, the answer came to him: Adélies had evolved so that just as the chicks' demand for food was peaking in January, krill stocks were at their summer high. So if chick hatching is delayed for a week or ten days, then the peak of krill abundance is often past, making it harder for parents to successfully forage for their chicks.

"It's a temporal mismatch," said Fraser. "The chicks' energy needs will be greatest at a point in time when krill abundance is already decreasing. So the parents are working a little harder to find the krill, and they may not find enough."

In good times, survival rates for fledged Adélie chicks that head out to sea can be as low as 10 to 15 percent, so environmental factors that cut down on those odds—such as increased snowfall, which can flood nests and lead to delayed nesting—can quickly push a population of Adélies into a precarious position. (In recent years, Fraser has documented a general decline in weights of fledged chicks, even those whose hatching was not delayed by snow. This evidence has persuaded him that a decline in krill may be the key factor affecting Adélies and their chicks along the northwestern Antarctic Peninsula.)

Fraser's studies in the penguin colonies yielded other evidence that a major reason Adélie populations were nose-diving in the region was the loss of young birds at sea. By closely monitoring the penguins from hatching to fledging, Fraser determined that pairs of Adélie penguins in his study area successfully raised, on average, 1.3 chicks to fledging. This is quite a high rate, roughly twice as high as in many other areas of the continent. At first glance, the success of Palmer's Adélies at raising chicks seemed counterintuitive: If so many chicks are raised to fledging, shouldn't Palmer's Adélie populations be increasing?

But the more Fraser thought about it, the more he realized that the coupling of the high rate of fledging success with the crashing Adélie populations made sense. These seemingly contradictory statistics clearly showed that the Adélie chicks were heading into the sea but not making it back. And Fraser soon understood that the reason Palmer's Adélies were so good at rearing chicks was that the breeders were almost all older, experienced adults, which have more success raising chicks than do younger Adélies. The Ross Sea Adélies had a lower rate of fledging success because their young birds were returning to breed, which naturally led to fewer of their chicks making it to the fledging stage and entering the sea.

"Our long-term breeding success at Palmer is increasing substantially, yet our populations are collapsing," said Fraser. "This high breeding success is actually an indicator of just how bad recruitment of new penguins into the population is, because new breeders do very badly—they always screw up. So they tend to lose their clutches of eggs or their chicks."

In effect, the Palmer Adélies are champion parents, but environmental factors have been decimating the chicks they have produced.

HAS MORE SNOW been falling along the western Antarctic Peninsula? Records from a station near Palmer, as well as two ice core drillings farther south, show that it has. The nearby Faraday/Vernadsky base—operated by the British Antarctic Survey before being turned over to the Ukrainians—recorded a pronounced increase in snowfall, with the number of days of precipitation (primarily snow) increasing at a rate of twelve days per decade from 1950 to 1999. Four hundred miles south of Palmer Station, on the Dyer Plateau, the renowned American glaciologist Lonnie Thompson drilled an ice core that revealed the snowfall and temperature record for the last five hundred years. That ice core showed a warming trend of 3.5°F in the twentieth century and a significant increase in snowfall in recent decades. Still farther south, at the base of the peninsula, another ice core record showed a doubling of snowfall since the 1850s, with an acceleration of snow accumulation in recent decades.

Palmer Station's precipitation records date only to the 1980s and show no clear trend. But as the importance of snow became clear to Fraser in the early 1990s, he and his team began keeping their own snow records, measuring snow depths on transect lines on the five penguin islands closest to Palmer Station. What that short data record has shown is increased spring snowfall, which is lingering longer in many colonies. That snow deposition then interferes with the Adélies as they are building their nests and incubating eggs.

As the 1990s progressed, Fraser became convinced that snowfall was increasing in the Palmer area; the overall record showed it, and he knew it anecdotally, from his own observations since 1974. Although counterintuitive, more snow was consistent with a marine environment that was seeing sea ice shrink. With less ice blanketing the Southern Ocean along the western Antarctic Peninsula, more open water was exposed, leading to increased evaporation. That moisture then formed as precipitation, which tended to fall as snow along the Antarctic Peninsula. The region was also experiencing an influx of warmer air and storms from the north, which brought more snow. As he continued to study the impact of deeper snows on Adélie penguins, it became increasingly clear to him that it was interfering with their ability to successfully hatch eggs and rear healthy chicks.

"As counterintuitive as it may sound, Adélie penguins are a snow-intolerant species," Fraser told me. "They evolved in a polar desert. And these birds' life histories are so finely tuned to the environment that tiny, tiny differences can affect their survival. If they don't have snow-free habitat by the end of November, their breeding success is catastrophic. You would think the Adélies would delay their breeding a bit because of the snow, but they can't. The birds are just hardwired and they don't adjust. They are hardwired into oblivion."

Spending 40 percent of the year at Palmer Station, Fraser continued to unravel the mystery of what was killing Palmer's Adélies. And by the mid-1990s, it was clear that Adélie populations in the region were starting to drop precipitously. After falling gradually from about 15,000 pairs on the five core islands in the early 1970s, to around 13,000 pairs in the 1980s, to roughly 11,000 pairs in the early 1990s, Adélie populations took a dive in the 1993–94 season, dropping to 8,000 pairs. They have fallen steadily ever since. (Fraser wondered whether a spill of light diesel fuel from an Argentine ship, the *Bahia Paraiso,* that hit a reef roughly a mile off Palmer Station in January 1989 might have affected the Adélie populations. The slick, covering about half a square mile, killed roughly 300 Adélies and hundreds of blue-eyed shags, which spend a great deal of time on the water and were susceptible to the slick. But the next season, the Adélie populations around Palmer were at their highest level in several years. And when Fraser tracked the Adélie populations on Dream Island and Biscoe Point— both miles from Palmer and unaffected by the spill—these rookeries showed the same steep downward trajectory as the rookeries near the station.)

Fraser was convinced that he had teased out one cause for the decline: the harmful impact of increased snowfall. He viewed this as a mechanism that worked on a micro level, affecting the ability of Adélies to reproduce on some islands more than others, and even on some portions of islands more than others—such as the south part of Torgersen. The trend toward greater snowfall was regional, but its effects were often highly localized.

He was aware, however, that much larger, often global forces were at play on the western Antarctic Peninsula—forces that had made the region among the fastest-warming places on the planet. He and his colleagues from the Long Term Ecological Research program—which *LTER* began at Palmer Station in 1990—were closely monitoring these changes as they attempted to piece together a cohesive portrait of an ecosystem undergoing a stunningly swift transformation. Fraser thought of many of these forces as being on the macro level—changes, such as the rapid disappearance of sea ice, that were fundamentally altering an ecosystem that had evolved over millions of years.

"There's this gigantic puzzle and you have all these pieces and it takes years to figure it out," said Fraser. "The most dangerous thing you can do is assume that one factor is causing these changes when many factors are playing a part. Someone once said that science is like a perpetual crime investigation in which all these pieces of the puzzle are forever rotating around in your head, and all of a sudden you pick up a clue that suddenly aligns three or four pieces."

As the pieces have fallen into place, the picture that has emerged has proven both fascinating and unsettling to Fraser and his colleagues.

"A century ago this was basically a polar environment," said Fraser. "This area embodied Antarctica. It was the dominion of Adélie penguins and there was much more sea ice. Now we have this subantarctic system impinging on this polar system. I've watched the confrontation here over the last thirty years. The polar system has really disintegrated at Palmer. It's gone to hell. I am in awe that it has taken such a short time to happen. Lesson Number One for me has been the realization that ecology and ecosystems can change"—he snapped his fingers—"like that. In geological time, it's a nanosecond."

CHAPTER 11

THE MELTING

If present trends in fossil fuel consumption continue . . .
a critical level of warmth will have been passed in high
southern latitudes 50 years from now, and deglaciation of
West Antarctica will be imminent or in progress. . . . One
of the warning signs that a dangerous warming trend is
under way in Antarctica will be the breakup of ice shelves
on both coasts of the Antarctic Peninsula, starting with
the northernmost and extending gradually southward.

—John H. Mercer,
Ohio State University, 1978

Bill Fraser hasn't needed a thermometer to tell him that the northwestern Antarctic Peninsula has warmed dramatically in recent decades. He sees evidence of that warming at Palmer Station everywhere he looks. It manifests itself in the Marr Ice Piedmont, which once abutted the station and has since retreated roughly fifteen hundred feet. He sees it when he stands next to the station and looks back at the Marr's massive dome of ice, which has lost so much height that Fraser can now gaze at mountaintops on the interior of Anvers Island that the Marr once blocked from view. He sees it in the gaping hole in the Marr Ice Piedmont that leads to Loudwater Cove, and he sees it as he rides in a Zodiac to penguin rookeries and notices an ever-expanding number of exposed points and islands once covered by the glacier. He sees it in the sea ice, or lack thereof, which once reliably blanketed the surrounding ocean three or four out of every five winters and now forms solidly every one or two. And he sees it most of all in the Adélie rookeries, which were once home to tens of thousands of penguins but are now shrinking so swiftly that Fraser believes Adélies will become locally extinct in the Palmer region in his lifetime.

Were Fraser to feel the need to consult a thermometer, there is a reliable one nearby, providing one of the longest-running temperature records in Antarctica. It is located about thirty miles to the south, at the Akademik Vernadsky base, which is now operated by the Ukrainians. Around Palmer Station, Vernadsky is known chiefly as the place from which fearless Slavic scientists and support staff occasionally set out in Zodiacs to make the long and risky trip to the American station—and not for scientific purposes. They come when they run out of cigarettes or are looking for some fresh food, which they will obtain by trading the homemade vodka they produce at Vernadsky.

The Ukrainians perform important work at Vernadsky in geophysics and meteorology, and none more so than continuing to maintain a detailed temperature record that dates to 1951. That record was begun by the British, who ran the base from 1947 to 1996—the United Kingdom's longest continuously operated Antarctic station—before turning it over to the Ukrainians in an effort to streamline British Antarctic operations. Under the British, the station eventually came to be known as Faraday, in honor of the English scientist Michael Faraday. About the size of Palmer Station, Faraday is located in the Argentine Islands at 65°15′ S—several miles off the coast of the Antarctic Peninsula—and commands a spectacular, close-up view of the peninsular range and the great rafts of icebergs that aggregate near the mainland.

The Faraday/Vernadsky record tells a simple and dramatic story: From 1951 to the present, the annual average air temperature in the region has increased by nearly 3°C, or 5°F. Winter temperatures have risen far more sharply, soaring by 11°F over the past six decades. And if you compare the average July temperatures for the decade of the 1950s with the decade from 1999 to 2008, the increase is even more extreme—an astronomical 13.6°F, from 8.8°F to 22.4°F. Other scientific stations on both sides of the Antarctic Peninsula also have recorded significant temperature increases. The longest continuous temperature record in the Antarctic—kept by the Argentines since 1904 in the South Orkney Islands, off the northern tip of the Antarctic Peninsula—shows a rise in temperatures for more than a century. Today, the northwestern Antarctic Peninsula is warming faster—at least in winter—than the other two hot spots of global warming, the Yukon basin, in Canada and Alaska, and the east-central Siberian lowlands.

With the earth warming 1.4°F over the past century—an increase overwhelmingly attributable, according to the Intergovernmental Panel on Climate Change, to humanity emitting greenhouse gases into the atmosphere—the heating of the northern Antarctic Peninsula is obviously well above the norm. But recent studies show that much of West Antarctica (the region on the Pacific Ocean side of the Transantarctic Mountains) is also warming significantly. In 2009, the most comprehensive study to date of Antarctic temperatures—which used a combination of land-based temperature data and infrared satellite analysis—showed that since 1950, temperatures in West Antarctica had risen on average by 1.5°F. Perhaps the most surprising part of the study, published in the journal *Nature*, was its finding that Antarctica overall had warmed by roughly 1°F from 1957 to 2006, refuting earlier, less comprehensive studies indicating that Antarctica might be cooling slightly while the rest of the world warms.

Conducted by scientists from several universities and NASA, the study showed that the warming over West Antarctica extended more than eight hundred miles from the coast and reached all the way to the Transantarctic Mountains, just several hundred miles from the South Pole. Some of these inland areas experienced temperature increases of 2.7°F in the past fifty years—hardly a large enough jump to melt ice in the center of the continent, where temperatures can easily reach −60°F in winter. But temperature increases of that magnitude—and far greater—along the Antarctic Peninsula are already fundamentally altering an ecosystem where a few degrees of warmth can make the difference between sea ice forming or not, and can bring about the disintegration of large ice shelves.

Another, often overlooked element in the discussion of the precipitous temperature increases along the Antarctic Peninsula is the temperature of the sea. Even small increases in ocean temperatures can have enormous impacts, as is already the case along the peninsula and in West Antarctica, where an upwelling of warmer water onto the continental shelf is eating away at huge floating ice shelves and at glaciers grounded deep under the ocean. That influx of warmer water, its temperature in the low 30s, vents a huge volume of heat into the frigid atmosphere and is the primary reason for soaring winter temperatures in the environs of Palmer Station.

Bill Fraser and his colleagues contend that the changes sweeping down the Antarctic Peninsula are a prelude—and a warning—of things to come worldwide. Contained in this extreme temperature increase are several sobering messages. One is that when man begins pouring greenhouse gases into the atmosphere as a result of an unprecedented burning of fossil fuels, regional and global changes can occur abruptly and unpredictably. A second message is that even though the continent proper—that vast ice cap three miles thick in places—is showing only small signs of warming, the changes hitting the peninsula represent the first breach in this citadel of ice and snow. The warming of the Antarctic Peninsula also has global implications, for already the heat that has poured over the region has led to the breakup of eight ice shelves. The most notable has been the Larsen B Ice Shelf, a floating sheet of ice—once the size of Connecticut—that disintegrated in 2002, in turn enabling the land-based glaciers held in place by the shelf to accelerate their slide into the sea. The warming air and ocean also are destabilizing large ice sheets and glaciers up and down the peninsula and in West Antarctica. And should West Antarctica's land-based glaciers and ice sheets begin to seriously melt, sea levels worldwide could rise sixteen feet.

So it is best, perhaps, to think of what is happening in Bill Fraser's world this way: Global warming is now nibbling at the edges of the greatest repository of ice on the planet, a continent so large and so frozen that it plays a pivotal role in world climate. Should mankind continue to emit ever-larger quantities of greenhouse gases into the atmosphere, leading to temperature increases of 2°C to 5°C (3.6°F to 9°F) in the next century, then global warming will no longer be gnawing at the edges of Antarctica. It will be taking large bites, bringing about changes that could destabilize the ice shelves, the ice sheets, and the sea ice that define the continent and that support the tens of millions of penguins, seabirds, seals, and other creatures whose life histories have evolved inside the unique world of the Antarctic Convergence. Such disruption would be felt far beyond the bounds of the Southern Ocean as it leads to a significant rise in sea levels worldwide and alters the global climate system.

THE WARMER AIR that has been funneled into the icy world of the Antarctic Peninsula in recent decades has arrived, in part, because of a shift in atmospheric currents. Two main reasons lie behind this change. The first is that the global buildup of greenhouse gases has warmed air in the tropical and temperate regions to the north of the Antarctic Peninsula, creating a stronger contrast with the frigid temperatures of Antarctica.

"You have this excess of heat delivered to the tropical regions and you have this deficit of heat in the polar regions and you get this temperature gradient," said Douglas Martinson, an oceanographer, a senior research scientist at Columbia University's Lamont-Doherty Earth Observatory, and a member of the Palmer Long Term Ecological Research team. "And one of the fundamental laws of thermodynamics is that heat always goes from warm to cold. Climate is nothing more than Mother Earth trying to redistribute the heat from warm to cold, and the stronger the gradient, the stronger the winds."

This growing contrast may be responsible for altering a Southern Hemisphere climatic pattern known as the Southern Annular Mode, or SAM. The SAM has kicked into high gear in recent decades, which has strengthened westerly winds around Antarctica and pulled in warmer, moister air from the north. Although the Antarctic and the Arctic are structured entirely differently—one is a continent of ice ringed by sea, and the other is an ice-covered ocean surrounded by land—significant shifts in atmospheric circulation patterns have played a role in causing both regions to warm more rapidly than other parts of the planet. In the Arctic, an atmospheric circulation pattern known as the Arctic Oscillation, or the Northern Annular Mode (the NAM, as opposed to the SAM), kicked into a positive pattern in the 1970s. And the positive phase of the Arctic Oscillation pumped warmer air into the Arctic from lower latitudes.

In the Antarctic, another factor—also brought about by man's activities—has tightened and strengthened the winds whirling around the continent, further adding to the heat being sucked down to the Antarctic Peninsula while actually cooling some other parts of Antarctica. That is the destruction of stratospheric ozone. In the mid- to late twentieth century, the widespread use of refrigerants containing chlorofluorocarbons began to destroy ozone, an important component of the atmosphere that absorbs and blocks harmful ultraviolet radiation. The chemical reaction that leads to the destruction of ozone is intensified at colder temperatures, and in the 1980s scientists discovered that an enormous ozone hole was opening up every spring over Antarctica. Ozone absorbs the sun's ultraviolet, or short-wavelength, radiation, thus warming the stratosphere—the layer of the planet's atmosphere that extends from about five to thirty miles above the surface of the earth. The destruction of Antarctica's ozone layer, which has led to the seasonal loss of 80 to 90 percent of the continent's heat-absorbing ozone, means that the air high above Antarctica and the South Pole has cooled by more than 10°F in recent decades. This colder dome of air brought about by the loss of ozone has served to strengthen the polar vortex, or polar jet stream, that roars around Antarctica because it has intensified the tropical-polar temperature gradient that drives climate. That, in turn, has drawn even more warm air down onto the Antarctic Peninsula.

"Think of it as a merry-go-round that's moving faster and faster," said Eugene Domack, a geologist and climate expert at Hamilton College who has studied the past twenty thousand years of the Antarctic Peninsula's climate history. As the polar vortex has spun more rapidly around Antarctica, west to east, it has changed shape somewhat, bulging out to the west of the Ross Sea—roughly two thousand miles to the southeast of Palmer Station—and dragging more frigid air off the polar plateau. As a result, sea ice is actually growing in that section of the continent.

With the 1989 treaty banning ozone-destroying chlorofluorocarbons—which can linger in the stratosphere for fifty to one hundred years—the ozone hole over the Antarctic is expected to close up around midcentury. The polar vortex should then weaken, a seemingly auspicious event since it signals man's victory in the battle to rid the world of ozone-destroying substances. But the closing of the ozone hole and the weakening of the polar vortex are now on the worry list of some scientists. They reason that the tighter, stronger polar jet stream has actually served to further insulate most of Antarctica—with the exception of the Antarctic Peninsula—from more extreme global warming. As the vortex weakens, they fear, the continental fortress of ice will become more pregnable to rising air temperatures.

Even more important than warming air temperatures—especially in winter—has been a rise in ocean temperatures on the continental shelf off West Antarctica. As atmospheric patterns have shifted in Antarctica, they also have affected the great stream of water that flows clockwise around the continent—the twelve-thousand-mile Antarctic Circumpolar Current, the most powerful on earth. Connecting the world's oceans, the Antarctic Circumpolar Current plays an important role in global ocean circulation and climate, as the cold water it transports around the most southerly continent—the Antarctic Bottom Water—sinks to the sea floor and then slowly creeps to the north, where it warms and rises to the surface hundreds of years later.

In recent years, as the Antarctic Circumpolar Current has rounded the Ross Sea and headed north up the west side of Antarctica, it has been channeled onto the continental shelf, in part because faster circumpolar winds are dispersing surface waters, allowing the warmer and deeper circumpolar water to rise. The temperature of that deep water has also increased in recent decades, most likely because of rising ocean temperatures globally. In winter, the deep water that surges onto the continental shelf in West Antarctica can be as warm as 37°F, which sounds cold but in fact is considerably warmer than the surface water and vastly warmer than the air temperatures. This huge volume of relatively warm water on the continental shelf is having an enormous impact, since water holds one thousand times more heat than air.

"This circumpolar current water is just blisteringly hot," said Martinson, speaking in relative terms. "This is essentially a freight train full of hot coals. It gets past the Ross Sea and heads north and all of a sudden, *slam*! It gets right on the continental shelf and scoots right along the shore. . . . The penguins down there will have to put on baggies and sunglasses!"

The effect of this surge of warmer water has been to increase sea surface temperatures off the western Antarctic Peninsula by more than 1°F in recent decades—a significant jump. Martinson believes that rising ocean temperatures have played the key role in the warming of the Antarctic Peninsula and the melting of ice shelves, glaciers, and sea ice.

No change has been more remarkable than the decline of sea ice along the length of the western Antarctic Peninsula. The most striking difference is not so much the extent of the seasonal sea ice coverage but its duration. Using satellite-based, passive microwave technology that can see through clouds and differentiate between sea ice and open water, Sharon Stammerjohn, an assistant professor of ocean sciences at the University of California, Santa Cruz, and also part of the Palmer LTER group, has shown that sea ice now blankets the Southern Ocean off the western Antarctic Peninsula for nearly three months less than it did in 1979. On average, sea ice now forms fifty-four days later in the autumn and retreats thirty-one days sooner in the spring. That means that, compared with three decades ago, sea ice now covers the Bellingshausen Sea for eighty-five fewer days a year—a huge drop in a region where the formation of sea ice is a signature event from which most living things take their cues for foraging, reproduction, and migration. In addition to sharply reduced duration, the extent of sea ice in the region also has declined slightly.

Hastening the loss of sea ice, and further warming the atmosphere, are what climate scientists refer to as "positive feedbacks," meaning that one event sets in motion a second one, which then intensifies the first one, each feeding upon the other in a vicious circle. Driving this in the Antarctic and the Arctic is the albedo effect. Albedo is the degree to which a surface reflects sunlight—and heat—back into space. Snow and ice have a very high albedo, with fresh snow reflecting roughly 80 percent of the sun's energy back into space. Charcoal reflects only 4 percent of sunlight back into space. The darker, open ocean also absorbs far more solar energy than does ice-covered ocean.

As sea ice disappears and the now-open ocean absorbs more heat, warmer ocean water in autumn leads to the delay of sea ice formation. The tardy formation means that the ice is less thick and therefore more likely to thaw earlier in the spring, which leads to further ocean warming. As Walt Meier, a sea ice specialist at the National Snow and Ice Data Center, told me, "The ocean falls behind and never gets a chance to catch up."

Such is the case in the Arctic, where the sea ice reached a record low extent in 2007, falling 40 percent below the long-term average between 1979 and 2000. The remaining sea ice has also thinned dramatically. In 2008, for the first time in recorded history, both the famed Northwest Passage, in Canada, and the Northern Sea Route, across Siberia, were navigable. Whereas scientists once predicted that the Arctic Ocean would be ice-free in summer sometime in the latter half of the twenty-first century, many researchers now say that summer sea ice could largely be gone within a decade, perhaps two.

As FRASER AND his colleagues contemplate the influx of heat by air and sea, they see one overarching effect rippling through this universe of ice: temperatures crossing the threshold between freezing and melting. "The whole system revolves around the freezing point, so a slight change in the positive direction has major implications for the entire food web," Fraser said. "The freezing point is truly a threshold."

Said Hugh Ducklow, head of the Palmer LTER study, "Sea ice is like an on-off switch. We warm a little bit, and then we don't get sea ice anymore, and then everything changes."

Ducklow and his colleagues in the LTER program are studying the impact of disappearing sea ice on life-forms ranging from the very smallest (single-celled diatoms) to predators at the top of the food chain (Adélie penguins). They do this from Palmer Station and on an annual January cruise along the Antarctic Peninsula, during which they methodically cover a grid 250 miles by 125 miles in the Southern Ocean. One group of species that appears to be in decline in the northwestern Antarctic Peninsula is the ice-dependent phytoplankton. Sea ice contains very little salt, since most of it is leached out of the ice through brine channels and sinks to lower depths. In the spring, as the sea ice melts, a lens of fresher water forms on top of the sea. This lens acts as a kind of cap on the ocean and resists mixing with the saltier water below. Diatoms and phytoplankton reside in this relatively stable, less salty lens, where sunlight strikes the organisms and creates massive, seasonal plankton blooms throughout the spring and summer. Krill then feed on the plankton, and virtually everything else—penguins, seabirds, seals, and whales—feeds on the krill.

But a recent study by Ducklow and some of his colleagues has shown that as sea ice duration has declined sharply along the northwestern Antarctic Peninsula, phytoplankton production has plummeted, as well. Using satellite images that measure concentrations of chlorophyll (the green photosynthetic pigment in plants), researchers have estimated that in places phytoplankton abundance in the northwestern Antarctic Peninsula has fallen by about 90 percent since 1978. The picture 250 miles to the south, around Marguerite Bay, is completely reversed. There, in areas that often were covered in ice nearly year-round—and therefore had low phytoplankton production because the ice blocked the sun's rays—melting sea ice has increased phytoplankton abundance by 67 percent. Of course, if Marguerite Bay's sea ice eventually disappears, ice-dependent phytoplankton there will decline, as well.

Ducklow says one thing is clear: As the sea ice disappears, the food web that evolved around the seasonal formation of the ice is changing, sundering the links—from phytoplankton, to krill, to penguins—that have supported flourishing populations of Adélies. Different organisms may replace the ice-dependent species, but the natural system that evolved around sea ice will be on its way out.

"We are seeing the creation of a new ecosystem for which there is no precedent," said Ducklow. "There is an entire, distinct ecosystem just living in and on the ice. So as sea ice begins to decline and then fails to form, as is now happening very rapidly, all these organisms that depend on the timing and the existence and the extent of sea ice for their successful feeding and breeding will be high and dry. If the warming continues, we are eventually going to get to a point where sea ice won't form anymore, and that would be catastrophic to the system."

No species is more dependent on sea ice—or forms a more crucial link in the Antarctic food chain—than the Antarctic krill, *Euphausia superba*. Reaching a length of two-and-a-half inches, related to crustaceans such as shrimp, and foraging by constantly paddling their six pairs of legs to form a feeding basket that channels phytoplankton into their mouths, Antarctic krill constitute an enormous biomass whose size is estimated at more than a billion metric tons. Sea ice plays an integral role in the life history of *Euphausia superba,* as the krill in their juvenile stage swarm under the ice and rake out algae and phytoplankton frozen in the surface of the sea. Sea ice also provides the krill with protection from predators and a stable environment in which they can drift.

As sea ice declines along the western Antarctic Peninsula, populations of Antarctic krill—one of a dozen krill species, or euphausiids, found in the Southern Ocean—also appear to be dwindling. One study, which compared 11,978 net hauls of krill from the years 1926 to 1939 and 1976 to 2003, said that since 1976 krill populations had tumbled by 80 percent in the southwestern Atlantic sector of Antarctic waters and that they are being replaced by salps, a cylindrical, filter-feeding organism known as a tunicate. Some krill experts, however, say that study may have overstated the decline of a creature whose populations are extremely hard to measure, since their reproductive success is cyclical and their concentrations vary wildly across the Southern Ocean. Few scientists doubt, however, that as sea ice disappears, so will Antarctic krill.

Antarctic krill usually experience two good spawning years followed by three to four poor spawning years, and these spawning peaks appear to be declining, according to Langdon Quetin, a krill specialist who worked for many years on the Palmer LTER team. "If we don't get enough sea ice, we will not have the krill recruitment," Quetin said.

Bill Fraser began to glean the sea ice's importance to krill as far back as the late 1980s. As he sampled Adélie diets, Fraser noticed that after heavy sea ice years, the penguins would be eating large numbers of smaller krill in the next year or two. Krill scientists were just beginning to piece together the importance of sea ice to juvenile krill, but Fraser was seeing it—in the form of regurgitated krill—as he lavaged the stomachs of Adélies: Lots of sea ice meant healthy krill populations.

Fraser is now convinced that the loss of sea ice is one of two factors—the other being increased snowfall—rapidly driving Palmer Station's Adélie penguins into oblivion. In Fraser's view, the reduction of sea ice is hurting the Adélies in two ways.

First, it means fewer krill overall. Fraser sees evidence of this in the duration of Adélie foraging trips. Using radio transmitters attached to the backs of Adélies on Humble Island, Fraser and his team measure how long adult Adélies stay at sea catching krill for their chicks. Over the past fifteen years, typical foraging trips have gone from roughly eight to thirteen hours according to preliminary data. This is a sign, says Fraser, that krill are scarcer, forcing the Adélies to spend more time filling their stomachs with krill for themselves and their offspring.

The drastic reduction in sea ice duration has also deprived Adélie penguins on the northwestern Antarctic Peninsula of a crucial platform needed to reach rich feeding grounds for much of the year. In winter, Adélie penguins throughout Antarctica must have access to areas of open water. In the depths of winter, those foraging areas must also be to the north of the Antarctic Circle so the penguins have sufficient light to see their prey. The most productive areas tend to be at the heads of deep undersea canyons, where upwelling brings nutrients and warmer water to the surface, forming open areas in the ice known as polynyas. When a lack of ice prevents the Adélies from easily reaching these feeding grounds, their winter survival rates begin to fall.

Fraser reached this conclusion over several years after placing satellite tags on roughly 150 Adélies along the western Antarctic Peninsula, in summer and in winter. He wound up with thousands of locations showing the foraging areas of Adélies in three main spots: off Palmer Station; Renaud Island, eighty miles south of Palmer; and Marguerite Bay, several hundred miles south of Palmer. The Adélies took off from land or ice and fed at the head of deep undersea canyons.

"There's no question Adélies use canyons as key areas to find prey in wintertime," said Fraser. "The evidence we have is unequivocal: Without enough sea ice, these birds can't reach what must be very productive areas of the ocean during wintertime. This is removing the Adélies' ability to exploit the areas they were able to exploit at one time. That's probably why these chicks aren't surviving."

Indeed, Fraser thinks many recently fledged chicks aren't even surviving until winter's onset. A larger percentage of chicks are lighter than their cohort of several decades ago, which means their caloric reserves will be exhausted if they don't quickly find krill or fish. Thirty years ago, sea ice often began advancing from the south in March, providing the chicks with a feeding platform. Today, with the onset of sea ice formation delayed by nearly two months, the safe haven of the ice is often not there at a crucial time in the young birds' lives.

Fraser noted that in heavy sea ice years, chick survival was generally good, according to his studies of chicks with flipper bands. In very light sea ice years, chick survival tended to be poor. Penguin expert David Ainley agrees that contracting sea ice will inevitably have an impact on these ice-dependent seabirds. "It just shrinks their habitat," he said. "I'll use the analogy of cutting down trees and songbirds disappear, even though there are still a lot of insects around to feed on."

The decline of sea ice is taking a toll on Adélies in yet another way, as Fraser has discovered through penguin diet sampling dating back to the mid-1970s. Three decades ago, up to half of Adélie penguin diets in the Palmer Station area consisted of Antarctic silverfish, *Pleuragramma antarcticum*. The life history of these fish is intertwined with sea ice, as their fertilized eggs rise to the underside of the sea ice and hatch; there they are partially protected from predation. As sea ice has waned around Palmer Station, so, too, have the silverfish, and today Fraser rarely finds silverfish in the diets of Adélies or other seabirds. (The presence of silverfish is determined by Adélie diet sampling and by the otoliths Fraser and his team find in Adélie guano traps and in South Polar skua droppings.) Farther south, where a Fraser field team studies Adélie penguins in the more frigid realm of Marguerite Bay, silverfish are still abundant and are common in Adélie diets.

What this means is that thirty years ago, if krill were in short supply, Adélies around Palmer Station could switch to silverfish—which grow to a length of ten inches—and eat their fill. Today, they do not have that option. "Adélies are almost exclusively eating krill, and that may be one of the reasons they're doing so poorly," said Fraser. "There was a time when Adélies here could prey-switch. They can't do that anymore. It's krill or nothing for them."

The upshot of all these precipitous changes—the increased snowfall on the nesting grounds, the loss of sea ice, the decline of krill, the near disappearance of Antarctic silverfish—is that the Adélies at Palmer Station simply cannot keep pace with large-scale environmental shifts and are dying out. Having evolved to exist in an environment with low snowfall, abundant sea ice, and prey species linked to sea ice, the Adélie penguins of the northwestern Antarctic Peninsula now find that another climate regime has, in the space of decades, nudged out the ecosystem to which they had become adapted.

"Climate change," noted Fraser, "disrupts evolved life histories."

Another way to look at it, said Fraser, is through the prism of an old ecological concept: "match-mismatch dynamics." More recently, some scientists and writers have taken to calling it "global weirding." On the most basic level, it simply means that a species gets out of sync with its environment. Already, as the planet warms, species of birds, butterflies, and other creatures are beginning to suffer from match-mismatch dynamics. The iconic example is the polar bear, which is in decline as it loses the sea ice platform it uses to hunt its preferred prey, ringed seals. Another well-known example involves the Edith's checkerspot butterfly (*Euphydryas editha*), found in western North America. Camille Parmesan of the University of Texas has done extensive research showing that the brightly colored Edith's checkerspot is going locally extinct in large parts of its southern range because a warming climate means that the butterfly larvae's host plants, which provide it with nectar, are turning brown earlier and thus are unable to support the larvae.

"A particular ecosystem is not just a collection of organisms," Ducklow told me. "It's a group of organisms coadapted over a long period of time to live together. Each of these organisms has its own preferred tolerances and preferences. As an ecosystem changes, organisms may not move as a mass. You may well put together a new system of organisms that won't be well adapted together. Each individual population has its own response to climate change."

ALTHOUGH THE RETREAT of the sea ice has most strongly affected the creature that is the main object of Fraser's work—the Adélie penguin— the other changes he and his colleagues have witnessed have been no less dramatic.

"The landscape side of it is incredible—glaciers retreating, ice shelves disintegrating—and it fits with what we're seeing happening to the penguins," Fraser told me one day at Palmer Station. "There is no longer any sector of this coast that looks anything like it looked thirty years ago. With the retreat of the glaciers, there's got to be at least two dozen islands and points that were not here thirty years ago. And when I'm up in the States and I hear arguments from people who dismiss global warming, or tell me that warming is going to be great for the planet, that's sort of what's running in the background when I see these kinds of changes. The changes here are so massive that it doesn't leave any doubt in my mind that the earth is warming."

A photograph from 1975 underscores Fraser's observations. The picture appears in the book *Antarctic Birds*, written by Fraser's mentor, David Parmelee. Looking north, it shows the station in the middle distance and, behind it, the high, unbroken sweep of the Marr Ice Piedmont flowing onto Norsel Point. Standing today where Parmelee snapped the picture thirty-five years ago—a place known as Gamage Point—you can easily see how the view has changed dramatically. Where once there was an imposing ramp of ice, now there is a large gap, several hundred feet wide, connecting Arthur Harbor to Loudwater Cove. The once-healthy glacial finger covering much of Norsel Point is melting away.

During my stay at Palmer Station, a Canadian documentary film crew aboard the *Sedna IV* paid a visit to the base. They were using a standard chart of Arthur Harbor that dates back to 1963—fine for identifying the reefs and nearby islands, but highly disorienting when you're attempting to gauge your position from a map depicting a coastline that has fallen back nearly a third of a mile. "When we arrived we had to take thirty minutes just to try to understand the landscape," said Captain René Turenne. "It was completely different."

According to that chart—and to black-and-white aerial photographs taken by the U.S. Navy in 1963—the Marr Ice Piedmont once nearly abutted Palmer Station. Station records, now kept using a GPS device, show that the glacier has retreated roughly fifteen hundred feet behind the station since 1963. In the 1970s and 1980s, Fraser and others used to hike and ski atop large portions of the Marr Ice Piedmont. That is virtually impossible now, as the thinning glacier is riven by many more crevasses and is falling back from the coastline in scalloped chunks. You can still hike to the top of the glacier just behind the station, but the path has become increasingly narrow as the Marr Ice Piedmont has contracted. Tattered black flags atop wooden poles mark the safe route, which constricts to a few hundred feet in some places. It seems only a matter of time before glacial retreat renders the much-used—and much-loved—route up the Marr impassable.

The steady regression of the Marr Ice Piedmont mirrors a trend up and down the western and northeastern Antarctic Peninsula. Roughly 90 percent of 244 glaciers along the western Antarctic Peninsula have retreated since 1940, according to a study by the British Antarctic Survey and the U.S. Geological Survey. Published in the journal *Science* and based on more than two thousand aerial photographs, the survey shows that from 1945 to 1954, two-thirds of the glaciers were still advancing, but as warming swept down the peninsula, rapid recession became the rule.

Around Palmer Station, one effect of glacial retreat has been the colonization of exposed ground by Antarctica's only two species of vascular plants, the hair grass *Deschampsia antarctica* and the cushion plant (or pearlwort) *Colobanthus quitensis*. Plant specialists Thomas (Tad) Day, of Arizona State University, and Chris Ruhland, of Minnesota State University, tracked the terrestrial changes around Palmer Station from 1994 to 2006 and found an explosive growth of plant life on many recently deglaciated areas. One of their study sites near Palmer Station, known as Point 8, had fewer than 100 hair grass plants in 1999. By 2006, 16,000 hair grass plants had sprouted on the point. Warming temperatures are speeding up growth and increasing the flowering of the two species, whose expansion is also aided by the abundant nitrogen—in the form of bird guano—present in the area. "Some areas," said Ruhland, "look like a hayfield."

The birding team's Brett Pickering, who has witnessed a significant transformation in a single decade, said, "These changes are so dramatic—it's not like roses blooming a week earlier in Europe. This is the disappearance of a portion of glaciers and a whole island population of breeding Adélies on Litchfield. It's the migration of gentoos that weren't here previously. I mean it's in-your-face, big changes—more so than anywhere else I've been or read about."

IF THE GLACIERS of the Antarctic Peninsula and West Antarctica continue to retreat, the biggest global impact will be on the sea level. Scientists are paying particularly close attention to some large glaciers in West Antarctica—especially the Pine Island and Thwaites glaciers at 75° S—that are flowing more rapidly into the sea than any other ice streams in Antarctica. Their swift movement has been triggered, scientists believe, by the same phenomenon that has partially contributed to declining sea ice in West Antarctica: the channeling of warmer Antarctic Circumpolar Deep Water up onto the continental shelf.

"We're firmly of the opinion that ocean heat is getting to the ice and causing these major changes," said Robert Bindschadler, one of the researchers studying the Pine Island Glacier's speedy slide into the sea. "So even if you isolate Antarctica on the surface from global warming, there's this back door—that [ocean] heat is still getting to this part of the ice sheet."

Bindschadler, the former chief scientist of NASA's Hydrospheric and Biospheric Sciences Laboratory and a senior fellow at the Goddard Space Flight Center, has led fifteen Antarctic field expeditions. He and his colleagues are now in the midst of an international, multiyear study of the Pine Island Glacier.

Like much of West Antarctica, the Pine Island Glacier is a huge river of ice that mainly rests on the bottom of a vast submarine basin. The thickest part of the West Antarctic Ice Sheet is nearly three miles deep, about 60 percent of which is actually under sea level. Formed over the course of millions of years, the ice has gradually expanded outward, displacing vast quantities of ocean water. Near its edge, it reaches a point where the ice becomes thin enough that it actually starts to float on the surface of the sea. That floating part is known as the Pine Island Glacier Ice Shelf. The glacier itself is about 190 miles long and 30 miles wide, while the ice shelf is roughly 25 miles long by 22 miles wide.

Bindschadler is convinced that the warmer waters flooding the ice shelf are causing parts of the submerged underside of the shelf to melt. In places, the ice shelf is thinning at a rate of 160 feet a year. Melting is most intense where the grounded glacier becomes the floating ice shelf, a point known as the grounding line. In effect, this has loosened the glacier's hold on the seabed, weakening a buttress and allowing the vast river of ice behind it to accelerate into the sea.

Today, the Pine Island Glacier is charging into the Amundsen Sea at a rate of more than a foot an hour, or about two miles a year. Should the ice of the floating Pine Island Ice Shelf melt, sea levels would not increase, just as melted ice cubes do not increase the level of liquid in a glass. But the glacier itself is so thick, with so much ice above sea level, that were the glacier to melt and slide into the ocean, sea levels *would* increase. Already, the volume of ice that the Pine Island Glacier is losing every year is staggering: 46 billion tons.

Bindschadler and his colleagues estimate that if all the ice from the ice streams that feed the Pine Island and Thwaites glaciers were to flow into the Southern Ocean, global sea levels could increase by as much as five feet—enough to inundate many coastal areas, from Florida to Bangladesh. When I suggested to him that such a calamity would not likely occur anytime soon, the NASA scientist replied, "That [five feet] is an upper bound. But the time scale is what really matters, and you say that we won't see these ice shelves disappear in our lifetime—I'm not so sure. I think we might well."

"Are you kidding?" I asked.

"No," Bindschadler replied. "Not at all."

Should ocean and air temperatures continue to rise in West Antarctica, melting the entire West Antarctic Ice Sheet, global sea levels could eventually rise by sixteen to twenty feet, flooding large parts of the globe, including Washington, D.C.

The person who first sounded this alarm, more than thirty years ago, was the renowned earth scientist John H. Mercer, of the Institute of Polar Studies at Ohio State University. Writing in 1978 in the journal *Nature,* at a time when global warming was only beginning to receive greater attention from scientists, Mercer said that a doubling of carbon dioxide concentrations in the earth's atmosphere from preindustrial levels could increase temperatures to the point that the West Antarctic Ice Sheet would begin to melt. "If the CO_2 greenhouse effect is magnified in high latitudes, as now seems likely, deglaciation of West Antarctica would probably be the first disastrous result of continued fossil fuel consumption," Mercer wrote.

Mercer also correctly foresaw that the West Antarctic Ice Sheet would begin to warm and lose mass well before the larger, colder, and higher East Antarctic Ice Sheet, most of which sits on land. "Fortunately, serious depletion of the East Antarctic ice sheet is a distant threat," wrote Mercer. "Even if further warming gave it a severely negative mass balance, it would waste away only slowly over millennia." Were the East Antarctic Ice Sheet to melt in some hellishly hot, far-distant future, global sea levels would rise another 180 to 200 feet, inundating much of civilization.

These titanic processes of glaciation and deglaciation are controlled by the physics of ice on the planet. During glaciations, water is locked up in ice; at the peak of the last ice age, sea levels were about 270 feet lower than today. During warm, interglacial periods, some portion of the ice melts and boosts sea levels. Of course, sea level rises of hundreds of feet are unlikely in the coming centuries. But sea levels have increased drastically in very short periods of time in previous warming periods. The physicist Mark Bowen, in his book *Thin Ice,* noted that "various records show that about 14,000 years ago, as the Wisconsonian [glaciation] was coming to an end, a pulse of meltwater from the disintegrating polar ice caps sent sea levels up at the rate of three feet every twenty years for five hundred years."

More modest sea level increases from the melting of large glaciers, such as Pine Island, are likely, which is why Bindschadler and other ice experts expect sea levels to increase during this century by at least three feet, and possibly as much as six feet.

What is happening to the glaciers of West Antarctica and the

Antarctic Peninsula is not an anomaly. Indeed, glaciers worldwide—in the Andes, the Rockies, the Alps, the Himalayas, and the Arctic—are melting like ice cubes on hot pavement. The World Glacier Monitoring Service reports that the territory covered by glaciers in the Alps has shrunk by half since the 1850s and that close to 90 percent of the region's glaciers are now smaller than four-tenths of a square mile. The U.S. Geological Survey says that 99 percent of Alaska's 100,000 glaciers are shrinking. Andean glaciers are rapidly melting, threatening the water supplies of millions, and the ice cap atop Africa's Mount Kilimanjaro will likely be gone in the next decade. The region known as the Third Pole—the Himalayas and the Tibetan Plateau, which together harbor more ice than any place on earth, other than Antarctica and the Arctic—is experiencing swift melting of its glaciers. More than one billion people on the Indian subcontinent and in China depend, at least in part, on glacial meltwater that flows into rivers such as the Brahmaputra, Ganges, Yellow, and Yangtze.

IN THE AUSTRAL summer of 2002, on the opposite side of the Antarctic Peninsula from Palmer Station, an event occurred that brought home to Fraser, his scientific colleagues in Antarctica, and the world at large just how precipitously parts of the great southern continent were heating up. It was then, after a string of warm summers, that the Larsen B Ice Shelf—which had been fastened to the shoreline of the eastern Antarctic Peninsula for at least eleven thousand years—disintegrated in spectacular fashion. In just a few days, a section of the ice shelf the size of Rhode Island shattered into millions of pieces. Its collapse marked the near-disappearance of an ice shelf that once had been as large as Connecticut, covering 5,400 square miles.

Although only fifty to sixty miles separate the western coast of the Antarctic Peninsula from the eastern, the two sides are worlds apart. Insulated from warmer, westerly Pacific breezes by the mountains of the Antarctic Peninsula, the east coast of the peninsula and the Weddell Sea are generally 10°F colder than the western Antarctic Peninsula. Frigid air streaming off the polar plateau and sweeping across the Weddell Sea has led, over many millennia, to the formation of Antarctica's second-largest ice shelf—the Filchner-Ronne Ice Shelf, which is nearly as large as Sweden. (Only the Ross Ice Shelf is bigger.)

The Larsen Ice Shelf—named for Norwegian whaling Captain Carl Anton Larsen, who sailed into the Weddell Sea in 1893—once consisted of three sections: Larsen A, Larsen B, and Larsen C, running north to south. An ice shelf is nothing more than an extension of a glacier or ice sheet that has flowed off the land or out of a submarine basin and come to rest atop the sea. Though not among the very largest Antarctic ice shelves, the Larsen Ice Shelf was nevertheless an imposing structure, extending more than 60 miles into the sea, running more than 350 miles along the coast, and measuring more than one thousand feet thick in its more southerly sections. As with icebergs, most of the shelf was underwater.

In 1995, decades of steadily increasing temperatures led to the disintegration of the Larsen A Ice Shelf, the smallest of the three, and the neighboring Prince Gustav Ice Shelf. The breakup occurred after the warmest summer then recorded, and the mechanism that caused the disintegration of the shelf appeared to be related to the formation of large melt ponds on its surface. Such ponds, which look in satellite photographs like narrow lakes or canals, enable water to seep into crevasses in ice shelves. This water then forces its way down, its weight further expanding fissures in the ice. If melt pond formation occurs across hundreds of square miles, as it did on the Larsen A, the ice shelf becomes eaten through with ponds and water-filled crevasses. Then the shelf can shatter like a plate glass window. (Warmer ocean waters circulating beneath the ice shelf thinned and weakened it, as well.)

The crumbling of the Larsen A—and the future disintegration of the Larsen B—occurred because steadily rising temperatures had crossed a threshold beyond which ice shelves cannot long survive. When mean summer air temperatures remain below 29°F, the formation of melt ponds is uncommon and ice shelves are more stable, according to Ted Scambos, the lead scientist at the National Snow and Ice Data Center in Boulder, Colorado, and an authority on ice shelves. Records at nearby Argentine bases show that before 1977, summers where mean temperatures exceeded 29°F in the northern Weddell Sea were extremely rare.

But in the 1980s and 1990s, air temperatures in the northwestern Weddell Sea began to increase by an average of 1°F per decade. More and more summers saw mean temperatures exceeding the 29°F threshold. Once regions along the Antarctic Peninsula cross this summer temperature threshold, ice shelf collapse usually occurs within ten years, Scambos said. John Mercer noted that the northwestern Antarctic Peninsula, where Palmer Station is located, had no ice shelves because sea and air temperatures were too high to sustain the floating ice sheets.

From September 2001 through February 2002, robust winds from the northwest—carrying warmth and moisture—blew across the northern half of the Antarctic Peninsula, causing air temperatures to increase 3.5°F above recent mean temperatures. In January, the Argentine base at Marambio, located to the north of the Larsen B on Snow Hill Island, experienced a heavy rain, a rare event on the Weddell Sea. (Several years later, Scambos also witnessed a freak rainstorm at Marambio, recalling, "You could hear the rain drumming on the roof. That whole evening was more like a summer in Maine than a summer in Antarctica.")

In February, from his offices at the National Snow and Ice Data Center in Boulder, Scambos received reports from Argentine colleagues that the summer continued to be exceptionally warm. Examining satellite photographs, Scambos was stunned to see that the surface of the Larsen B was riddled with deep blue melt ponds, their dark color absorbing sunlight and further melting the ice shelf. Soon, the front edge of the Larsen B began to crumble, and dozens of sliver-like icebergs broke away from the northern part of the shelf.

"In early March, we got an image that was just spectacular," Scambos said. "It showed a vast area had completely disintegrated to basically blue slush. The chunks had crumbled to the point where they didn't look like ice. Some process was going on that wasn't just breaking the ice shelves, but actually disintegrating them to a very fine scale."

A series of time-lapse images, carried by news organizations around the world, showed how, almost overnight, the shelf had dissolved into a turquoise raft of millions of chunks of ice.

What Scambos and other researchers have witnessed in the Weddell Sea in the past fifteen years is precisely what John Mercer of Ohio State had predicted in 1978: rapid warming, caused by man's emission of heat-trapping greenhouse gases into the atmosphere, leading to the breakup of ice shelves on both coasts of the Antarctic Peninsula, steadily moving from north to south. With the Larsen A and B gone, the Larsen C—more than one thousand feet thick and twice as large as Massachusetts—is thinning in places at a rate of about eight feet a year. Scambos thinks the Larsen C will experience significant melt-pond formation and will probably begin to disintegrate along its northern edge in about ten years.

In the past several decades, eight ice shelves—including the Wordie, the Wilkins, and the Prince Gustav—have fully or partially collapsed along the Antarctic Peninsula. Their combined area once covered nearly ten thousand square miles.

The story of the disappearance of the Larsen B and other ice shelves often does not end with these spectacular collapses. Indeed, for those concerned about rising global sea levels, the demise of ice shelves is only the beginning.

After the loss of the Larsen B, scientists began monitoring the large glaciers that flowed out of the mountains of the Antarctic Peninsula and onto the coast to which the ice shelf had been affixed. What they found was that the Larsen B had acted as a buttress or a dam, significantly slowing the flow of the ice sheets into the sea. Once that buttress was removed, the glaciers behind the Larsen B Ice Shelf began moving far more rapidly to the Weddell Sea, dumping ice that had once been on land into the ocean, and thereby raising sea levels. A study by Scambos and several colleagues showed that in the year following the collapse of the Larsen B, four major glaciers that fed the ice shelf sped up by a factor of two to six times. After a steep initial acceleration, the rate of movement slowed somewhat over time, but the glaciers behind the Larsen B are still losing mass, thinning, and delivering more ice to the ocean than is being created anew every year on land.

"We are already at the point where the changes we're seeing in this part of Antarctica are unprecedented throughout the entire period of human civilization," said Scambos.

THE PERIOD OF which Scambos speaks is the latest geologic epoch, known as the Holocene, from the Greek words *holos,* or entire, and *kainos,* or new. Scholars talking about climate change and the Holocene—which began about 11,500 years ago—often note that it is the era in which human civilization rose and flourished. They bring this up for a reason: The Holocene has been a period of relative climatic stability, which, scientists say, is a major reason why human society has advanced as far as it has. Climate scientists are quick to point out that the reason for that relative climatic stability is that the concentration of carbon dioxide in the atmosphere remained at a fairly steady level of about 280 parts per million until the Industrial Revolution gathered momentum in the second half of the nineteenth century.

Many climate scientists now believe we have entered a new geologic period, the Anthropocene; the term comes from the Greek word for human, *anthropo*. They say this because mankind—by combusting ever-larger quantities of fossil fuels and degrading a growing portion of the planet—is increasingly shaping the earth's climate. From the preindustrial level of 280 parts per million, humanity has elevated carbon dioxide levels to nearly 390 parts per million. The real explosion in greenhouse-gas production has occurred since 1950, with carbon dioxide emissions soaring from roughly 5 billion tons a year to 30 billion tons today. Now, as America continues to produce massive quantities of greenhouse gases, as China has surpassed America in emitting carbon dioxide, and such other nations as India and Brazil rapidly industrialize and raise their standards of living, carbon dioxide emissions have reached unprecedented levels, rising by 2 parts per million a year.

Hugh Ducklow has a handy way of describing the current situation. Over the course of hundreds of millions of years—when the earth was steamy, dinosaurs roamed, and unfathomable quantities of vegetation grew, decayed, and were stored underground—the planet laid down enormous quantities of fossil fuels. As all that carbon became locked underground in the form of coal and oil, levels of carbon dioxide slowly declined, and the earth cooled. Now, in the space of a century or two, all of us—by driving, flying, heating and lighting our homes, and enjoying the amenities of modern civilization—are pulling that long-stored carbon out of the ground and burning it. That reinjects carbon dioxide into the atmosphere, and since carbon dioxide traps heat, temperatures are on the rise.

Anyone who doubts that explanation need only examine the latest science from Antarctica. There, on the polar plateau of East Antarctica, two teams—the Russians at Vostok Station and the Europeans at Dome C—have taken deep ice core samples. Gas bubbles trapped in those ice cores reveal both atmospheric levels of carbon dioxide and air temperature, dating back hundreds of thousands of years. The latest ice coring—taken at Dome C to a depth of more than two miles, just a few feet above Antarctic bedrock—shows that atmospheric concentrations of carbon dioxide are now higher than at any time in at least the last 800,000 years. Graphs of carbon dioxide levels from both Dome C and Vostok show them rising and falling in roughly 100,000-year cycles, with low carbon dioxide levels corresponding with glacial periods and high carbon dioxide levels corresponding with warm, interglacial periods. Not once, going back 800,000 years, have atmospheric carbon dioxide levels ever exceeded 300 parts per million. But a graph of carbon dioxide in the atmosphere shows its levels steadily rising in the late nineteenth and early twentieth centuries and then, since 1950, rocketing straight up.

Throughout its 4.5-billion-year history, the earth has experienced wild swings in climate. It is believed that during the "Snowball Earth" period, about 630 million to 800 million years ago, the entire planet was covered in ice for some time. At the other extreme, during the Cretaceous period of 65 million to 145 million years ago, the planet was warm, dinosaurs were abundant, and sea levels were high.

Antarctica has experienced similarly wild swings. In the late Cretaceous period, when Antarctica was part of Gondwana and still attached to Australia and South America (and located farther to the north), forests of conifers and beech trees grew on the continent. From the earliest days of the discovery of Antarctica, explorers and scientists have come across carbonized wood and countless fossils: leaves from trees of the genus *Nothofagus,* or the southern beeches, which still grow in South America today; giant ferns; palm trees; and a 40-million-year-old opossum jaw. Even after Antarctica broke away from Gondwana, settled at the bottom of the earth, and began to ice over, it still experienced periods of warmth during which flowering plants and trees grew. Fossils of these plant species have been found that date back 3 to 5 million years.

Roughly 2 million years ago, however, the earth entered a cooler period known as the Pleistocene, and Antarctica's great ice sheets thickened and grew. During glacial periods, ice spilled far off the continent, even covering the South Shetland Islands. Periods of glaciations and warmer, interglacial periods came and went in roughly 100,000-year cycles, attributable primarily to changes in the earth's tilt on its axis and its orbit, which allowed more—or less—sun to strike the radiation-absorbing landmasses of the Northern Hemisphere and cool or warm the planet. (The effects of the earth's movements on periods of glaciation and deglaciation are known as Milankovitch cycles, named after the Serbian mathematician Milutin Milankovitch, who discovered this mechanism.) Antarctic ice cores vividly illustrate this periodicity, with the rising and falling of temperature closely linked to increases and decreases in atmospheric carbon dioxide. Temperature and carbon dioxide feed off each other. When the earth enters glacial periods because the tilt of its axis reduces the amount of solar radiation striking the planet, the cooler temperatures lead to a decline in carbon dioxide, because colder ocean waters absorb more carbon dioxide. Likewise, rising temperatures can increase carbon dioxide levels because warming oceans absorb less. But emissions of carbon dioxide into the atmosphere—whether from a huge volcanic eruption or massive combustion of fossil fuels—also directly affect climate, with temperatures rising as atmospheric concentrations of carbon dioxide increase. The planet has generally experienced 20,000 years of warmer, interglacial periods followed by slow, 80,000-year processions into a global ice age. The last glacial maximum was about 20,000 years ago, which was followed by a 10,000-year return to warmth, which was in turn followed by the relative warmth and stability of the past 10,000 years.

Now we should be gradually returning to a cooler global climate and, in about 80,000 years, another ice age. People seeking comfort in the prospect that natural cooling will offset man-made warming are deluding themselves, however, according to the geologist and ice sheet expert Richard Alley of Pennsylvania State University. He has noted that the slide into an ice age means about .01°F degree of cooling per century, and human-induced warming is heating up the planet at least one hundred times faster. When Alley and other climate scientists look at the experiment that man is performing on the earth today—pumping carbon stored over millions of years back into the atmosphere in mere decades— they are concerned, above all, about the unpredictability of our actions. Although the Holocene has been reasonably stable, ice cores tell researchers that the climate can change drastically in dozens or hundreds of years. In his book *The Two-Mile Time Machine*, Alley writes about climate "wobbling wildly" or advancing in a "drunken stagger." More than being a dial, he suggests, climate can be like a switch, changing drastically, especially when unprecedented "forcings"—such as current levels of carbon dioxide emissions—act on the planet's complex climate system. In the past, temperatures have risen sharply in a few decades and massive ice sheets and ice shelves have melted and disintegrated in a few hundred years. The geological record shows, for example, that about 129,000 years ago, the rapid melting of Greenland's ice sheet caused global sea levels to rise roughly sixteen feet.

LIKE OTHER SCIENTISTS who work at the poles, Bill Fraser has been in a position to witness how swiftly natural systems can change. He is keenly aware that the earth's climate has often seesawed in the past, but he is worried most of all by two things. First, that man's burning of fossil fuels is the main engine driving global warming, and, second, that the world will soon be home to seven billion people and is likely to hold nine billion by midcentury. In previous eras of climate change, such as the last glaciation, 15,000 to 20,000 years ago, the earth had so few people as to be essentially uninhabited compared to today's teeming planet.

"There's no question whatsoever that every time this planet has warmed and cooled in the past it has had ecological consequences," Fraser told me. "The thing that's important is that the earth is beginning to warm and ecosystems are changing and at no point in history has this happened with 6.5 billion people on the planet who are dependent on these ecosystems. Never has change like this taken place with so many people on earth who need these systems to survive. When I look at these incredible changes here, that's what's running in the back of my mind."

CHAPTER 12

DEPARTURE

Here you have this unbelievably tough little animal, able to deal with anything, succumbing to the large-scale effects of our activities. And that's the one thing they can't deal with, and they're dying because of it.

—BILL FRASER,
Torgersen Island, 2006

As FEBRUARY WOUND DOWN, THE SCENE IN THE PENGUIN colonies was more Western Front than Antarctic. The carcasses of dead Adélie chicks were arrayed across a bleak landscape composed of shades of blacks, grays, and browns. By the third week of the month, the healthy Adélie chicks had all slipped into the pebbled shallows and disappeared into the Southern Ocean. At the two largest rookeries, on Torgersen and Humble islands, a handful of chicks remained in the colonies, but they were half-fledged runts that were soon picked off by brown skuas.

Most of the adult Adélies had long since left the colonies to seek out ice floes or islands, where they would stand, nearly motionless, for several weeks, fasting as they shed their old feathers for new ones in the annual molt. The molt is an essential stage in the Adélies' yearly cycle, for without replenishing their plumage the birds would not survive in the Antarctic. Polar penguins—Adélies and emperors—have the densest feathers of any birds on the planet, with up to 250 per square inch, overlapping in shingle-like fashion to insulate the birds from the bitter cold.

About thirty adults remained on Humble Island and ninety on Torgersen, resting in the lee of hills and ridges. Their bodies were puffed up from the blood and new feathers under their skin. Fraser warned us to stay far away from the Adélies, as the molt was a stressful and painful period for the birds, already exhausted from months of nesting and feeding chicks. Many Adélies lose a third of their body weight during the eighteen to twenty days of molting.

On the southeast side of Torgersen Island, several dozen adults stood silently near the shore. Their white breast feathers drifted to the ground like cherry blossoms. Feathers piled up at their feet, looking as if someone had cut open a down pillow and dumped it out. "Unhappy" is not a word you would normally use to describe the aspect of Adélie penguins—"amusing," "cantankerous," or "determined" more readily come to mind—but during the molt, the Adélies look decidedly out of sorts. "These unfortunates stood about in such poor shelter as they could find—the picture of misery, with their moth-eaten-looking garments hanging in rags about them," wrote Robert Falcon Scott's photographer, Herbert Ponting.

One afternoon, I asked Fraser what happened in the colonies after the molt. I knew from earlier conversations with him that immediately upon growing a new set of feathers, the Adélies embark on a two-week feeding binge to replenish the resources they expended during the past seven months of migration, mating, nesting, incubating eggs, and feeding their chicks. After the postmolt binge, I had assumed that the Adélies immediately took off on the first leg of their winter journey. Fraser said, however, that April can be a magical month in the colonies, with hundreds of penguins returning to their home territories—now covered in a chaste layer of snow—for a final farewell before embarking on their winter migration.

"You see them leave as spent, skinny parents who have just been harassed to death by their chicks for the past fifty days, and then you see them return to their breeding sites as these absolutely gorgeous, fat birds that have undergone the molt," said Fraser. "And they have a totally different temperament. In peak season the Adélies will pay absolutely no attention to you, but in April they're more curious and a lot more tolerant of you being around them."

One April, Fraser and the paleoecologist Steven Emslie excavated a penguin colony to date the penguin remains from earlier centuries. Engrossed in their work, the two men were paying little attention to their surroundings. Something caught their eye, however, and when they looked up they had visitors.

"All of a sudden," recalled Fraser, "there were thirty or forty Adélies surrounding us in a circle, just watching us."

WITH THE PENGUIN work over, Fraser and the team turned full-time to banding and monitoring southern giant petrels, brown skuas, and South Polar skuas, all of which were still rearing their chicks on Anvers and surrounding islands. Parmelee and his students had begun banding South Polar skuas thirty years before, and for roughly two decades Fraser had been monitoring the reproductive success of South Polar skuas on Shortcut Island, located a mile southeast of the station. During the three previous seasons, the 60 pairs of South Polar skuas on Shortcut had by February suffered total reproductive failure as hungry adults devoured their own—and their neighbors'—chicks. But during the 2005–06 season, most of Shortcut's South Polar skuas had managed to keep at least one chick alive until mid-February, and some had reared two chicks to this stage.

By late February 2006, however, the team began to find the remains of chicks, some apparently eaten by their own parents, some by other South Polar skuas. We had been tracking the chicks since the South Polars had laid their eggs in early December, first weighing and measuring the eggs and then weighing the downy chicks and measuring their beaks every few days. Near the end of February, after finding the remains of another dead, freshly eaten South Polar chick, Fraser turned to me and said, "Things are tightening up. These birds are getting hungry."

Although South Polar skuas are known to experience periods of reproductive failure, Fraser noted that in the past fifteen years reproductive failure had become the norm. In the Palmer Station area, South Polar skua populations have fallen from a peak of 1,000 pairs three decades ago to roughly half that today. Fraser attributes the birds' deteriorating reproductive success to one main factor, tied to a warming climate: the near disappearance of ice-dependent Antarctic silverfish.

"South Polar skuas provided us with the very first evidence that the food web in this area has changed dramatically in the last fifteen years," Fraser said one day as we sat on the rocks by the boat landing on Short-cut and ate lunch. "South Polar skuas were completely dependent on silverfish in their diet. The skuas used to bring so many silverfish to their chicks that there were fish oil slicks around the nests from the birds not eating them."

Two decades ago, pairs of South Polar skuas raised an average of 1.5 chicks to fledging. Today, even in good years, rearing one chick to fledging is considered a success. During the 2005–06 season, only 54 chicks—out of 113 chicks hatched from 64 pairs—survived to fledging.

THE OUTLOOK FOR one seabird species at Palmer Station—the south-ern giant petrel—is anything but bleak. And for the past eighteen years, Fraser's wife, Donna Patterson, has conducted an exhaustive study of this bird, *Macronectes giganteus*. To do so, Patterson and Fraser have pulled off one of the most successful efforts ever recorded at habituat-ing a seabird to humans, a feat all the more remarkable because south-ern giant petrels have a fearsome reputation. But as I learned at Palmer Station, that reputation is in many ways undeserved. Indeed, one of the most touching aspects of my time in Antarctica was helping Fraser and his team handle the giant petrel eggs and chicks, an experience that brought us in close contact with their parents.

Southern giant petrels are members of the Procellariiformes order of seabirds, which also includes fulmars, prions, shearwaters, and other species of petrels. This group of birds also is known as tubenoses, for the cylindrical, ivory-like structures atop their beaks that enable them to extract salt from seawater. Twenty-three species of the Procellariidae family breed in the Antarctic and subantarctic, of which the southern

giant petrel—also sometimes referred to as the <u>southern giant fulmar—
is the largest</u>.

Southern giant petrels—which Patterson and Fraser refer to as "gipes" (pronounced "Jeeps")—migrate throughout much of the Southern Hemisphere, and gipes banded at Palmer Station have been spotted or recovered in Australia, New Zealand, South Africa, and various parts of South America. Gipes have long had a reputation as repulsive scavengers, which has earned them nicknames such as "stinkpot," "sea vulture," and "glutton." Their infamy as aggressive predators and scavengers has not been helped by the fact that the eyeballs, tongues, hearts, and feet of penguins are often found at their nests; that they are commonly pictured with their blood-drenched heads and beaks emerging from the innards of a seal carcass; that they appear in large numbers on subantarctic islands in early spring to feast on the placentas of newborn seals; that they prey on lambs in the Falkland Islands; that they have been seen knocking other birds out of the sky, then battering and drowning them at sea; and that they stalk penguin chicks on land with their long wings outstretched as they crab-walk across stony beaches before killing and eviscerating the smaller birds. In other words, even among the small number of people who are aware of the existence of southern giant petrels, the general impression is not that of a cuddly creature.

Among Antarctic explorers and sailors, the opinion of gipes has tended toward the abysmal. This is in part due to a few documented attacks by southern giant petrels on sailors who have been swept overboard or been shipwrecked—attacks that at the time were attributed to albatrosses but that Robert Cushman Murphy and others concluded, judging from the birds' behavior, almost certainly were caused by giant petrels. In one instance, the boatswain aboard James Clark Ross's *Erebus* fell overboard in the Southern Ocean in 1840 and almost immediately was set upon by southern giant petrels. The *Erebus* was unable to come about in time to rescue the boatswain, and the last glimpse his shipmates had of him before he sank beneath the waves came, wrote Murphy, as giant petrels "swooped at the man as he struggled to keep afloat, and appeared to strike him with their bills."

No wonder that even a seabird lover such as Murphy would call southern giant petrels "ungainly and uncouth" and that the renowned ornithologist Roger Tory Peterson would refer to gipes as "this rather ugly, rapacious predator." And unlike the universally beloved penguins and albatrosses, which have been extensively studied for more than a century, few scholars deigned to study southern giant petrels. When they did, said Patterson, some of them treated the seabirds more like varmints, subduing them by using a forked stick to pin their necks and heads to the ground while colleagues placed numbered bands on their legs.

This was the state of affairs when Patterson began working on Fraser's birding team in 1991. She was fascinated by the southern giant petrels, in part because the reviled bird of lore seemed to bear little resemblance to the large, almost regal creature—some gipes weigh more than fifteen pounds—she saw incubating eggs on nests around Palmer Station. When she spotted the chicks—tiny white or pale gray fuzzballs that she would eventually come to call "wooshies"—sticking out from under their parents, her desire to work with giant petrels took hold.

"I've come to realize that everything and everybody has a fan club," said Patterson. "They were the underdogs. Nobody wanted to do anything with them. Nobody knew anything about them, and there was no interest in them other than baseline numbers."

At Palmer Station, British scientists had begun banding some gipes in the mid-1950s. In the course of roughly two decades, David Parmelee and his students banded nearly two thousand gipes, most of them chicks. In 1985, Parmelee used harnesses to attach six satellite transmitters to male gipes on Humble Island; this is believed to be the first time seabirds had been outfitted with such devices.

Patterson spent the summer of 1991–92 walking around Humble Island, home to as many as 60 nesting pairs of gipes arrayed on low ridgelines in a roughly circular pattern; this would come to be known as the "gipe loop." She kept her distance from the giant petrels, noted when males and females were on the nests, and observed their interactions with their chicks, their mates, and other gipes. For the next couple of seasons, Patterson worked on Humble Island—largely on her own—and gradually began approaching the birds. If a gipe was skittish or acted aggressively—spreading its wings, opening its mouth, and emitting a guttural burst of air as if it were preparing to propel a stream of stomach oil her way—she would back off.

Soon she learned the temperaments of the different birds; gipes, like skuas, have distinctive personalities, ranging from utterly relaxed to implacably hostile. A sizable number of the giant petrels were reasonably docile, since the Humble gipes had enjoyed some contact with humans, in the form of occasional leg banding. Before long, she discovered that certain giant petrels would allow her to gently approach their nests as they incubated their eggs or brooded their chicks.

Eventually, many of the giant petrels became habituated to Patterson, tolerating her as she slowly approached them and allowing her to reach under them, remove their eggs or chicks, and weigh and measure them. She worked without gloves and initially received numerous gashes from their razor-sharp bills.

"If they're stressed out, I back away," said Patterson. "If they're not stressed, then I just do what I need to do, get up, and go. They don't want to get rubbed under the chin. These are not house pets. They really don't want you hanging around, but they tolerate you. And I've found that if the parents are habituated enough that they don't show fear, then fear is never passed on to the chicks."

Some gipes even displayed behavior toward Patterson that looked an awful lot like affection. During the 1998–99 season, as she and some team members were putting a satellite transmitter on one of the calmest gipes, the bird began acting very "broody," edging closer and closer to Patterson. Soon, the giant petrel crawled into her lap, where it sat calmly as a team member attached the transmitter to its back. In the ensuing years, other gipes did the same thing with her.

"Historically, people have been skeptical that these birds have become so habituated to us," Fraser told me one day as we finished walking the gipe loop. "There were two ornithologists lecturing on a tourist ship, and we brought them out here and Donna put a satellite tag on this bird and it crawled into her lap and she put it back on the nest, and they said, 'Okay, we give up.' We have managed to habituate a species that up until recently was thought to be very difficult to work with. I know from personal experience that the birds recognize us. They sometimes become agitated when we bring strangers to the nest."

Walking the gipe loop, which we did every few days through much of the season, soon became one of my favorite field activities at Palmer

Station. The giant petrels laid their eggs in early to mid-November and incubated them for two months, until hatching began after the first of the year. The males and females took turns on the nest, occasionally sitting side by side but usually remaining alone on the territory while their partners—to whom they can remain faithful for years—were foraging at sea. Approaching the parents, Fraser would crouch down and gently insinuate his hand under the bird. The Humble gipes almost invariably issued a staccato grunting call and swung their lowered heads back and forth in greeting. Fraser then extracted the newly hatched chick—gipes produce only one egg per pair—and cradled it in his hand as he measured its beak and then weighed it in a mesh bag dangling from a scale. I occasionally did the weighing and measuring, and the first time I slid my cold, gloveless hand under the compliant adult to extract a tiny chick from the sauna-like warmth of the brood patch, I was astonished. The downy chicks had a pleasantly earthy scent, which some team members compared to Doritos, though others detected the aroma of a newborn baby. I associated the aroma most closely with the scent of my dog's paws.

As I eased away, the giant petrels—most had gray and light brown feathers on their backs and mottled, off-white feathers on their breasts—eyed me without alarm. Their eyes are a striking silver or pale blue, with jewel-like facets. Their long bills are a shiny flesh color down to the tip, which is pale gray-green.

Before fledging and taking off on their own in May, the chicks grow at an exponential rate as they devour the regurgitated seal meat, whale meat, penguin flesh, fish, squid, and krill brought to them by their parents. By the time we left in mid-March, many chicks weighed ten to twelve pounds. Within three weeks of hatching, the gipe chicks are large enough to thermoregulate and both parents sometimes depart on foraging trips simultaneously, leaving the chicks unguarded. Not even as big as a chicken, the young giant petrels looked vulnerable sitting on their nests, but we never saw another gipe or skua attack a gipe chick. One reason, Fraser said, is that from the moment they are hatched, the chicks are capable of expelling a foul-smelling orange-red stomach oil, called "gack," that predators avoid at all costs. Fraser once saw a South Polar skua perish after being gacked on by an adult gipe; the petrel had unloaded so much of the oily substance on the skua that its feathers were matted and wet, causing the bird to eventually die of exposure.

As we made the rounds of the gipe loop, Fraser identified the birds by nest and, occasionally, by nicknames such as "Psycho" or "Hollywood Girl." He kept up a steady, reassuring monologue with the petrels: "How are you doing, sweetie pie? . . . Must be girls' night out—nothing but you males on these nests."

Reminders that these birds were indeed fierce predators and scavengers were frequently in evidence, from the penguin body parts left by their shell-and-rock nests to the blood caked on their necks and heads. Seeing one crimson-headed male glide in from the ocean, land, and walk to its nest to feed its chick, Fraser said, "No question what he's been doing."

The studies by Fraser and Patterson have added a wealth of knowledge to what little was known about southern giant petrels, including detailed data on chick growth rates. The long-lived banding program has provided extensive information about gipe migration and about their longevity. In 1998, for example, Patterson and Fraser spotted a gipe that had been banded by the British more than forty years before; Patterson is confident that some giant petrels can live more than fifty years.

The many satellite transmitters that Fraser and Patterson have placed on gipes have also provided rich details about their epic foraging trips. The Palmer record is held by a female who flew to Alexander Island and then far west, completing a fifteen-hundred-mile, round-trip journey in six days. (Females generally make the long foraging trips in order to avoid competing with males, which stick closer to home.) Giant petrels are able to cover such great distances by dynamically soaring low over the waves, using the energy of the constant winds rising off the swells to power their flight.

The ability of southern giant petrels to detect a whale or seal carcass from many miles away was on display while I was at Palmer Station. In mid-January, Fraser could see from satellite data that giant petrels were making quick trips lasting one or two days, flying to an area about a hundred miles south of Palmer Station. As he was contemplating this mystery, the answer came from Peter Horne and Kristen Gorman, who

were at that moment on the *Laurence M. Gould* making the annual
LTER cruise. The pair reported that hundreds of giant petrels were
feeding on a whale carcass near Renaud Island.

In late February and early March, we put leg bands on chicks at the
571 active gipe nests in Palmer's environs. Dealing with these unhabituated birds was a trickier business than monitoring the generally
docile giant petrels on the Humble gipe loop. The greatest danger was
gack, which the adults and chicks would occasionally expel in a long
stream. The birding team split into two groups. I generally approached
the chicks with a sheet or towel and quickly draped it over their heads,
the so-called gack rag ensuring—generally—that none of us would be
splattered with the noxious oil. Peter Horne's jacket was hit on a couple
of occasions, a far more desirable outcome than the experience he'd
had the previous season: He'd been gacked in the face. The smell never
came out of his beard, forcing him to shave it. Robert Cushman Murphy reported that giant petrel carcasses placed in museums would still
carry the unforgettable odor of gack decades later. I soon grew attuned
to the unmistakable warning sounds of an approaching gack attack.
The chick would lurch forward once or twice, open its mouth wide, and
make a sound that resembled Donald Duck imitating the crack of a
bullwhip.

The threat of occasionally being gacked added a touch of excitement
to the banding, which entailed hiking up and down the rocky southern
coastline of Anvers and nearby islands. Peter Horne kept the group
amused. When the chicks—with sheets or towels over the heads—began
jerking their legs away from Horne as he placed bands on the birds,
he remarked, "Doing the Elvis-leg here." Horne draped and undraped
the towels over the chicks' heads with the flourish of a matador.

Southern giant petrel populations around Palmer Station have more
than doubled in the past few decades, in contrast to many gipe populations in the Southern Hemisphere; with roughly 46,000 total breeding
pairs, the species is listed as vulnerable and declining. One major reason for the steady decline of gipe populations is longline fishing. Paying out lines that stretch for dozens of miles and are baited with tens
of thousands of hooks, longline boats account for the deaths of hundreds of thousands of seabirds every year; albatrosses, giant petrels,

shearwaters, and many other species are killed when they dive for the bait, are hooked, and drown.

Patterson and Fraser believe that the Palmer giant petrel populations are faring well because the adults forage mainly along the southern half of the western Antarctic Peninsula, where long-line fishing boats do not operate. Still, every season Fraser and his team find fishhooks embedded in giant petrels or lying around their nests. We discovered several while I was at Palmer, including a long hook protruding from the right breast of a male on Stepping Stone Island. Fraser returned twice in an attempt to remove the hook. He lay down next to the skittish bird but found it impossible to work the hook free without hurting the gipe. On that occasion, he cut the hook—a few feet of line were still dangling from it—close to the gipe's body. Returning a few days later, he once again attempted to remove the hook, to no avail. He then snipped off even more of it, confident that the small part that remained would either rust out or, at the very least, not hinder the bird's ability to fly.

BY EARLY MARCH, the days began to take on a chill not felt since the start of the season, and an inch or two of snow fell on the surrounding islands. Storms seemed to intensify, and several times gales relegated us to the station, with winds reaching 60 miles per hour. One day, on Litchfield Island, I watched as a nearly fledged brown skua chick attempted to lift off in high winds, flapping its wings and hovering a few feet in the air before being eased back to the ground by the wind. Other tidings of the late season also came to Litchfield Island, in the form of two hundred fur seals, which hissed and whimpered as they fled from us by pulling themselves swiftly across the stones. The seals wore doleful expressions reminiscent of Bert Lahr's lion in *The Wizard of Oz*, and their smell preceded them. From afar it sometimes reminded me of cooking onions, but the closer you got, the more their musky tang filled the air.

Darkness descended for several hours, and when the weather was clear I walked behind the station and gazed at the kite-shaped form of the Southern Cross. With few penguins around to eat, the leopard seals turned to attacking crabeater seals, and two appeared at the station with fresh scars from lep attacks. One five-foot crabeater plopped down on the stones just outside the birders' tent and took up residence for several days. A beautiful, velvety creature colored a soothing shade of taupe, the crabeater paid scant attention to the parade of people moving in and out of our tent and the lab building next door. The seal spent a considerable amount of time sleeping, sometimes twitching as it dreamed; its disturbed sleep reminded me of my dog's often-animated slumber. Indeed, there was something doglike about the crabeater's face and large brown eyes. One day, as we packed boxes and moved them out of the lab, the crabeater, its head resting on the stones, shot me the same put-out look that my aging golden retriever gives me when he is trying to rest by the front door and I am hauling something out to the car.

This particular crabeater was so composed and elegant that Peter Horne took to calling him Winston. "Crabeaters look like they ought to be wearing wire-rim glasses and reading a book," Horne said as he eyed the recumbent seal.

As our departure neared, my time at Palmer took on an elegiac feel. One sunny evening, I hiked up the glacier behind the station for the last time, walking on a thin layer of recent snow concealing the hard, icy surface that had become exposed as the season wore on. Pausing halfway to the top, I turned around and looked down on Arthur Harbor, filled with thick brash ice from the frequent calving of the Marr Ice Piedmont. A section of the glacier about seventy feet wide was colored a vivid sky blue where it had shed a large amount of ice the day before, in a spectacular series of cascades that had sent rumbles through the station.

I was alone when I reached the top, and I lingered there a long time. Swiftly moving dark clouds unloaded snow on the Bismarck Strait, and soon I was engulfed in a squall that released a fine, icy snow for fifteen minutes. Then the storm scurried away to the east and the sun shone on the islands around Palmer and the imposing summits of the peninsular range. I remembered the view from nearly five months before, when the sea had been blanketed with ice and the islands had been deep in snow. Now, even though a dusting of snow covered the islands, the glittering tableau of the spring had been replaced by a somber blue sea and gray islands. I strained to take in the vast panorama, hoping to etch into my memory this last glimpse of ocean, rock, and ice from the vantage point of the Marr.

THE WANING DAYS at Palmer must have had a powerful effect on Fraser, as well. Since the birth of his son in 2004, Fraser has come to Palmer less often, breaking the long string of years when he worked at the station season after season. (In the ensuing three seasons, he would leave the work at Palmer to his young field team, led by Jennifer Blum.) His work here was also tinged with nostalgia for the simple reason that his study subjects—Adélie penguins—were fast disappearing, foreshadowing the end of a life of research at Palmer Station.

On several occasions in our final weeks at Palmer, Fraser said that within a decade Adélie colonies would remain only on Torgersen Island and Dream Island, with perhaps a swiftly disappearing remnant on Humble Island.

"We're running out of birds near Palmer," he said. "The order of disappearance is going to be Litchfield, Cormorant, Christine, Humble, and Torgersen. Biscoe will fall somewhere in there—it's pretty close to vanishing." The last island to go, Fraser predicted, will be Dream, where 2,200 Adélie breeding pairs remain, down from about 11,000 pairs in the mid-1970s. If recent trends continue, he believes, Adélie penguins will disappear from Dream and the entire northwestern Antarctic Peninsula in about two decades.

"They're on a decline," he once said, "that has no recovery."

What will replace them? Mainly gentoo penguins, it seems. Chinstraps have been moving in as well, although their populations remain low in the Palmer area and have declined slightly in recent years. Adélies, gentoos, and chinstraps make up the genus of pygoscelid penguins, but only Adélies have evolved into an ice-dependent species. Gentoos, which customarily do not migrate, have been in the Palmer area in small numbers for much of the twentieth century and perhaps longer, establishing colonies on the Gerlache Strait, whose swiftly flowing waters leave the passage ice-free most of the year. But the steady decline of sea ice in the

Palmer area is creating increasingly propitious habitat for the gentoos, and their numbers are rising steadily.

Gentoos—the penguins with the trademark white patch above their eyes—have a number of advantages over Adélies. Gentoos are more flexible breeders and often lay their eggs three weeks later than Adélies, avoiding the problems of nesting in snow and snowmelt. Gentoos also are slightly larger than Adélies, weighing roughly a pound more and standing an inch or two taller. This enables them to dive more deeply and for longer periods of time, opening up a realm of prey species unavailable to Adélies. Finally, gentoos do not use ice as a feeding platform, instead preferring to spend their year on rocky coasts near open water. These advantages are clearly evident in the region's changing penguin demographics. While Adélie populations are inexorably heading toward zero around Palmer Station, gentoos have gone from no pairs on Biscoe Island in 1992 to 2,400 by 2010. On Petermann Island, home to the southernmost gentoo colony in the world, gentoo numbers have risen from about 75 pairs a century ago to 2,700 pairs in 2008. The gentoos often nest in colonies once occupied by Adélie penguins; Fraser believes that the arrival of increasing numbers of gentoos is not directly affecting Adélies, but that gentoos are merely filling the void left by the other species.

In effect, species that are obligates of sea ice—Adélie penguins, crabeater seals, and Weddell seals—are being replaced by species not associated with sea ice, such as gentoo penguins, elephant seals, and fur seals. Speaking of these major population shifts at a conference several years ago, Fraser said, "This is our equivalent of the collapse of the Larsen B Ice Shelf—absolutely major, unprecedented changes. Ice-dependent life history groups are being replaced by ice-intolerant life history groups over ecological [short-term] time scales."

IN THE FUTURE, if Fraser or his successors want to find large numbers of Adélie penguins to study along the Antarctic Peninsula, they're going to have to shift their work far to the south, where a system dominated by heavy sea ice still exists—at least for now. Indeed, in 1995, Fraser began studying Adélies on Avian Island, located about 250 miles closer to the pole, off the southern tip of Adelaide Island, in Marguerite Bay. On Avian Island, Adélie populations are actually growing as the region warms, and for a basic reason: Adélies thrive in an optimal mix of sea ice and open water. Too little sea ice—as is now the case around Palmer—and populations falter. Too much sea ice and Adélies have difficulty finding the polynyas and exposed water they need to forage. For a long time, Marguerite Bay had too much ice and not enough open water and was not optimal habitat for Adélie penguins. But as the bay has warmed—the Wordie Ice Shelf there was the first major ice shelf on the Antarctic Peninsula to disintegrate, beginning in the 1970s—there is more open water available for the Adélies, and populations have climbed.

Two members of Fraser's team spend a week on Avian every January as part of the LTER cruise, and their estimates place the number of Adélies on the small island at 50,000 to 75,000 pairs. Having studied the number of recently colonized areas on the island and earlier estimates of penguins there, Fraser believes Adélie populations have probably doubled on Avian in the past few decades. During the 2005–06 season, Peter Horne and Kristen Gorman carried out the research at Avian, and both were struck by the sharp contrast between the packed, thriving Adélie colonies on Avian Island and the increasingly sparse rookeries around Palmer. Sampling Adélie diets, they also were impressed by the large number of ice-dependent Antarctic silverfish the penguins were eating from the more polar seas of Marguerite Bay, compared to the krill-dominated diets at Palmer.

In Fraser's mind, no clearer evidence exists of the relationship between sea ice, prey species dependent on sea ice, and penguins than the contrast between the Adélie populations on Avian Island and in the Palmer region. "You suddenly pump a bunch of Adélie penguin stomachs," he said, "and you realize that deep in Marguerite Bay, which is still a polar system, the diet samples look like they did at Palmer thirty years ago, and you say to yourself, 'Holy shit. This is clear evidence that something major has happened to the food web at Palmer.'"

Bill Fraser's work has never hinted at the extinction of Adélie penguins, which now number 2.5 million breeding pairs in Antarctica, distributed among 160 colonies around the continent. What his work has shown is that local populations will go extinct, and that as warming increases, the threat to Adélie penguins will creep farther south. Indeed, Fraser believes that conditions for Adélies are optimal now in Marguerite Bay and that Avian's populations will soon begin to decline, as well.

"I'd say that we're picking up the peak of the Adélie population on Avian and then it will start to decrease, probably in about a decade or two," Fraser said. "If things continue warming, then what is happening here at Palmer will soon be happening in Marguerite Bay."

In the opinion of many scientists who have studied the warming of the Antarctic Peninsula, the southward progression of warming seems inevitable, given the quantity of greenhouse gases already released into the atmosphere and the continuing growth of global emissions. Significant warming could extend well beyond Marguerite Bay, hitting massive Alexander Island and reaching the base of the peninsula, at 74° S. Unlike the Palmer Station area, which has long been influenced by a more maritime climate, the southerly realms of the peninsula are truly polar and locked in ice year-round. That may change this century.

The British Antarctic Survey's David Vaughan, who often works out of the Rothera base, in Marguerite Bay, summed things up this way: "We really should be expecting some quite dramatic changes in the Antarctic Peninsula in the next fifty years."

WHAT WILL BE the fate of ice-dependent Adélie and emperor penguins as the world—and Antarctica—continues to warm? One thing seems virtually certain: Rising temperatures will not be a wash for Adélies and emperor penguins, with populations falling in one area—Palmer Station—while increasing in another, such as Avian Island. In fact, the most comprehensive study to date projects that if global temperatures rise by 2°C (3.6°F) above preindustrial levels—which seems almost certain to occur this century—the impact on Antarctica's two truly polar penguin species will be profound.

The goal of many climatologists and policy makers is to drastically cut greenhouse-gas emissions in the coming decades in order to hold temperature increases to 2°C. But as the first decade of the twenty-first century ended, and carbon dioxide emissions continued to soar, that looked like an increasingly elusive target. Atmospheric concentrations of carbon dioxide could well rise from roughly 390 parts per million today to 500 by the second half of the century, meaning temperatures will almost certainly jump by more than 2°C.

Even if humanity begins to significantly reduce greenhouse-gas emissions, the carbon dioxide that we have already pumped into the atmosphere will continue to elevate temperatures for as long as a thousand years, according to a recent study by the atmospheric chemist Susan Solomon and her colleagues. Not only do carbon dioxide and other greenhouse gases trap heat for centuries, but that atmospheric warmth is then transferred to the ocean, which will continue to radiate that heat back into the air for centuries more. These facts are not a signal to throw up one's hands in despair, Fraser says, but, rather, an impetus to slash emissions as much as possible and thereby moderate future warming. Otherwise, temperatures could easily increase 3°F to 7°F this century, which would not bode well for the ice-dependent creatures at the poles, including Adélie and emperor penguins.

David Ainley and two fellow scientists forecast the impact on polar penguins if global temperatures rise 3.6°F above preindustrial levels. They concluded that Adélie and emperor penguin colonies north of 70° S—comprising half of Antarctica's 348,000 pairs of emperor penguins and three-quarters of the continent's 2.5 million pairs of Adélies—"are in jeopardy of marked decline or disappearance, largely because of severe decreases in pack-ice coverage and, particularly for emperors, ice thickness."

The thinning of the sea ice poses a particular threat to emperors—the world's largest penguin, featured in the film *March of the Penguins*—because of their unique natural history of establishing colonies and incubating eggs on sea ice. "The trends of decreasing sea ice and colonies currently seen along the west coast of the Antarctic Peninsula thus would broaden in geographic extent," said Ainley's paper, funded by the National Science Foundation and the conservation group WWF. "It appears that by the time Earth's troposphere [lower atmosphere] reaches 2°C above preindustrial levels . . . we can expect major reductions and alterations in the abundance and distribution of pack-ice penguins."

This is a sober conclusion from a highly respected penguin scientist who has cautioned his colleagues not to focus solely on climate as the cause for shifting penguin populations. Ainley believes that fishing in the Southern Ocean—much of it illegal—has also had an impact on penguin populations in some regions by reducing prey species. Ainley conducts his studies in the Ross Sea, where Adélie penguin populations have been growing slightly in recent decades. He attributes this in large part to the impact of increasing winds around the continent, which have opened up more polynyas in the Ross Sea through which Adélies can forage.

When I asked Ainley if it would be "many, many centuries" before rising temperatures begin to affect sea ice—and therefore Adélie and emperor penguins—in frigid regions such as the Ross Sea, he replied, "Nope." He added that if temperatures increase 3°C (5.4°F) above preindustrial levels or even more, "the whole Southern Ocean system starts falling apart," with widespread loss of sea ice.

Ainley has another concern: If the Antarctic sea ice continues to withdraw southward, closer to the pole, Adélies may find themselves in regions well below the Antarctic Circle, with little winter light in which to forage. "The Adélie penguins are going to have to cope with the dark of winter," said Ainley, and, because they hunt by sight, "they don't cope with the dark very well."

THESE ARE THE issues that scientists who work at the poles are grappling with, forced, as they are, to come to terms with global warming far earlier than the rest of us. Few global-warming skeptics exist among the coterie of researchers who have witnessed firsthand the loss of sea ice, the retreat of glaciers, the melting of ice sheets, and the collapse of ice shelves in the Arctic and along the Antarctic Peninsula. Fraser often says that Palmer Station's Adélies are like the canaries in the coal mine, stating this with the conviction of someone who believes the rest of the world is paying scant attention to the portents he and others have seen in polar regions.

He also is unsettled by the realization that the long arm of man's industrial activity has reached all the way to the last, largely untouched corner of the planet.

"I have real affection for Adélies," said Fraser, "but everything seems to be working against them. Here you have this unbelievably tough little animal, able to deal with anything, succumbing to the large-scale effects of our activities. And that's the one thing they can't deal with, and they're dying because of it. And that's the sad side of that story for the Adélies. It's such a long-distance effect. The industrial nations to the north are having an impact that Adélies are being subjected to down here. That's what sort of pisses me off about the whole picture, that these incredible animals have to take it in the neck because a bunch of humans can't get together to decide what to do about the planet."

As we talked on Torgersen Island one afternoon, Fraser remarked that at least Adélie penguins live in an environment upon which man has scarcely impinged, and thus have a better chance of adapting as Antarctica warms. "But that's not the case for the rest of the planet, where we have already taken species in some ecosystems to the verge of extinction," he added. "You've got species clinging to mountaintops, species clinging to small freshwater lakes and deserts. Those species have no place to go. Their habitat has already been compromised by human activity. I think there's going to be bad news for many, many species."

Although Fraser and I talked frequently about many things, most were related to his work at Palmer Station. We seldom discussed larger issues of global warming. But that afternoon—standing on the quiet, nearly penguin-free south side of Torgersen Island—he spoke with emotion about his changing Antarctic backyard, and how it presages changes that are coming to all our beloved places.

"There is no question that the earth is warming and that the poles are very sensitive barometers of that warming," he said. "All you have to do is look back thirty years at what was here and see what is here now. To me this is foretelling the future across major parts of the planet. What we're looking at here is an entire ecosystem that is changing, and it's not changing in hundreds of years, which is what we used to be taught. It's changing in thirty to fifty years—it's changed so quickly that it has encompassed the research lives of a few people who have spent a lifetime here. No one would have ever believed thirty years ago that this sort of change would have occurred. But I do think that here we're looking at the future of large parts of the globe in terms of how ecosystems are going to change. So all those places we cherish are going to change. Some may change in positive ways. But I think the majority of them will be catastrophic changes unless we do something."

I LEFT PALMER Station shortly after ten A.M. on Sunday, March 12, aboard the *Laurence M. Gould*. It was a fitting Antarctic scene as the birding team departed, with winds gusting 20 to 25 miles per hour and a light snow falling. Hero Inlet, where the *Gould* had been tied up, was clogged with brash ice, but that did not deter eight hardy souls from clambering atop the rubber bumpers at the dock and jumping into the jade-colored waters that opened up in the wake of the *Gould*. Standing on the stern of the ship and watching my fellow station members dodge chunks of brash ice as they did cannonballs into the 33°F water, I found myself deeply moved, in large part because I knew I would almost certainly never again work in such a magical place with such a fine group of people.

The *Gould* steamed out of Arthur Harbor and passed Torgersen Island, where I caught my last glimpse of Palmer's Adélies—a few dozen stalwart, molting penguins standing on the island's east side. I watched as the station grew smaller, a cluster of inconsequential structures squatting on bare, charcoal-gray rock. The Marr Ice Piedmont rose above the station, its mass scalloped with fissures and tinged, in places, a light brown from glacial till.

Scheduled to pick up a small group of penguin researchers on Petermann Island, the *Gould* swung east into the Bismarck Strait, cruising parallel to the southern shore of Anvers Island. A southern giant petrel flew over the ship, heading south to foraging grounds, and a South Polar skua cut through the air on the high winds. Ahead lay the black, razorback peaks of the peninsular range, their sheer surfaces laced with ice and snow, their highest summits shrouded in clouds. Behind the range a faint streak of blue appeared, but otherwise everything in sight was shades of gray, black, and white. Even the sea had surrendered its blue color and assumed a flat gray hue.

The ship passed Shortcut, Christine, and Cormorant Islands, where we had spent many hours working with Adélie penguins and South Polar skuas. We traveled past the low, white domes of the Wauwermans Islands and then headed south into the Lemaire Channel, a narrow passage between Booth Island and the Antarctic Peninsula that is flanked by sheer mountains looming overhead. The Lemaire is one of the most breathtaking spots on the Antarctic Peninsula, but we encountered a ghostly scene, with clouds and fog drifting across the faces of the ice-encrusted mountains and car-sized icebergs—discharged by the ice ramps that spilled between the nearby peaks—bumping along in the channel. The mountains were covered in a layer of fresh snow that drifted gently down into the channel on puffs of wind. The scene was bleak yet beautiful, emblematic of what James Clark Ross called the "awful grandeur" of the continent. "To me those peaks always did and always will represent silent defiance," wrote Edgar Evans, a member of Scott's last expedition. "There were times when they made me shudder."

The stop at Petermann Island—the winter home of the French explorer Jean-Baptiste Charcot a century before—was brief. Leaving the island, we turned northwest and motored through French Passage. The wind picked up, stirring the surface of the sea with whitecaps, and snow began to fall once again, this time heavier than in the morning. On our starboard side, we passed small islands veiled in fog. I walked to the stern, gazed back at the peninsula, and took in a final view of Antarctica—a mosaic of dark mountain facades broken by massive streams of ice. Soon, the peaks dissolved in a blur of snowflakes and mist.

"There was great beauty here," Admiral Richard E. Byrd once wrote, "in the way that things which are also terrible can be beautiful."

WE CRUISED UP the peninsula in foul weather. The next day, with the sea churned by 35-mile-per-hour winds, we passed to the west of King

George Island and entered the Drake Passage in the afternoon. The air and sea temperature began to rise gradually, and sometime later that day or early the next we crossed the Antarctic Convergence. On Tuesday, March 14, with winds gusting to 58 miles per hour, the sun came out and I stood on deck for a very long time, watching fifteen-foot waves smash into the ship, propelling sheets of spray—shimmering with rainbows in the sunlight—the full length of the *Gould*. Black-and-white pintado petrels escorted us north, as did black-browed albatrosses, which rode the winds so close to the ship that I could clearly see their dark eyes. Toward evening, I donned rain gear and walked onto the stern of the *Gould*, awash with waves, to release a probe that would measure temperature and salinity as it dropped to the bottom of the Drake Passage. As I stood near the side of the boat, the waves loomed high overhead, their wind-whipped crests colored turquoise.

By the next day we had passed through the Drake and were in sight of the Isla de los Estados, off Tierra del Fuego. The air temperature hit 55°F and the sea 50°F as we sailed through the South Atlantic, the mountains of Tierra del Fuego on our port side. The following day we entered the Strait of Magellan under partly cloudy skies. I stood on the bow and, for the first time in nearly five months, felt real warmth in the air. Black-and-white Commerson's dolphins played in our wake, and Magellanic penguins bobbed on the water's surface like ducks. We passed isolated ranches and an oil refinery and gazed at a dun-colored shoreline broken by patches of green shrubs and stunted trees. There was an unaccustomed smell in the air—the scent of warm breezes blowing over earth.

"That was a wonderful day to all of us," Ernest Shackleton wrote in 1909 upon returning to New Zealand after his *Nimrod* expedition. "For over a year we had seen nothing but rocks, ice, snow, and sea. There had been no color and no softness in the scenery of the Antarctic; no green growth had gladdened our eyes, no musical notes of birds had come to our ears. We had had our work, but we had been cut off from most of the lesser things that go to make life worthwhile. No person who has not spent a period of his life in those 'stark and sullen solitudes that sentinel the Pole' will understand fully what trees and flowers, sun flecked turf and running streams mean to the soul of man."

We docked in Punta Arenas at 1:45 P.M. on March 16, under overcast skies. Creeping up the low ridges in front of us were houses with gaily colored roofs of red, blue, and green. I checked into my hotel and, opening the window, breathed in the smell of flowers and city life. Later, I sat for a while amid the trees and flowers of the town's picturesque central square, with its bronze statue of Magellan.

The birding team, Hugh Ducklow, and others from Palmer Station met that night for drinks and dinner. We consumed large quantities of pisco sours and wine and talked about the months in Antarctica. Everyone was thinking of home, and at one point Ducklow turned to Fraser and asked, "Do you have transition problems when you go home?"

"Well," replied Fraser, "I don't talk to anyone but Donna and Christopher for three weeks."

"I guess that's a yes," said Ducklow.

Within a day, the members of the birding team had said good-bye to each other and headed back to their separate lives. I soon understood what Fraser had meant about reentry into twenty-first-century American life. For the first several weeks at home, I did little but putter around my office, attend my daughters' sports games, prepare family dinners, and avoid most people. After many months at Palmer Station, I had grown accustomed to spending my days outdoors amid the seabirds, seals, rocks, sea, and ice. It was a rhythm I had come to love, and it took me a while to adjust to a world in which wilderness played little part and the horizon no longer seemed without limits.

Now, SEVERAL YEARS later, I sit behind my computer and watch images from Antarctica progress across the screen. The photographs, particularly from the early season, glow with a cool blue purity. There is something about snow and ice that brings comfort and joy to humans; it must have to do with the chasteness of the frozen world, a quality that pulls us out of our daily routine and transports us to a place that seems somehow better, or at least extraordinary.

The Antarctic Peninsula had that, of course, in abundance, and when I glance these days at my photographs, I am transported back to that world: penguins standing on two feet of snow as they prepare to construct their nests; the sea, frozen to the horizon; the soaring, glaciated peaks of the peninsular range; the great white mass of the Marr; the immense, tabular slabs of ice shelves that broke off many miles to the south and became embedded in the frozen ocean around Palmer Station.

The constant in all these photographs is ice—ice in all directions, in unfathomable quantities, lighting up this unearthly place.

ACKNOWLEDGMENTS

I AM DEEPLY grateful to Bill Fraser and his wife, Donna Patterson, for their generous cooperation during the six years that it has taken to bring this book to life. Not only did they answer countless questions and submit to lengthy interviews as I reported on their work and their lives, they also agreed to take me on as a member of their birding team and supported my application to live and work at Palmer Station under the auspices of the National Science Foundation. Without Bill and Donna's help, there would have been no book.

I am also indebted to the other members of Bill and Donna's birding team during the 2005–2006 field season, especially to team leader Peter Horne, who showed remarkable patience and good humor as he schooled me on everything from knot-tying to how to hold a penguin. I also want to thank the other team members—Jen Blum, Kristen Gorman, and Brett Pickering—for their kindness and forbearance. It was a true pleasure to spend months in the field with this group of young scientists.

Hugh Ducklow, the head of the Palmer Long Term Ecological Research (LTER) project, also played a key role in helping me write this book. I am extremely thankful to Hugh for sharing his knowledge of the rapidly changing environment along the western Antarctic Peninsula, and especially for reading the manuscript and offering numerous suggestions as to how it could be improved.

Thanks also to LTER members Doug Martinson of Columbia University's Lamont Doherty Earth Observatory and to Sharon Stammerjohn of the University of California, Santa Cruz, for their extensive interviews and for reading portions of the manuscript. I also want to thank other scientists who worked at Palmer Station, including Langdon Quetin, Robin Ross, Tad Day, Wally Ruhland, and Maria Vernet. In addition, I am grateful to Robert Bindschadler of the Goddard Space Flight Center and Ted Scambos of the National Snow and Ice Data Center for speaking with me and for reviewing portions of the manuscript.

Palmer Station is an unusually collegial place to work, and I am grateful to many people there. At the top of the list are the station managers during my stay, Bob Farrell and Joe Petit, who did so much to make me feel welcome at their Antarctic outpost. I am also very grateful to science technician Glenn Grant for his help with research, computer experts Curt Smith and Sarah Kaye for patiently answering my many questions, laboratory supervisor Cara Sucher for help with scientific inquiries, and boating coordinator Toby Koffman. And I want to thank the station's wonderful chefs—Wendy Beeler, Marge Bolton, and Susan Novak—for their delicious cooking, which did so much to keep morale high.

Special thanks also to George Westby, for taking the author photo for this book, and to David Huang, for allowing me to use his Palmer Station videos on the book's Web site.

Two organizations were instrumental in the making of this book. The first is the National Science Foundation, which I would like to thank for selecting me to participate in their Antarctic Artists and Writers Program, under which I was able to live and work at Palmer Station for nearly five months. I particularly want to thank Kim Silverman of the

Artists and Writers Program, as well as Polly Penhale and Dave Bresnehan for their support.

In addition, I am extremely grateful to the John Simon Guggenheim Memorial Foundation, whose generous grant upon my return from Antarctica enabled me to spend many months doing research for the book.

I also want to thank David Remnick and the editors at the *New Yorker* who did a superb job of adapting the book for the magazine. David has been a loyal friend and supporter for many years, and his enthusiastic response to the manuscript was a great boost at a time when I wondered if the book was ever going to be completed. He offered excellent editing suggestions that gave me the impetus to cut the manuscript down to size. Katherine Stirling did a masterful job of culling the book for material for the excerpt and worked patiently with me on the article. I am also grateful to Dorothy Wickenden and Daniel Zalewski for their seamless editing. Thanks also to Siobhan Devine for her diligent fact-checking.

Many thanks also to Oliver Payne and Bob Poole of *National Geographic* magazine for giving me the assignments that led to this book.

I would like to warmly thank my friend Dominique Browning, who read the manuscript in its early stages and offered many good suggestions about how it could be improved. Thanks also to Steve Rifkin and Michelle Buhler for their help with the cover design. Many thanks, as well, to Nicole Browning, Buzz Bissinger, and Lisa Smith for their friendship and support.

At Yale University, I am indebted to my colleagues at the online magazine *Yale Environment 360*. Most of all I would like to thank Roger Cohn, who waited patiently as work on the book ran far behind schedule. I also want to thank Ted O'Callahan for his research assistance at various Yale libraries and Kevin Dennehy for his advice on promoting the book online.

I am profoundly grateful to my editor at Henry Holt, Jack Macrae, for his patience, superb editorial advice, and unflagging support and good cheer. Jack's knowledge, skill, and passion are unparalleled in the publishing world, and it has been an honor to do this book with him. I also want to thank his assistants, Kirsten Reach and Supurna Banerjee, for their hard work. Many thanks, also, to Bonnie Thompson for her excellent copy editing, and to Lisa Fyfe and Rebecca Seltzer for their skill and patience as we worked on the jacket design.

I also want to thank Michael Carlisle for finding a home for this book at Henry Holt, and Alice Martell for all her support and hard work as the book made its way into print.

While I was at Palmer Station, my sister-in-law, Constance Laibe Hays, died after a long struggle with cancer. Connie was a loving—and much beloved—mother, wife, and daughter. She was also a fine journalist and author. She has been sorely missed by her large family and her many friends.

Finally, I want to thank my wife, Laurie Hays, and our daughters, Claire and Nuni, for their love and support. Five months in Antarctica was a long time to be away, but that separation was followed by several years in which I spent countless weekends working on this book. I am so grateful to Claire and Nuni for their understanding. My debt to Laurie—for her love, her patience, her thoughtful critique of the manuscript, and her tireless efforts to support the family while I plunged deeper into this project—is immense. The heart of this family, she has somehow managed to do it all.

BIBLIOGRAPHY

Ainley, David G. *The Adélie Penguin: Bellweather of Climate Change*. New York: Columbia University Press, 2002.

Ainley, David G., et al. *Breeding Biology of the Adélie Penguin*. Berkeley and Los Angeles, California: University of California Press, 1983.

———. "Adélie Penguins and Environmental Change." *Science* 300, no. 5618 (2003): 429–30.

———. "Competition Among Penguins and Cetaceans Reveals Trophic Cascades in the Western Ross Sea, Antarctica." *Ecology* 87, no. 8 (2006): 2080–93.

———. "Paradigm Lost, or Is Top-down Forcing No Longer Significant in the Antarctic Marine Ecosystem?" *Antarctic Science* 19, no. 3 (2007): 283–90.

———. "The Fate of Antarctic Penguins When Earth's Tropospheric Temperature Reaches 2°C Above Pre-Industrial Levels." http://assets.panda.org/downloads/wwf_climate_penguins_final.pdf (Accessed 2008).

Alexander, Caroline. *The Endurance: Shackleton's Legendary Antarctic Expedition*. New York: Alfred A. Knopf, 1999.

Allen, K. Radway, et al. *Antarctica: Great Stories from the Frozen Continent.* Sydney: Reader's Digest, 1985.

Alley, Richard B. *The Two-Mile Time Machine.* Princeton, NJ: Princeton University Press, 2000.

Alley, Richard B., et al. "Ice-Sheet and Sea-Level Changes." *Science* 310 (2005): 456–60.

Amundsen, Roald. *Roald Amundsen's* Belgica *Diary.* Edited by Hugo Decleir. Bluntisham, UK: Bluntisham Books / Erskine Press, 1999.

Arctowski, Henryk. "The Antarctic Voyage of the *Belgica* During the Years 1897, 1898, and 1899." *Geographical Journal* 18, no. 4 (1901): 377–88.

Atkinson, Angus, et al. "Long-term Decline in Krill Stock and Increase in Salps Within the Southern Ocean." *Nature* 432 (2004): 100–103.

Austin, Oliver L. *Antarctic Bird Studies.* Washington, DC: American Geophysical Union, 1968.

Bagshawe, Thomas Wyatt. *Two Men in the Antarctic: An Expedition to Graham Land: 1920–1922.* New York: The Macmillan Company, 1939.

———. "Notes on the Habits of the Gentoo and Ringed or Antarctic Penguins." *Transactions of the Zoological Society of London* 24, part 3, no. 1 (1938): 185–291.

Barbraud, Cristophe, and Henri Wiemerskirch. "Emperor Penguins and Climate Change." *Nature* 411 (2001): 183–86.

Baughman, T. H. *Before the Heroes Came: Antarctica in the 1890s.* Lincoln and London: University of Nebraska Press, 1994.

Begley, Sharon. "For Family Survival, Penguins Play a Game of 'Name That Tune.'" *Wall Street Journal*, September 9, 2005.

Bellingshausen, Thaddeus. *The Voyage of Captain Bellingshausen to the Antarctic Seas, 1819–1821.* Volumes 1 and 2. Edited by Frank Debenham. London: The Hakluyt Society, 1945.

Bindschadler, Robert. "Future of the West Antarctic Ice Sheet." *Science* 282 (1998): 428–29.

Bowen, Mark. *Thin Ice: Unlocking the Secrets of Climate in the World's Highest Mountains.* New York: Henry Holt and Company, 2005.

Brandt, Anthony, ed. *The South Pole: A Historical Reader.* Washington, DC: National Geographic Adventure Classics, 2004.

British Antarctic Survey. "Antarctic Tragedy." Press Release, July 23, 2003.

Byrd, Richard E. *Alone.* Washington, DC: Island Press / Shearwater Books, 2003.

Cameron, Ian. *Antarctica: The Last Continent.* Boston: Little, Brown and Company, 1974.

Campbell, David G. *The Crystal Desert: Summers in Antarctica.* Boston: Houghton Mifflin Company, 1992.

Carrick, Robert, et al., eds. *Biologie Antarctique.* Paris: Hermann, 1964.

Chapman, Walker. *The Loneliest Continent: The Story of Antarctic Discovery.* Greenwich, CT: New York Graphic Society Publishers Ltd., 1964.

Charcot, Jean-Baptiste. *Towards the South Pole Aboard the Français: The First French Expedition to the Antarctic, 1903–1905.* Norwich and Bluntisham, UK: The Erskine Press / Bluntisham Press, 2004.

Charcot, Jean. *The Voyage of the "Pourquoi Pas": The Journal of the Second French South Polar Expedition, 1908–1910.* Hamden, CT: Archon Books, 1978.

Cherry-Garrard, Apsley. *The Worst Journey in the World.* New York: Carroll and Graf Publishers, 2003.

Clarke, Andrew, et al. "Introduction: Antarctic Ecology from Genes to Ecosystems. The Impact of Climate Change and the Importance of Scale." *Philosophical Transactions of the Royal Society: Biological Sciences* 362 (2006): 5–9.

———. "Climate Change and the Marine Ecosystem of the Western Antarctic Peninsula." *Philosophical Transactions of the Royal Society: Biological Sciences* 362 (2007): 149–66.

Collier, Graham. *Antarctic Odyssey: In the Footsteps of the South Polar Explorers.* New York: Carroll and Graf Publishers, 1999.

Cook, A. J., et al. "Retreating Glacier Fronts on the Antarctic Peninsula over the Past Half Century." *Science* 308 (2005): 541–44.

Cook, Frederick A. *Through the First Antarctic Night: 1898–1899.* Pittsburgh: Polar Publishing Company, 1998.

Cook, James. *A Voyage Towards the South Pole and Round the World.* Volumes 1 and 2. London: BiblioBazaar, 2007.

Crawford, Richard D. "Non-Breeding Adélie Penguins Feeding Chicks." *Notornis* 21, no. 4 (1974): 381–82.

Croxall, J. P., et al. "Southern Ocean Environmental Changes: Effects on Seabird, Seal and Whale Populations." *Philosophical Transactions of the Royal Society: Biological Sciences* 338 (1992): 319–28.

———. "Environmental Change and Antarctic Seabird Populations. *Science* 297, no. 5586 (2002): 1510–14.

Davis, Lloyd Spencer. *A Season in the Life of the Adélie Penguin.* San Diego: Harcourt Brace and Company, 1994.

Davis, Lloyd Spencer, and Martin Renner. *Penguins.* New Haven, CT: Yale University Press, 2003.

Davis, Lloyd S., et al. "Satellite Telemetry of the Winter Migration of Adélie Penguins (*Pygoscelis adeliae*). *Polar Biology* 16 (1996): 221–25.

Dawson, Elliot W. "Adélie Penguins and Leopard Seals: Illustrations of Predation—History, Legend, and Fact." *Notornis* 21 (1974): 36–69.

De Angeles, Hernán, and Pedro Skvarca. "Glacial Surge After Ice Shelf Collapse." *Science* 299 (2003): 1560–62.

Debenham, Frank. *Antarctica: The Story of a Continent.* New York: The Macmillan Company, 1961.

Decleir, Hugo, and Claude De Broyer, eds. *The* Belgica *Expedition Centennial: Perspectives on Antarctic Science and History.* Brussels: Brussels University Press, 2001.

De Gerlache, Adrien. *Fifteen Months in the Antarctic.* Banham, Norfolk: The Erskine Press, 1998.

Delaca, T. E., et al. "Encounters with Leopard Seals (*Hydrurga leptonyx*) Along the Antarctic Peninsula." *Antarctic Journal* 9, no. 3 (1975): 85–91.

di Prisco, Guido, E. Pisano, and A. Clarke. *Fishes of Antarctica: A Biological Overview.* Milan: Springer-Verlag, 1998.

Domack, Eugene, et al., eds. *Antarctic Peninsula Climate Variability: Historical and Paleoenvironmental Perspectives.* Antarctic Research Series 79. Washington, DC: American Geophysical Union, 2003.

———. "Stability of the Larsen B Ice Shelf on the Antarctic Peninsula During the Holocene Epoch." *Nature* 436 (2005): 681–85.

Doyle, Alister. "Rain Speeds Antarctic Peninsula Glacier Melt." Reuters, January 16, 2009.

Ducklow, Hugh, et al. "Marine Pelagic Ecosystems: The West Antarctic Peninsula." *Philosophical Transactions of the Royal Society: Biological Sciences* 362 (2007): 67–94.

Dufek, George J. *Operation Deepfreeze.* New York: Harcourt Brace and Company, 1957.

Eastman, Joseph T. *Antarctic Fish Biology: Evolution in a Unique Environment.* San Diego: Academic Press, Inc., 1993.

Fahnestock, Mark. "An Ice Shelf Breakup." *Science* 271 (1996): 775–76.

Emlen, J. T., and R. L. Penney. "Distance Navigation in the Adélie Penguin." *The Ibis* 106, no. 4 (1964): 417–31.

———. "The Navigation of Penguins." *Scientific American* 215, no. 4 (1966): 105–114.

Emslie, Steven D. "Radiocarbon Dates from Abandoned Penguin Colonies in the Antarctic Peninsula Region." *Antarctic Science* 13, no. 3 (2001): 289–95.

Emslie, Steven D., and Jennifer D. McDaniel. "Adélie Penguin Diet and Climate Change During the Middle to Late Holocene in Northern Marguerite Bay, Antarctic Peninsula." *Polar Biology* 25 (2002): 222–29.

Emslie, Steven D., et al. "Abandoned Penguin Colonies and Environmental Change in the Palmer Station Area, Anvers Island, Antarctic Peninsula." *Antarctic Science* 70, no. 3 (1998): 257–68.

———. "A 45,000-year Record of Adélie Penguins and Climate Change in the Ross Sea, Antarctica." *Geology* 35, no. 1 (2007): 61–64.

Eppley, Zoe A., and Margaret A. Rubega. "Indirect Effects of an Oil Spill: Reproductive Failure in a Population of South Polar Skuas Following the *Bahia
Paraiso* Oil Spill in Antarctica." *Marine Ecology Progress Series* 67 (1990):
1–6.

Ferrigno, Jane G., et al. *Coastal-change and Glaciological Map of the Palmer Land
Area, Antarctica: 1947–2009*. U.S. Geological Survey Geologic Investigations
Series Map I–2600–C, 2009.

———. *Coastal-change and Glaciological Map of the Larsen Ice Shelf Area, Antarctica: 1940–2005*. U.S. Geological Survey Geologic Investigations Series
Map I–2600–B, 2008.

Flegg, Jim, with Eric and David Hosking. *Poles Apart: The Natural Worlds of the
Arctic and Antarctic*. London: Pelham Books / Stephen Greene Press, 1990.

Fox, Adrian J., and David G. Vaughan. "The Retreat of the Jones Ice Shelf, Antarctic Peninsula." *Journal of Glaciology* 41, no. 175 (2005): 555–60.

Fraser, William R. *Aspects of the Ecology of Kelp Gulls* (Larus dominicanus) *on
Anvers Island, Antarctic Peninsula*. PhD thesis, University of Minnesota, 1989.

Fraser, William R., and Eileen E. Hoffmann. "A Predator's Perspective on Causal
Links Between Climate Change, Physical Forcing and Ecosystem Response."
Marine Ecology Progress Series 265 (2003): 1–15.

Fraser, William R., and Donna L. Patterson. "Human Disturbance and Long-term
Changes in Adélie Penguin Populations: A Natural Experiment at Palmer Sta-
tion, Antarctic Peninsula." In *Antarctic Communities: Species, Structure and
Survival*, edited by B. Battaglia, 445–52. Cambridge: Cambridge University
Press, 1997.

Fraser, William R., and Wayne Z. Trivelpiece. "Factors Controlling the Distribution of Seabirds: Winter-Summer Heterogeneity in the Distribution of Adélie
Penguin Populations." *Antarctic Research Series* 70 (1996): 257–72.

Fraser, William R., et al. "Increases in Antarctic Penguin Populations: Reduced
Competition with Whales or a Loss of Sea Ice Due to Environmental Warming?" *Polar Biology* 11 (1992): 525–31.

———. "Using Kite-based Aerial Photography for Conducting Adélie Penguin
Censuses in Antarctica." *Waterbirds* 22, no. 3 (1999): 435–40.

Geisz, Heidi N., et al. "Melting Glaciers: A Probable Source of DDT to the Antarctic Marine Ecosystem." *Environmental Science & Technology* 42, no. 11
(2008): 3958–962.

Gorman, James. *Ocean Enough and Time: Discovering the Waters Around Antarctica*. New York: HarperCollins Publishers, 1995.

———. *The Total Penguin*. New York: Prentice Hall Press, 1990.

Greenland, D., et al. *Climate Variability and Ecosystem Response at Long-Term
Ecological Research Sites*. New York: Oxford University Press, 2003.

Grikurov, G. E. *Geology of the Antarctic Peninsula.* Moscow: Nauka Publishers, 1973.

Gurney, Alan. *Below the Convergence: Voyages Toward Antarctica 1699–1839.* New York: W. W. Norton Company, 1997.

——. *The Race to the White Continent: Voyages to the Antarctic.* New York: W. W. Norton Company, 2000.

Hansen, James, et al. "Global Temperature Change." *Proceedings of the National Academy of Sciences* 103. no. 39 (2006): 14, 288, 293.

Hansen, J., et al. "Dangerous Human-made Interference With Climate." *Atmospheric Chemistry and Physics* 7 (2007): 2287–2312.

Heacox, Kim. *Antarctica: The Last Continent.* Washington, DC: National Geographic Society, 1998.

——. "A Brutal Reputation." *National Geographic.* November 2006: 72–73.

Henry, Thomas R. *The White Continent: The Story of Antarctica.* New York: William Sloane Associates, 1950.

Herbert, Wally. *A World of Men: Exploration in Antarctica.* New York: G. P. Putnam's Sons, 1969.

Horwitz, Tony. *Blue Latitudes: Boldly Going Where Captain Cook Has Gone Before.* New York: Henry Holt and Company, 2002.

Hosking, Eric, with Bryan Sage. *Antarctic Wildlife.* New York: Facts on File, Inc., 1982.

Hulbe, Christina. "How Ice Sheets Flow." *Science* 294 (2001): 2300–01, 2001.

Jenouvrier, Stéphanie, et al. "Demographic Models and IPCC Climate Projections Predict the Decline of an Emperor Penguin Population." *Proceedings of the National Academy of Science* 106 (2009): 1844–47.

Jouventin, Pierre. *Visual and Vocal Signals in Penguins, Their Evolution and Adaptive Characters.* Berlin: Verlag Paul Parey, 1982.

Kennett, J. P., et al. "Development of the Circum-Antarctic Current." *Science* 186, no. 4159 (1974): 144–7.

Landis, Marilyn J. *Antarctica: Exploring the Extreme.* Chicago: Chicago Review Press, 2001.

Lansing, Alfred. *Endurance: Shackleton's Incredible Voyage.* New York: Carroll and Graf Publishers, 1986.

Laseron, Charles, and Frank Hurley. *Antarctic Eyewitness.* Sydney: Angus & Robertson / HarperCollins, 1999.

Lee, Charles. *Snow, Ice and Penguins: A Cavalcade of Antarctic Adventures.* New York: Dodd, Mead and Company, 1950.

Levick, G. Murray. *Antarctic Penguins: A Study of Their Social Habits.* London: William Heinemann, 1914.

Lewis, Richard S. *A Continent for Science: The Antarctic Adventure.* New York: The Viking Press, 1965.

Linden, Eugene. *The Winds of Change: Climate, Weather, and the Destruction of Civilization.* New York: Simon and Schuster, 2006.

Loeb, V., et al. "Effects of Sea-ice Extent and Krill or Salp Dominance on the Antarctic Food Web." *Nature* 387 (1997): 897–900.

Luthi, Dieter, et al. "High-Resolution Carbon Dioxide Concentration Record 650,000–800,000 Years Before Present." *Nature* 453 (2008): 379–82.

Lynch, Wayne. *Penguins of the World.* Buffalo, NY: Firefly Books, 1997.

Marret, Mario. *Antarctic Venture: Seven Men Amongst the Penguins.* London: William Kimber, 1955.

Martinson, Douglas G., et al. "Western Antarctic Peninsula Physical Oceanography and Spatio-Temporal Variability." *Deep Sea Research II* 55 (2008): 1964–87.

Massom, Robert A., et al. "Extreme Anomalous Atmospheric Circulation in the West Antarctic Peninsula Region in Austral Spring and Summer 2001/02, and Its Profound Impact on Sea Ice and Biota." *Journal of Climate* 19 (2006): 3544–71.

———. "West Antarctic Peninsula Sea Ice in 2005: Extreme Ice Compaction and Ice Edge Retreat Due to Strong Anomaly with Respect to Climate." *Journal of Geophysical Research* 113 (2008): 1–23.

Mathews, Eleanor. *Ambassador to the Penguins: A Naturalist's Year Aboard a Yankee Whaleship.* Boston: David R. Godine, 2003.

Matthews, L. Harrison. *Penguins, Whalers, and Sealers: A Voyage of Discovery.* New York: Universe Books, 1978.

Matthiessen, Peter. *End of the Earth: Voyages to Antarctica.* Washington, DC: National Geographic Society, 2003.

McClintock, James, et al. "Ecological Responses to Climate Change on the Antarctic Peninsula." *American Scientist* 96 (2008): 302–10.

McGonigal, David, and Lynn Woodworth. *Antarctica: The Blue Continent.* Buffalo, NY: Firefly Books, 2003.

Mercer, J. H. "West Antarctic Ice Sheet and CO2 Greenhouse Effect: A Threat of Disaster." *Nature* 271: 321–25, 1978.

Miller, Jonathan. "March of the Conservative Penguin Film as Political Fodder." *New York Times,* September 13, 2005.

Miller, Richard Gordon. *History and Atlas of the Fishes of the Antarctic Ocean.* Carson City, Nevada: Foresta Institute for Ocean and Mountain Studies, 1993.

Mitrovica, Jerry X., et al. "The Sea-Level Fingerprint of West Antarctic Ice Collapse." *Science* 323 (2009): 753–55.

Mitterling, Philip I. *America in the Antarctic to 1840.* Urbana: University of Illinois Press, 1959.

Montes-Hugo, et al. "Recent Changes in Phytoplankton Communities Associated with Rapid Regional Climate Change Along the Western Antarctic Peninsula." *Science* 323 (2009): 1470–73.

Murphy, Robert Cushman. *Logbook for Grace.* Chicago: Time-Life Books, Inc., 1982.

———. *Oceanic Birds of South America,* Volumes 1 and 2. New York: The American Museum of Natural History, 1936.

Naveen, Ron. *Learning to Fly.* New York: Quill, William Morrow, 1999.

———. *The Oceanites Site Guide to the Antarctic Peninsula.* Chevy Chase, MD: Oceanites, Inc., 2005.

Naveen, Ron, with Colin Monteath, Tui de Roy, and Mark Jones. *Wild Ice.* Washington, DC: Smithsonian Institution Press, 1990.

Neider, Charles, ed. *Antarctica.* New York: Random House, 1972.

———. *Beyond Cape Horn: Travels in the Antarctic.* San Francisco: Sierra Club Books, 1980.

Nicklen, Paul. "Deadly Beauty." *National Geographic,* November 2006: 68–91.

Nordenskjold, Otto, and Joh. Gunnar Anderson. *Antarctica, or Two Years Amongst the Ice of the South Pole.* Hamden, CT: Archon Books, 1977.

Oulié, Martha. *Charcot of the Antarctic.* New York: E. P. Dutton and Company Inc., 1939.

Parfet, Michael. *South Light: A Journey to the Last Continent.* New York: Macmillan Publishing Company, 1985.

Parmelee, David Freeland. *Antarctic Birds: Ecological and Behavioral Approaches.* Minneapolis: University of Minnesota Press, 1992.

———. "Banded South Polar Skua Found in Greenland." *Antarctic Journal of the United States* 3, no. 2 (1976): 11.

Parmelee, David Freeland, and J. M. Parmelee. "Revised Penguin Numbers and Distribution for Anvers Island, Antarctica." *British Antarctic Survey Bulletin* no. 76 (1987): 65–73.

Parmesan, Camille, and Gary Yohe. "A Globally Coherent Fingerprint of Climate Change Impacts Across Natural Systems." *Nature* 421 (2003): 37–42.

Patterson, Donna L., et al. "The Effects of Human Activity and Environmental Variability on Long-term Changes in Adélie Penguin Populations at Palmer Station Antarctica." In *Antarctic Biology in a Global Context.* Edited by Huiskes, A. H. L., et al., 301–7. Leiden, the Netherlands: Backhuys Publishers, 2003.

Penney, Richard L. *Territorial Behavior and Social Interactions by the Adélie Penguin.* PhD thesis, Madison: University of Wisconsin, 1964.

———. "Territorial and Social Behavior in the Adélie Penguin." In *Antarctic Bird Studies.* Washington, DC: American Geophysical Union, 1968.

———. "Molt in the Adélie Penguin." *The Auk* 84 (1967): 61–71.

———. "Some Practical Aspects of Penguin Navigation-Orientation Studies. *Bioscience* April (1965): 268–70.

Penney, Richard L., and J. T. Emlen. "Further Experiments on Distance Navigation in the Adélie Penguin." *Pygoscelis adeliae. Ibis* 109 (1976): 99–109.

Penney, Richard L., and George Lowry. "Leopard Seal Predation of Adélie Penguins." *Ecology* 48, no. 5 (1967): 878–82.

Peterson, Roger Tory. *Penguins.* Boston: Houghton Mifflin Company, 1979.

Petit, J. R., et al. "Climate and Atmospheric History of the Past 420,000 Years from the Vostok Ice Core, Antarctica." *Nature* 399 (1999): 429–36.

Philbrick, Nathaniel. *Sea of Glory. America's Voyage of Discovery, the U.S. Exploring Expedition.* New York: Penguin Books, 2003.

Phillips, R. A., et al. "Movements, Winter Distribution and Activity Patterns of Falkland and Brown Skuas: Insights from Loggers and Isotopes." *Marine Ecology Progress Series* 345 (2007): 281–91.

Pietz, Pamela Jo. *Aspects of the Behavioral Ecology of Sympatric South Polar and Brown Skuas Near Palmer Station, Antarctica.* PhD thesis, Minneapolis: University of Minnesota, 1984.

Poncet, S., and J. Poncet. "Censuses of Penguin Populations of the Antarctic Peninsula." *British Antarctic Survey Bulletin* no. 77 (1987): 109–29.

Ponting, Herbert G. *The Great White South.* New York: Cooper Square Press, 2001.

Porter, Eliot. *Antarctica.* New York: E. P. Dutton, 1978.

Preston, Diana. *A First Rate Tragedy: Robert Falcon Scott and the Race to the South Pole.* Boston: Houghton Mifflin Company, 1997.

Pyne, Stephen J. *The Ice: A Journey to Antarctica.* Iowa City: University of Iowa Press, 1986.

Quetin, Langdon B. and Robin M. Ross. "Episodic Recruitment in Antarctic Krill *Euphausia superba* in the Palmer LTER Study Region." *Marine Ecology Progress Series* 259 (2003): 185–200.

Quigg, Philip W. *A Pole Apart: The Emerging Issue of Antarctica.* New York: McGraw-Hill Book Company, 1983.

Reeves, Randall R., Brent S. Stewart, and Stephen Leatherwood. *The Sierra Club Handbook of Seals and Sirenians.* San Francisco: Sierra Club Books, 1992.

Reilly, Pauline. *Penguins of the World.* Oxford: Oxford University Press, 1994.

Rignot, E. J. "Fast Recession of a West Antarctic Glacier." *Science* 281 (1998): 449–51.

Rignot, Eric, and Stanly S. Jacobs. "Rapid Bottom Melting Widespread Near Antarctic Ice Sheet Grounding Lines." *Science* 296 (2002): 2020–23.

Rignot, Eric, and Robert H. Thomas. "Mass Balance of Polar Ice Sheets." *Science* 297 (2002): 1502–6.

Root, Terry L., et al. "Fingerprints of Global Warming on Wild Animals and Plants." *Nature* 421 (2003): 57–60.

Rosove, Michael H. *Let Heroes Speak: Antarctic Explorers.* New York: Berkley Books, 2002.

Ross, Robin M., Eileen E. Hofmann, and Langdon B. Quetin, eds. *Foundations for Ecological Research West of the Antarctic Peninsula*. Antarctic Research Series 70. Washington, DC: American Geophysical Union, 1996.

Rymill, John. *Southern Lights: The Official Account of the British Graham Land Expedition, 1934–1937*. London: The Travel Book Club, 1939.

Salihoglu, Boris, et al. "Factors Affecting Fledging Weight of Adélie Penguin (*Pygoscelis adeliae*) Chicks: A Modeling Study." *Polar Biology* 24 (2001): 328–37.

Scambos, et al. "The Link Between Climate Warming and Break-Up of Ice Shelves in the Antarctic Peninsula." *Journal of Glaciology* 46, no. 154 (2000): 516–30.

———. "Glacier Acceleration and Thinning After the Ice Shelf Collapse in the Larsen B Embayment in Antarctica." *Geophysical Research Letters* 31 (2004): L18402.1–L18402.4.

Schafer, Kevin. *Penguin Planet: Their World, Our World*. Minnetonka, MN: NorthWord Press, 2000.

Scher, Howie D., et al. "Timing and Climatic Consequences of the Opening of the Drake Passage." *Science* 312 (2006): 428–30.

Scott, R. F. *Scott's Last Expedition*. New York: Dodd, Mead and Company, 1913.

Shackleton, Ernest. *The Heart of the Antarctic: The Farthest South Expedition, 1907–1909*. New York: Signet, 2000.

———. *South: The Endurance Expedition*. New York: Signet, 1999.

Shepherd, Andrew, et al. "Inland Thinning of Pine Island Glacier, West Antarctica." *Science* 291, no. 5505 (2001): 862–64.

Shepherd, Andrew, and Duncan Wingham. "Recent Sea Level Contributions of the Antarctic and Greenland Ice Sheets." *Science* 315 (2007): 1529–32.

Shirihai, Hadoram. *A Complete Guide to Antarctic Wildlife*. Degerby, Finland: Alula Press, 2002.

Simpson, George Gaylord. *Penguins: Past and Present, Here and There*. New Haven, CT: Yale University Press, 1976.

Sladen, William J. L. *The Pygoscelid Penguins*. Falkland Islands Dependencies Survey Scientific Reports, No. 17. London: 1958.

———. "Ornithological Research in Antarctica." *BioScience* April 1965: 264–68.

Smith, Raymond C., et al. "The Palmer LTER: A Long-Term Ecological Research Program at Palmer Station, Antarctica." *Oceanography* 8, no. 3 (1995): 77–86.

———. "Marine Ecosystem Sensitivity to Climate Change." *BioScience* 49, no. 5 (1999): 393–404.

———. "Palmer Long-Term Ecological Research on the Antarctic Marine Ecosystem." *Antarctic Research Series* 79 (2003): 1–11.

Solomon, Susan. *The Coldest March: Scott's Fatal Antarctic Expedition*. New Haven, CT: Yale University Press, 2001.

Solomon, Susan, et al. "Irreversible Climate Change Due to Carbon Dioxide Emissions." *Proceedings of the Natural Academy of Sciences* 106 (2009): 1704–1709.

Soper, Tony. *Antarctica: A Guide to the Wildlife.* Guilford, CT: The Globe Pequot Press, 2004.

Sparks, John, and Tony Soper. *Penguins.* New York and Oxford: Facts on File Publications, 1987.

Spears, John R. *Captain Nathaniel Brown Palmer: An Old Time Sailor of the Sea.* Stonington, CT: The Stonington Historical Society, 1996.

Speirs, Elizabeth A. H., and Lloyd S. Davis. "Discrimination by Adélie Penguins, *Pygoscelis adeliae*, Between the Loud Mutual Call of Mates, Neighbours and Strangers." *Animal Behavior* 41 (1991): 937–44.

Spufford, Francis. *I May Be Some Time: Ice and the English Imagination.* New York: St. Martin's Press, 1997.

Stammerjohn, S. E., et al. "Ice-Atmosphere Interactions During Sea Ice Advance and Retreat in the Western Antarctic Peninsula Region." *Journal of Geophysical Research* 108 (2003): 3329–44.

———. "Trends in Antarctic Annual Sea Ice Retreat and Advance and Their Relation to El Nino—Southern Oscillation and Southern Annular Mode Variability." *Journal of Geophysical Research* 113 (2007).

———. "Sea Ice in the Western Antarctic Peninsula Region: Spatio-Temporal Variability from Ecological and Climate Change Perspectives." *Deep Sea Research Part II: Topical Studies in Oceanography* 55, no. 18–19 (2008): 2041–58.

Steig, Eric J., et al. "Warming of the Antarctic Ice-Sheet Surface Since the 1957 Geophysical Year." *Nature* 457 (2009): 459–62.

Stone, Gregory. *Ice Island: Expedition to Antarctica's Largest Iceberg.* Boston: New England Aquarium Press, 2003.

Stonehouse, Bernard. *Penguins.* London: Arthur Barker Limited, 1968.

———. *Animals of the Antarctic: The Ecology of the Far South.* New York: Holt, Rinehart and Wilson, 1972.

Stonehouse, B., ed. *Encyclopedia of Antarctica and the Southern Oceans.* Chichester, England: John Wiley and Sons, Ltd., 2002.

Thomas, R., et al. "Accelerated Sea-level Rise from West Antarctica." *Science* 306 (2004): 255–8.

Thomas, Elizabeth R., et al. "A Doubling in Snow Accumulation in the Western Antarctic Peninsula since 1850." *Geophysical Research Letters* 35, L01706.

Thompson, David W. J., and Susan Solomon. "Interpretation of Recent Southern Hemisphere Climate Change." *Science* 296 (2002): 895–9.

Trewby, Mary, ed. 2002. *Antarctica: An Encyclopedia from Abbott Ice Shelf to Zooplankton.* Buffalo, NY: Firefly Books, 2002.

Tripati, Aradhna, et al. "Coupling of CO2 and Ice Sheet Stability Over Major Climate Transitions of the Last 20 Million Years." *Science* 326, no. 5958 (2009): 1394–97.

Trivelpiece, Wayne Zebulon. *Ecological Studies of Pygoscelid Penguins and Antarctic Skuas.* PhD thesis, Syracuse: State University of New York, 1981.

Trivelpiece, Wayne Z., et al. "Ecological Segregation of Adélie, Gentoo, and Chinstrap Penguins at King George Island, Antarctica." *Ecology* 68, no. 2 (1987): 351–61.

———. "Adélie and Chinstrap Penguins: Their Potential as Monitors of the Southern Ocean Marine Ecosystem." In *Antarctic Ecosystems: Ecological Change and Conservation.* Berlin: Springer-Verlag, 1990.

Turner, J., et al. "Significant Warming of the Antarctic Winter Troposphere." *Science* 311 (2006): 1914–7.

Turner, John, et al. *Climate Change and the Antarctic Environment.* Cambridge, England: Scientific Committee on Antarctic Research, 2009.

Van Der Does, Willem. *Storms, Ice, and Whales: The Antarctic Adventures of a Dutch Artist on a Norwegian Whaler.* Grand Rapids, MI, and Cambridge: William B. Eerdmans Publishing Company, 2003.

Vaughan, David G., et al. "Recent Rapid Regional Climate Warming on the Antarctic Peninsula." *Climatic Change* 60 (2003): 243–74.

Vaughan, David G., and Robert Arthern. "Why Is it Hard to Predict the Future of Ice Sheets." *Science* 315 (2007): 1503–4.

Victor, Paul-Émile. *Man and the Conquest of the Poles.* New York: Simon and Schuster, 1963.

Votier, Stephen C., et al. "The First Record of Brown Skua *Catharacta Antarctica* in Europe." *Ibis* 146, no. 1 (2003): 95–102.

Walton, D. W. H., ed. *Antarctic Science.* Cambridge: Cambridge University Press, 1987.

Warham, John. "The Biology of the Giant Petrel *Macronectes Giganteus.*" *The Auk* 79, no. 2 (1962): 139–60.

Weiss, Rick. "Molecular Action May Help Keep Birds on Course." *Washington Post.* May 5, 2008.

Wheeler, Sara. *Terra Incognita: Travels in Antarctica.* New York: The Modern Library, 1999.

Wilson, Edward. *Diary of the Discovery Expedition to the Antarctic Regions, 1901–1904.* London: Blandford Press, 1966.

———. *Diary of the Terra Nova Expedition to the Antarctic, 1910–1912.* New York: Humanities Press, 1972.

Woehler, Eric J. *The Distribution and Abundance of Antarctic and Subantarctic Penguins.* Cambridge: Scientific Committee on Antarctic Research, 1993.

Woehler, Eric J., et al. *A Statistical Assessment of the Status and Trends of Antarctic and Subantarctic Seabirds*. Cambridge: Scientific Committee on Antarctic Research, 2001.

Young, Euan. *Skua and Penguin: Predator and Prey*. Cambridge: Cambridge University Press, 1994.

INDEX

ABOUT THE AUTHOR

FEN MONTAIGNE is a journalist and author whose work has appeared in *The New Yorker, National Geographic, Outside, Smithsonian,* and *The Wall Street Journal.* A former Moscow bureau chief of *The Philadelphia Inquirer,* he is the author of *Reeling in Russia* and has coauthored two other books. For his work on *Fraser's Penguins,* Montaigne was awarded a Guggenheim Fellowship in 2006. He now works as senior editor of the online magazine *Yale Environment 360.*